Credit to California Winemakers

"I wonder often what vintners buy one-half so precious as the stuff they sell," questioned Omar Khayyam, the great poet of Persia about 1100 A.D.

I often wonder what vintners could possibly eat away from home one-half so delicious as the food they consume at home.

Because of the wonderful dishes served at their family tables, I asked winemakers, their wives and their winery associates to send me these recipes. The result is a collection of recipes that are easy to prepare, and each includes some one of the winemakers' products — wine, Champagne, Vermouth or Brandy.

Wine has been recognized for centuries around the world as a food and food ingredient, as well as a healthful and temperate beverage especially suited to be an accompaniment to meals. It harmonizes the flavors in food and when its alcohol evaporates during cooking, tantalizing flavors and aromas remain.

Some of the recipes were concocted in the kitchens of the senders, for wine people know that it is easy to create new exotic combinations by experimenting with the addition of small amounts of the more than four score different wine types produced in California.

Many of the recipes are not original. They were chosen on the basis of how good they were to the taste.

"A meal without wine is like a day without sunshine," in the words of a great French author. Believing this, I asked each contributor to give a personal choice of the wine type to accompany each main dish. The selections show that those who know aroma and flavors are not bound by so-called rules such as "white wine with white meat" but rely on their sense of taste to guide them in specifying delightful wine and food combinations. The most valid guide for each individual is to drink what tastes best to him.

We express sincere thanks to the donors of these recipes for sharing them with us and with you.

Wine Advisory Board
D. C. TURRENTINE, MANAGER

EASY RECIPES

of California Winemakers

A NEW COLLECTION OF RECIPES GATHERED
AND PUBLISHED BY THE WINE ADVISORY BOARD
SAN FRANCISCO

Production Editor: FRANCES W. HEWLETT

Editor: MARJORIE KENT JACOBS

Designer and Illustrator: NANCY J. KENNEDY

Food Consultants: MARJORIE LUMM and DOROTHY CANET

Editorial Assistant: DIANE L. SCHWEITZERHOF

The Universal Ingredient

by Marjorie Jacobs

Wine is the one element which makes itself welcome in any dish, blending with all foods — sweet, sour, savory, bitter, fat, lean, simple or complicated. It enhances the flavor of every meat, red or white, fresh or smoked. It melds with gravies and sauces and makes them far better than they would be alone. White wine, even red wine, provides smooth or piquant and perky taste to fish, from salt water or fresh; and lobsters and crabs bask in its flavorous warmth.

The Hunter's Friend

Wild game? Wine makes venison become tender, wild boar tame. Sherry sophisticates a rabbit stew and is on familiar terms with pheasant. Quail and squab turn golden and tender, enveloped in a buttery wine sauce.

But don't leave vegetables out! Wine is at home with artichokes, loves spinach, turns carrots into gourmet fare. Potatoes succumb to its seduction; turnips become regal. And once a chef uses wine vinegar in a salad, it is almost certain that no other type of vinegar will be permitted in salads thereafter, so great are the gastronomical wonders it works.

Wines to the Sweet

White, Rosé, Sherry, Port — all refresh fruits in their different ways. Enjoy them all — peach, fig, melon, pear, nectarine, orange, cherry — cold and sweet, bathed in a compatible blend of fruit juice and wine. Wine, this magic ingredient, makes a creamy pudding richer, and cakes rise to new heights of delicacy and flavor. Or takes a commonplace gelatin dessert and turns it into something memorable with wine used in place of water.

Then, after wine has made your cooking delectable, fragrant, irresistible, there is the pleasure awaiting of pouring golden, ruby red, tawny, pale-bubbled, green-gold, or rosy California wines into sparkling crystal to savor with the meal.

Shakespeare said, "O, thou invisible spirit of wine!" Wine is indeed mysterious, a living entity with myriad personalities, a different one in each bottle, unlimited in its usefulness, and central to healthy enjoyment of the pleasures of the table.

Even Cereal?

It is difficult to think of a single food that wine would not go with. . .Oatmeal, perhaps? No, on second thought, how about plumping raisins in a little Sherry, adding them to the hot cooked cereal and serving with brown sugar and fresh cream? This would be a good dish for Sunday brunch. Yes, there are endless possibilities for combining wines with foods.

The vintner and the grape are good friends to man, as good as anyone or anything that lives and grows on earth. We hope you will find pleasure in this book, that wine graces your table, enlivens the menu, makes your hospitality genial and you and your guests happy.

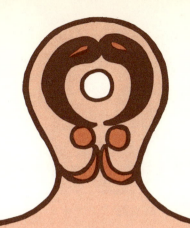

CONTENTS

RECIPES

Little Known Facts

Wine Cookery

The recipes in this book call for modest amounts of wine in the belief that no one ingredient should dominate the flavor. However, the many people who enjoy a pronounced wine flavor can add more wine just before serving. A generous splash of red wine over a pot roast, or even a hamburger, at the last minute greatly enhances the meat. Wine can always be added during the final minutes of heating to bring gravies or sauces to the required thickness, again with richer flavor resulting. Also the Sherry bottle can be passed to guests for individual addition to soups, creamed or clear, whether or not this classic accompaniment to the soup course is served to drink at the beginning of the meal.

Alcohol Disappears

When you use wine in cooking, the alcohol disappears after a few minutes at simmering temperatures just as the alcohol in vanilla or lemon extract disappears. All that is left is the flavor. Calorie counters, relax! When the alcohol from a dry wine in a recipe boils off, most of the calories go with it because they are contained principally in the alcohol.

Dryness and Sweetness in Wine

In the language of wine, "dry" means the opposite of sweet because the yeast, during the fermentation process, has converted the natural sugar in the grape into wine alcohol and carbon dioxide gas. A wine becomes completely "dry" when all the sugar has been consumed by fermentation.

California's benign climate is ideal for ripening grapes. Indeed, their sugar content develops so well and so consistently that winemakers have no difficulty complying with a California regulation which prohibits the addition of cane sugar to natural wines. The regulation makes an exception in the production of sparkling wines to allow addition of a small amount of sugar to produce the necessary secondary fermentation.

Approximate Servings

When a "bottle of wine" is referred to without stating size, the capacity is understood to be 4/5 quart (25.6 ounces, or 1/5 gallon), or six average-size (4-ounce) servings. In giving a dinner party, count on opening at least one bottle for every four guests.

Chilling Wine

Chilling wine is a matter of one's own personal taste. As a general guide, white and rosé table wines are chilled one or two hours before serving. Traditionally, red table wines are served at cool room temperature, somewhere between 60° and 70°. If you prefer them chilled, your own taste should govern. Muscatel, Sherry and appetizer wines are usually chilled; Port, however, seems to be preferred at cool room temperature. Champagne and other sparkling wines are served coldest of all. There is a good reason for chilling Champagne and other sparkling wines more than other wines — two or three hours. It is the low temperature that enables sparkling wines to retain their natural carbon dioxide gas that gives these wines their bubbles. If sparkling wines aren't chilled sufficiently, upon opening, the bubbles may rise too forcefully, resulting in the loss of some of the precious liquid.

Wine In Gallon Jugs

Serve at Low Cost

Sound California wine served inexpensively from gallon or half-gallon jugs is appearing on more and more American dinner tables as couples discover that wine adds enjoyment to everyday meals far beyond its modest cost.

Many California wineries bottle table as well as appetizer and dessert wines in these larger containers. Buying wine in jugs can bring down the cost of serving wine to a few cents a glass. Wine experts recognize California wines sold by the jug as being among the world's best wine values.

Quality Good

Because of the great abundance of wine grapes in California, the State's wine growers are able to produce table and dessert wines of consistently good quality in great quantity. By bottling in gallon and half-gallon sizes, they can save on bottling and shipping costs and pass the savings on to the consumer.

Table Wines

A good variety of California wines is available in jugs. There are white wines such as Rhine wines, Sauterne and Chablis; red wines such as Burgundy, Claret, Chianti, Zinfandel and the more mellow Vino Rosso wines; and of course, the ever popular Rosés.

In addition to these table wines, some wineries also bottle their Sherries, Ports and Muscatel dessert wines in jugs.

The wine may be poured from the jug into a carafe or decanter for more convenient serving at the table. The remaining wine can be kept in the jug in the refrigerator for several days, with little, if any, change. But if longer storage is anticipated, the wine should be rebottled in smaller containers, once the jug has been opened. Air is an enemy of wine, so the less air space in the bottle, the less the wine will be affected.

Used screw cap fifth bottles are handy for home rebottling. They should be washed, thoroughly rinsed and then sterilized. When filled, the bottles should be closed tightly to prevent air from entering.

Can Be Used Generously

Jug wine has enjoyed an upsurge in popularity in the kitchen as well as in the dining room. Inexpensive enough to be used generously, it takes cooking with wine out of the luxury class. Wine makes an excellent substitute for other liquids as an agent to blend and improve flavors. One tremendously popular national television program on French cuisine suggests the use of California jug wines, both as an ingredient in cooking and for pouring with the meal.

But jug wine's major role is on the table. In the words of the American writer Crosby Gaige, "It is axiomatic that good wine and good food go hand in hand." With wine in the jug, it's very easy and inexpensive to maintain that relationship.

Memorable Experiences With Wine

We asked winemakers and their families to give us some of their most treasured memories of occasions when California wines added their unique qualities to the pleasure of those present. These happy stories follow.

ARE WOMEN BETTER THAN MEN?

We had a most interesting time one evening when each guest was blindfolded in turn and asked to identify a rosé, a white and a red wine. To our amazement, some couldn't tell the difference between the red and the white when blindfolded. Women did better than men. Two men of the six couldn't identify any of the wines while five of the six women identified all of them. *Mrs. E. A. Kirkman, Jr., Wente Brothers, Livermore*

Editor's Note: Some authorities say women are more perceptive at tasting than men because they taste to adjust flavors, seasonings, etc. in cooking. However, both men and women who have done little tasting, can become capable tasters quite rapidly, when they sip wines attentively with the purpose of learning what they can about appearance, aroma, bouquet and flavor.

SO — WE MADE OUR OWN

A few years ago, I was fond of a wine purchased at a local store. As a joke, my husband told me the wine was too expensive and he would thereafter make it himself. I requested a few changes — not quite as herby, a little lighter in color, more cocoa flavor. The result was more delicious than the original. Guests were so pleased by its richness and satisfying flavor that we began to produce the wine commercially and are continuously increasing production. It contains a trace of egg and other flavors which make it one of the creamiest and smoothest dessert types I have ever tasted.
Mrs. Joseph Filippi, Jr., Thomas Vineyards, Cucamonga

CALIFORNIA GOES TO GERMANY

When my husband, Sam, third generation winemaker, and I, native of Ireland and novice wine drinker, were first married, we were stationed in Germany with the U.S. Army. We celebrated our arrival by dining in a fine restaurant. When the waiter asked my husband if we would like wine with our dinner, Sam surprised him and me by producing a bottle of California wine from his coat and asked the waiter to serve it; naturally, Sam paid the waiter the same as if we had purchased the local wine, and we had a wonderful time feasting on native German dishes, accompanied by our fine California wine.
Mrs. Sam Sebastiani, Samuele Sebastiani Winery, Sonoma

EXPERTS WERE STUMPED

My greatest experience with wine took place in London at a blind tasting of all wines selling there in the price category of the wines of our company. All of the experts present incorrectly identified our California Emerald Riesling as a German Moselle. I was the only one who correctly identified it. *Mrs. Otto Meyer, Paul Masson Vineyards, Saratoga*

BETTY FURNESS

At our most outstanding evening of wine, we hosted Betty Furness, then assistant to President Johnson on consumer affairs, and several other guests. Champagne preceded dinner under the grapevine arbor in our patio, an outstanding Pinot Noir and Cabernet Sauvignon accompanied filet mignon followed by melon balls in Pink Champagne. Without moving chairs, we picked grapes hanging from the arbor to eat with a delightful Port to conclude a memorable feast marked by sparkling conversation and good companionship. *Mr. and Mrs. Vincent Petrucci, Fresno State College, Fresno*

CHRISTMAS TURKEY BASTE

One of our most exciting wine flavor surprises occurred one Christmas when preparing a turkey. After the turkey was thoroughly browned, we basted it with our apricot wine every half hour. This was truly the best tasting turkey I ever prepared. I have since found this wine to be a delicious baste for chicken, cornish hen, rabbit and baked ham. I really believe use of this wine will improve the flavor of any food. *Mrs. John M. Filice, San Martin Vineyards Co., San Martin*

A DINNER TO REMEMBER

During a football weekend in Miami, I was invited to join a congenial group for dinner. I accepted and immediately hastened to remove from my traveling bag two bottles of fine Livermore Valley Sauterne. When this extremely smooth Sauvignon Blanc-Semillon blend was sampled with the pheasant entrée, it was received with enthusiastic accolades. This spontaneous meal became a memorable affair with this excellent white wine from California. *Mr. Don Rudolph, Cresta Blanca Winery, Livermore*

WINES BEYOND COMPARE

At a private wine tasting party the guests, all semi-professional wine tasters, recognized the first 12 wines presented without labels, but were stumped by two wines of unique and interesting character. The winemaster finally confessed that these smooth and utterly delicate wines, both from our winery, had been aged in white oaken casks for 20 years. They were suave, mellow, beyond compare — one a Golden Muscat, the other a superb Tokay. *Mr. R. J. Hannah, Bargetto's Santa Cruz Winery, Soquel*

THE WORLD'S LARGEST WINE COOLER

On a trip to the beach, the car was packed with a hearty repast, but when we were almost at our destination, someone remembered that we had neglected to bring a beverage. I suggested wine, but was reminded that we had no cooler with us and the warmth of the day necessitated chilled wine. I persisted, however, and purchased two bottles of California Riesling. At the beach, I waded out a few yards into the cold waters of the Pacific and secured the bottles in the sand under water. When the picnic was ready, the wines were well chilled and served as a perfect complement to the food. *Mr. Larry Cahn, Wine Institute, San Francisco*

Wine and Your Well-Being

by
SALVATORE P. LUCIA, M.D.
Professor Emeritus of Preventive Medicine
University of California

Wine has been enjoyed as an accompaniment to food for so many centuries that most of us are apt to forget that wine, in addition to its pleasurable uses, has an ancient and honorable history as a substance with definite health values. Modern medical research, in this country and abroad, continues to reveal sound scientific reasons for the beneficial uses of wine in health and in illness.

Wine is the simple and natural product of luscious fruit. However, modern research has shown us that wine is also an extremely complex liquid, and that its unique composition makes it valuable as an aid to health. We know, for instance, that all grape wines contain consistent and measurable quantities of the B vitamins in sufficient amounts to add substantially to the daily vitamin intake.

As for minerals, wines contain, in some degree, all thirteen of the elements that are necessary for the maintenance of human life: calcium, phosphorus, magnesium, sodium, potassium, chlorine, sulfur, iron, copper, manganese, zinc, iodine and cobalt.

SOURCE OF ENERGY

Wine is a valuable aid to digestion. Of all dietary alcoholic beverages, wine in particular aids in the digestion of fat. And, without being overloaded with calories (4 ounces of table wine contain, on the average, about 95 calories), it is a source of quick energy. For this reason it is being used in the recovery rooms of many hospitals for patients who have just undergone surgery, and who cannot yet stand the thought of solid foods.

According to modern clinical thinking, the problems of both over-eating and under-nourishment are often the result of anxiety and emotional tension. Where such emotional factors are involved, even though symptoms are strikingly different, wine may be beneficially employed.

The appropriate use of wine can contribute to an anti-obesity program by making it easier for the patient to adhere to a prescribed diet. The amount indicated for this purpose is approximately a four-ounce serving with the major meal of the day. Also, its use before bedtime has a tendency to reduce insomnia, lessen the craving for a nocturnal meal, and discourage "refrigerator raiding." Another important point is the fact that when a dry wine is incorporated into a reducing diet, most persons naturally tend to decrease their carbohydrate intake.

The unbiased scientist and physician must admit that wine is more than just a beverage containing alcohol. If properly used, wine stimulates appetite and excites gastro-intestinal secretory functions. For this reason, wine is also useful for the person whose problem is lack of appetite. A dry table wine, in moderate amounts, not only eases the emotional tension that is often the cause of a harmful loss of appetite, but it also provides, in itself, a source of energy and food.

ANTIBIOTIC EFFECT

The pigments which give wine its color also destroy certain bacteria, including those which cause food poisoning. It has been demonstrated that the bacteria-killing action of wine is three times greater than that of water containing the same amount of alcohol.

USE IN DIABETES

A dry table wine can be included in the diet of most diabetics. The control of diabetes has been made easier — and certainly more pleasant — by the prescribed dietary use of wine. The difficulty for a diabetic is that his body cannot readily convert sugar into energy. This is a serious problem because sugar, as a carbohydrate, gives the body the ready fuel it needs for maintaining energy. For many centuries, wine has been recommended by physicians as an important part of the diabetic diet. Research has shown that the alcohol in wine provides ready energy for the body, and does not require insulin as a converting agent.

ANXIETY DIMINISHED

We are living in an era that has been aptly termed the Age of Anxiety. Emotional tension is so widespread today that it easily ranks as one of our major health problems. Relaxation is necessary to health, but the frenzied pace of modern life too often makes relaxation impossible. There is no question that the general tension experienced by the average person at the end of a wearisome day diminishes after having enjoyed a glass of wine.

For 40 centuries, wine has been used as a safe agent to lessen anxieties and induce relaxation and sleep. The fact that most tranquilizing agents can cause side effects induces physicians to use them with caution and knowledge. In contrast to drugs, wine provides a safe, gentle, natural tranquilizer when used moderately.

Wine is unquestionably the most healthful dietary alcoholic beverage used by man.

NOTES ON THIS BOOK

In most cases we have listed the wives who contributed recipes as being associated with their husband's winery or firm, at the California town where the organization is located.

There is no duplication of recipes or features with those appearing in any of the four previous Wine Advisory Board cookbooks. This book, in combination with the above-mentioned four, is believed to comprise the largest collection of wine cookery recipes in existence.

All of the recipes have been prepared and tested by our home economists to insure use of uniform measurements, modern cooking terms and ease and speed of preparation — all for your cooking convenience.

Punches for weddings and wine drinks for all occasions are featured in the Beverage Section.

Where the word "NOTE" appears under recipes, the comments that follow are the editor's. Other comments, unless otherwise indicated, are by recipe donors.

This book is designed to let you look while you cook. You can open it flat on table or counter, or stand it up, slipping a rubber band around each side to keep the pages in place. Keep the covers clean by simply wiping with a damp cloth.

BEVERAGES

"The landlord fills the flowing bowl/Until it doth run over." As good as wine is alone, it mixes delectably with other wines and flavors, as the California winegrowers demonstrate with these recipes. Servings are four ounces each, before adding ice. Remember one large block of ice will chill your punch with less dilution than cracked ice, which should be reserved for beverages of high potency. Freeze ice in refrigerator trays without dividers and with the addition of fruits, leaves and flowers you can produce beautiful molds for a spectacular punch bowl; but a tall glass of chilled wine and soda is just as hospitable, for wine graces any occasion.

Citrus Champagne

(35 servings)

Brother Timothy, The Christian Brothers, Napa

- 1 (6 oz.) can frozen orange juice concentrate
- 1 (6 oz.) can frozen lemonade concentrate
- 1 (30 oz.) can pineapple juice
- 2 (4/5 qt.) bottles California Sauterne
- 2 (4/5 qt.) bottles California Brut Champagne

Combine fruit juices and simmer 10 minutes over low heat. Cool and chill. At the time of serving pour this base over chunk of ice in punch bowl. Add the chilled wines and stir gently. Garnish with thin orange slices or strawberries as desired.
NOTE: If a sweeter punch is desired, this can be accomplished by the addition of white corn syrup, honey, or simple syrup (half sugar, half water) to taste, to the fruit juice mixture.

Frappé Roshar

(1 serving)

Mrs. Frank Franzia, Jr., Franzia Brothers Winery, Ripon

- 1/2 cup California Rhine Wine
- 1/2 cup club soda
- 1/4 teaspoon sugar
- Juice of 1 slice of lime

Fill a tumbler with crushed ice, add above ingredients, stir well and serve.

Morning Sherry Tang

(1 serving)

Mrs. John Daddino, Guild Wine Co., Fresno

This is an excellent drink for company brunch and can be prepared with minimum effort.

    1   juice glass Tang instant breakfast
        drink, made with cold water
1-1/2   ounces California Cream Sherry
        Twist of lemon peel

Blend, stir well, and serve "on the rocks", or well chilled from refrigerator.

Green Bird

(8 servings)

Mr. Hal Cutler, E. & J. Gallo Winery, Modesto

Editor's note: This refreshing drink looks as good as it tastes.

     1   pint firm lime sherbet
    12   ounces California Citrus-Flavored
         Wine, well chilled

Combine wine and sherbet in blender at high speed. Mound into chilled glasses and serve with short straws. Sprinkle with nutmeg, if desired.

Bubbling Fruit Punch

(86 servings)

Mrs. Bill Warddrip, California Wine Association, San Francisco

    3   (4/5 qt.) bottles California Vin Rosé
    4   quarts grapefruit-flavored
        sparkling water
    6   (4/5 qt.) bottles California
        Pink Champagne

Chill all ingredients well before mixing. Pour over large chunk of ice in punch bowl. Garnish with fruits in season and to taste.

Fishermen's Coffee

(1 serving)

Brother Timothy, The Christian Brothers, Napa

    1/4   jigger Cointreau
    3/4   jigger California Brandy
      2   cloves
      1   slice lemon peel, twisted

To a cup or mug of good hot coffee, add above ingredients. You may vary the amount of Cointreau to California Brandy to suit your taste.

NOTE: The standard jigger measures 1-1/2 ounces.

LEMON SHERRY is a refreshing variation of Sherry on the Rocks. Mrs. Roy W. Mineau of Roma Wine Co., Fresno, freezes 1 quart lemonade made of frozen concentrate or fresh lemons in ice trays and places a maraschino cherry in half the cubes. She suggests putting 2 or 3 cubes, including one with cherry in glasses and filling with your favorite California Sherry. Garnish with sprig of mint.

California Sherry Fizz

(6 servings)

Mr. Evins R. Naman, Wine Institute, San Francisco

      1   egg
    1/2   cup orange juice
    1/2   cup milk
    1/2   cup California Sherry
      2   tablespoons sugar
      1   cup ice

Put all ingredients in blender and mix at high speed for about 30 seconds. Pour into small glasses and garnish with maraschino cherries.

NOTE: This makes an excellent introduction to a Sunday brunch.

Café Brûlé

(1 serving)

Mrs. E. A. Mirassou, Mirassou Vineyards, San Jose

          Hot coffee
      1   cube sugar for each cup
    2-1/4 ounces California Brandy

Fill cup 3/4 full of very hot coffee and place spoon in it until thoroughly heated. Drain and dry spoon and rest over cup. Place cube of sugar in spoon and pour about one-third of Brandy over sugar. Ignite Brandy and sugar. As it burns continue to pour Brandy over sugar a little at a time. When flame goes out, stir sugar into coffee and add whatever Brandy remains.

Party Punch

(36 servings)

Mrs. Sam Sebastiani, Samuele Sebastiani Winery, Sonoma

This must always be made just before serving because it loses its taste if bubbly ingredients become flat. It's delightful, no matter what the season, and warms whoever drinks it, although it's light enough to serve at a bridge luncheon or a bridal or baby shower.

- 2 cups California Port
- 1 cup California Brandy
- 2 cups California Sherry
- 1 cup sugar syrup (1/2 cup sugar melted over low heat with 1/2 cup water)
- 2 (4/5 qt.) bottles California Champagne
- 3 pints ginger ale

Combine all ingredients except Champagne and ginger ale. Chill in refrigerator for several hours. Just before serving, place in punch bowl with block of ice, add chilled Champagne, ginger ale and garnish with 3 lemons or oranges sliced thin.

NOTE: Mrs. Sebastiani adds, to be festive the punch can be served in a hollowed out watermelon and maraschino cherries can be frozen in the ice.

DELIGHTFUL CUP is a favorite of Mrs. John Franzia, Sr., Franzia Bros. Winery, Ripon. She adds about 3 tablespoons of California Claret or Burgundy to a cup of good hot tea, sweetened with a teaspoon of sugar, and floats a slice of lemon in it. The addition of wine really makes for the "cup that cheers."

Reception Punch

(60 servings)

Mr. Joseph Ghianda, Ghianda Winery, Oroville

This punch is served with fancy open face sandwiches, mosaics, pinwheels and others.

- 2 (6 oz.) cans frozen lemonade concentrate
- 4-1/2 cups cold water
- 2 (46 oz.) cans pineapple juice
- 1 (12 oz.) can papaya nectar
- 1 (4/5 qt.) bottle California Champagne
- 1 (4/5 qt.) bottle California Vin Rosé
- 2 (24 oz.) bottles 7-Up

Combine lemonade concentrate, water, pineapple juice and papaya nectar, freeze to a slush and put in punch bowl. Add chilled wines, 7-Up, stir and serve immediately.

NOTE: Mr. Ghianda also suggests filling a mold (or molds, depending on size) half full with fruit juice mixture. After it is frozen, arrange a wreath of grapes and grape leaves on frozen surface, add enough juice combination to fill, and refreeze. This mold makes a beautiful presentation for the Reception Punch. If desired, this recipe can be doubled successfully.

Ice Cream Egg Nog

(28 servings)

Mrs. Tillie Snyder, California Wine Association, Lodi

Editor's note: This mild version of the traditional egg nog is delicate and different.

- 8 eggs, separated
- 1/2 to 1 cup sugar, according to taste
- 1 teaspoon nutmeg
- 1/2 teaspoon cinnamon
- 1 quart vanilla ice cream
- 2 cups California Sherry
- 1/2 cup California Brandy
- 1 quart milk

Beat egg yolks well. Beat in sugar, nutmeg and cinnamon. Add ice cream, beat in Sherry and Brandy and stir in milk. Fold in stiffly beaten egg whites. Refrigerate overnight and stir well before serving.

Pineapple Punch

(20 to 25 servings)

Brother Frederick, The Christian Brothers, Napa

Editor's note: This is a delicious combination, just sweet enough and the pineapple is rich with flavor.

- 1 quart diced pineapple, fresh or canned
- 2 tablespoons powdered sugar
- 1 pint California Brandy
- 3 (4/5 qt.) bottles California Champagne

Have all ingredients well chilled. Place diced pineapple with its juice in large glass bowl, sprinkle with sugar and add Brandy. Let stand in refrigerator for 3 to 4 hours. When ready to serve, add large chunk of ice and pour Champagne over it. Stir lightly and serve in punch glasses.

Royal Ruby Punch

(32 servings)

Mrs. Doris K. Larson, Wine Institute, Detroit

- 2 (6 oz.) cans frozen pineapple-raspberry drink
- 2 (6 oz.) cans frozen lemonade concentrate
- 4 cups water
- 1 (4/5 qt.) bottle California Burgundy
- 1 (4/5 qt.) bottle California Sparkling Burgundy
- 1 (24 oz.) bottle ginger ale

Place concentrated lemonade and punch drink into large pitcher or pan. Dilute with water. Stir until thawed. Strain ingredients into punch bowl or storage container. Add chilled Burgundy, Sparkling Burgundy and ginger ale. Stir and add chunk of ice.

NOTE: If desired, the first four ingredients can be blended ahead of time and stored in refrigerator. The chilled Sparkling Burgundy and ginger ale are added at time of serving. This recipe can be doubled or tripled. Also, frozen Hawaiian Punch concentrate can be substituted if the pineapple-raspberry concentrate is unavailable.

Diplomat Punch

(15 servings)

Mrs. Tillie Snyder, California Wine Association, Lodi

The flavor of this remarkable punch improves with age — if you can keep it that long.

- 2 cups California Sweet Sherry
- 2 cups California Dry Vermouth
- 2 cups California Brandy
- 1 teaspoon angostura bitters
- 1/4 cup grenadine syrup
- 1 cup water

Combine all ingredients and chill in refrigerator overnight. Serve over plenty of crushed ice.

Waldmeister Riesling

(36 servings)

Mr. Walter E. Schmitter, The Christian Brothers, Reedley

Editor's note: If fresh Waldmeister (also known as sweet Woodruff) cannot be found, it is frequently available dried from herb dealers or pharmacies.

- 6 bunches fresh Waldmeister (4 oz. dried)
- 2/3 cup powdered sugar
- 1 cup California Brandy
- 4 (4/5 qt.) bottles California Riesling
- 2 (4/5 qt.) bottles California Champagne
- 1 cup fresh strawberries

Wash herb and shake out excess water. Place in large bowl with sugar, Brandy, 1 bottle Riesling. Cover and let stand overnight. To serve, strain mixture, using fine sieve if dried herb is used, pour over ice in large punch bowl, and add remaining Riesling and Champagne. Float strawberries in punch.

Hawaiian Punch

(42 servings)

Mr. Mario J. Lanza, Wooden Valley Winery, Suisun

- 1 (6 oz.) can frozen lemonade concentrate
- 1 (46 oz.) can Hawaiian Punch
- 1/2 gallon California Dry White Wine
- 2 (4/5 qt.) bottles California Champagne

Pour over large chunk of ice in punch bowl. If desired, garnish with can of crushed pineapple, chilled.

Baccari Festival Punch

(60 servings)

Mrs. Alessandro Baccari, Baccari Wine Festival, San Francisco

Editor's note: When you are faced with entertaining a large mixed group on a warm day, this punch is ideal because it is tasty and inexpensive.

About 8 trays of ice cubes
1 pound sugar cubes
1 (4/5 qt.) bottle California Haut Sauterne
1 (4/5 qt.) bottle California Vin Rosé
1 (4/5 qt.) bottle California Medium Sherry
3 cups California Sweet Vermouth
1 (46 oz.) can grapefruit and pineapple juice drink
1 quart ginger ale
1 quart soda water
1 quart orange soda
3 bananas, sliced (small, or 2 large)
4 oranges, sliced thinly (medium thin-skinned)

Place ice in punch bowl. Pour sugar cubes over ice and add wines, juice and chilled ginger ale, soda and orange soda. Float sliced fruit in punch before serving.

Blossom Hill Pink Delight

Mrs. E. Jeff Barnette, Martini & Prati Wines, Santa Rosa

Editor's note: This is a versatile recipe and with these basic proportions you can make any amount.

> 1 part California Chianti, Cabernet Sauvignon or other Red Table Wine
> 1 part simple syrup
> 1 part lime or lemon juice
> 2 parts California Brandy

For cocktails: combine all ingredients with a generous portion of cracked ice, shake well and serve.

For punch: mix all ingredients, refrigerate several hours or overnight. Pour over large piece of ice, or ice cubes, in chilled punch bowl.

Silver Champagne Punch

(38 servings)

Mrs. Elaine Filippi, J. Filippi Vintage Co., Mira Loma

A Champagne punch may be served at weddings, showers, birthdays, holidays, etc. This punch was originated by one of our tasting room managers. It has been used over and over and is a favorite for any gathering.

> 2 (4/5 qt.) bottles California Champagne
> 1/2 gallon California Sauterne
> 1 cup California Brandy
> 1 quart 7-Up

Chill all ingredients for at least 6 hours before mixing together. Pour over large block of ice in chilled punch bowl. Bowl may be cushioned in container of crushed ice to maintain chill.

NOTE: For a pink punch use above ingredients, substituting Pink Champagne for the white.

Simple Champagne Punch

(28 servings)

Mr. C. A. "Cap" Percy, Brookside Vineyard Co., Guasti

This punch is like drinking straight champagne, and so simple to prepare. For large weddings, etc., it can cut the expense in half and avoids the messiness when guests remove fruit slices and other ingredients from drinks.

> 2 (4/5 qt.) bottles Extra Dry California Champagne
> 1 (4/5 qt.) bottle California Haut Sauterne
> 1 quart club soda
> 1/4 cup California Brandy

Pre-chill ingredients and pour over block of ice in punch bowl. The Sauterne retains champagne flavor and club soda preserves effervescence. Brandy simply replaces alcohol that was diluted by adding soda and, being a grape product, blends perfectly.

Brandanis

(1 serving)

Mr. Vincent E. Petrucci, Fresno State College, Fresno

This is a delightful after dinner drink, particularly following lamb or chicken.

> 1 ounce California Brandy
> 1/2 ounce Anisette

Fill cocktail glass 3/4 full with crushed ice, add Brandy and Anisette and garnish with mint leaf.

Rose Bowl

(6 servings)

Brother Timothy, The Christian Brothers, Napa

This recipe was given to me by Dr. Dennison Morey, President of General Bionomics (rose hybridizers) Santa Rosa. The location, Santa Rosa, is particularly appropriate since it was named for Saint Rose.

> 1 (4/5 qt.) bottle California Sauterne or Sauvignon Blanc
> 1 quart fresh rose petals (carefully trimmed with basal portion cut away)*
> 1/2 to 3/4 cup sugar

*Use only rose petals that have not been treated with pesticides. Combine wine and roses. Add sugar and refrigerate covered for several days to blend flavors. Strain out petals. Serve chilled, over cracked ice, if desired. A few fresh rose petals make an attractive garnish.

NOTE: For a beautiful table decoration, Dr. Morey suggests a hollow stem glass to display a rose and a few rose leaves. Place a number of these along the center line of a banquet table. Dr. Morey also furnished Brother Timothy with the following verse:

> "Fill the bowl with rosy wine;
> Around our temples roses twine.
> And let us cheerfully awhile
> Like the wine and roses smile."

Abraham Cowley, English Poet, 1618-1667

Holiday Punch

(32 servings)

Mrs. John Franzia, Sr., Franzia Brothers Winery, Ripon

2 (4/5 qt.) bottles California Burgundy
or Zinfandel
1 (1 qt.) bottle apple juice
2 tablespoons lemon juice
1/4 cup sugar
1 large bottle ginger ale

Have all liquid ingredients well chilled and combine with lemon juice and sugar in punch bowl, stirring to dissolve sugar. Pour in ginger ale and stir to blend. Add ice and serve at once.

NOTE: One quart of apple-cranberry juice instead of the apple juice makes an attractive color and flavor variation of this recipe.

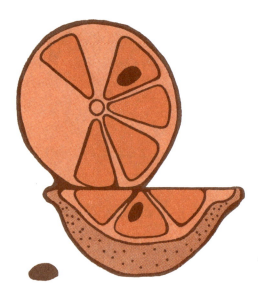

Special Occasion Punch

(45 servings)

Mrs. Louis W. Pellegrini, Sr., Italian Swiss Colony, Asti

1 (4/5 qt.) bottle California Sauterne
5 ounces California Brandy
5 ounces grenadine syrup
1 (4/5 qt.) bottle California Champagne
1 (24 oz.) bottle 7-Up
1 (46 oz.) can pineapple juice
1 (46 oz.) can grapefruit juice
2 cups fresh strawberries or 1 (10 oz.)
package frozen strawberries
Fresh mint leaves (optional)

Have all ingredients well-chilled. Place small block of ice in punch bowl and pour all liquid ingredients over it. Add strawberries last. Garnish with fresh mint leaves, if desired.

Mai Tai Punch

(60 servings)

Mrs. Herbert L. Grosswendt, Brookside Vineyard Co., Guasti

This is an inexpensive, tasty punch.

4 or 5 oranges, thinly sliced
1 gallon California Sauterne
1 cup California Malvasia Bianca
1 cup Mai Tai Mix
1/2 pint California Brandy
3 quarts soda water, chilled

Combine and chill in refrigerator for several hours. Just before serving, add large chunks of ice and soda.

NOTE: California Champagne may be substituted for all or part of soda water.

Grenache Punch

(9 servings)

Mrs. Armand E. Bussone, Almaden Vineyards, Los Gatos

We needed a tasty punch to serve guests during a swimming party. My husband whipped this up when he discovered he lacked the ingredients to make the punch planned. It was so well liked that it has become our favorite.

1 (4/5 qt.) bottle California
Grenache Rosé
1 (6 oz.) can frozen lemonade
concentrate
1/2 cup California Cream Sherry

Mix above ingredients thoroughly and pour over ice cubes in tall glasses. A slice of orange makes a pretty garnish.

San Franciscan

(26 servings)

Mrs. E. B. Nelson, Wine Institute, San Francisco

This is an easy way to serve a large group, whatever the occasion — right from the bottle on the rocks, or in a punch bowl over ice. It keeps well.

- 2 (4/5 qt.) bottles California Sherry (Dry, Sweet, or Cocktail)
- 1 (4/5 qt.) bottle California Sweet Vermouth
- 1 (4/5 qt.) bottle California Dry Vermouth
- 1/2 teaspoon angostura bitters
- 1/2 teaspoon maraschino syrup (optional)

Combine and pour mixture back into original bottles to store in refrigerator for 4 days. Garnish with any of the following: cherry, cocktail onion, olive, or mushroom.

California Punch

(22 servings)

Mrs. Catherine L. Menth, California Wine Association, Burlingame

For an attractive garnish you can freeze fruit or flowers in chunk of ice used to chill the bowl, or you can float fruit or flowers right in the punch.

- 1 (4/5 qt.) bottle California White Table Wine
- 1 cup California Brandy
- 1 (4/5 qt.) bottle California Champagne
- 1 quart lemon-lime sparkling water

Pre-chill ingredients. Mix white wine and Brandy in punch bowl. Add ice and pour Champagne and sparkling water in bowl simultaneously. Serve immediately.

NOTE: This dry, basic recipe can be varied by adding compatible frozen fruit juices, such as orange juice, pink lemonade, maraschino cherry juice or syrup.

Berry Champagne Punch

(15 to 18 servings)

Brother U. Gregory, The Christian Brothers, Napa

- 1 quart ripe strawberries, hulled
  Juice of 1/2 lemon
  Powdered sugar to taste
- 1 (4/5 qt.) bottle California Rhine Wine or Chablis
- 1 (4/5 qt.) bottle California Champagne
- 1 pint sparkling water

Place strawberries in punchbowl, sprinkle with lemon juice and powdered sugar. Pour 1/2 bottle of Rhine wine over this and refrigerate for 3 hours. Just before serving, place good size chunk of ice in bowl, add remainder of wine, Champagne and sparkling water. Stir lightly and serve in punch glasses, allowing a few strawberries to each glass.

Pink Parfait Punch

(6 to 8 servings)

Mrs. John A. Pedroncelli, John Pedroncelli Winery, Geyserville

This was concocted in our kitchen after much fun and experimentation. It makes a wonderful after-dinner drink because it's so delightful to see and sip.

- 1 quart vanilla ice cream, slightly softened
- 1 quart ginger ale, chilled
- 1 (4/5 qt.) bottle California Rosé or California Pink Champagne

Beat together ice cream and ginger ale until smooth. Combine with wine and serve immediately in tall glasses.

Wedding Punch

(36 servings)

Mrs. Roy H. Richardson, Paul Masson Vineyards, Saratoga

I use this punch for afternoon affairs when men are included. It's not too sweet. This recipe was chosen as favorite punch by the Culinary Artists group of Sunnyvale Newcomer's Club.

- 1/2 gallon California White Port
- 1 (4/5 qt.) bottle vodka
- 1 (46 oz.) can pink pineapple-grapefruit juice

Mix ingredients and chill thoroughly. When ready to serve, pour over ice in punch bowl. Garnish with fruit, if desired.

APPETIZERS

Appetizer Wines, an array of tasty bites and crisp crackers, will help to launch a memorable meal. However, taste buds should not be drowned at the cocktail hour, nor hunger satisfied. The following collection, ranging from a presentation worthy of Lucullus (ancient Rome's foremost gourmet) to simple dips, can be adapted to your needs. If you plan to serve several hors d'oeuvres, vary textures, temperature and flavors. All the California wine selections accompanying the tempting appetizers offered will fulfill their role of providing good fellowship and heightening appetites. Then — on to the table!

Seasoned Croutons

(4 cups)

Mr. E. A. Mirassou, Mirassou Vineyards, San Jose

Editor's note: The Sherry flavor in these croutons is subtle, but delightful. Mr. Mirassou uses sour dough French bread to make this dish. Where available, it makes especially fine croutons.

    1   stale (1 lb.) loaf of French bread
    1   cup (2 sticks) butter
    1   clove garlic
    1/4 teaspoon sage
    1/2 teaspoon oregano
    1   cup parsley, chopped
    1/2 teaspoon seasoned salt
    1/4 teaspoon seasoned pepper
    1/4 teaspoon ground celery seed
    5   ounces California Dry Sherry

Cut bread into 1/2-inch cubes. Put on a cookie sheet and bake in a moderate oven until light brown. Put aside in large mixing bowl. In a saucepan, melt butter and sauté garlic. When garlic is brown, discard. To remaining butter, add seasoning ingredients. Pour this over the toasted bread cubes and stir until butter and seasoning are evenly distributed. Sprinkle with wine. Return to oven and bake at 350° for about 20 minutes.
My choice of wine to accompany this dish:
CALIFORNIA MEDIUM OR DRY SHERRY
NOTE: These croutons can be used in soups or salads as well as for nibbling. Can be stored in refrigerator in air-tight jar. Remember to crisp them in oven before use.

Sherried Walnuts

(2 cups)

Mrs. A. C. Huntsinger, Almaden Vineyards, Los Gatos

These make wonderful snacks at any time.

    3/4   cup brown sugar
    2   tablespoons California Sherry
    1   tablespoon light corn syrup
    1-1/2 cups walnut meats

Combine sugar, Sherry and syrup in bowl. Add walnut meats and stir until well coated. Roll in sugar and put on wax paper to dry.
My choice of wine to accompany this dish:
CALIFORNIA PORT

Party Pâté

(3 generous cups)

Mrs. Anne Matteoli, Italian Swiss Colony Winery, Asti

This makes an inexpensive pâté to be spread on party crackers.

    1   (3 oz.) package frozen chicken livers
    1   (10-1/2 oz.) can consommé
 1/2 pound butter or margarine
    1   tablespoon unflavored gelatin
    2   tablespoons California Sherry
 1/8 teaspoon pepper

Thaw and chop livers coarsely. In a saucepan, heat consommé and butter. Gently poach livers in this liquid until they turn pale pink. In cup, combine gelatin and wine. When gelatin is soft, add to hot mixture and stir until dissolved. Add seasoning, turn into blender and blend at high speed until smooth. Pour into 4-cup mold and chill. When set, unmold in the center of large dish and surround with various types of crackers.

NOTE: A delicate accompaniment would be California Pale Dry Sherry or a Rosé.

Shrimp Sauterne

(15 servings)

Mrs. Elaine Filippi, J. Filippi Vintage Co., Mira Loma

This recipe is one of our favorites when entertaining dinner guests. The men especially enjoy it because it is always tasty and a little more filling than most appetizers.

 1/2 cup butter
    1   tablespoon lemon juice
    4   small cloves garlic, pressed
 3/4 cup parsley, finely chopped
 1/2 teaspoon green chili sauce
 1/2 cup California Sauterne
 1/2 teaspoon salt
 1/2 teaspoon pepper
    2   pounds medium-size shrimp, shelled and deveined

Melt butter in large frying pan and add all ingredients except shrimp. Stir and simmer for about 5 minutes. Add the shrimp in an even layer. Cover and simmer for 15 minutes, turning occasionally, until shrimp are evenly pink. Uncover and allow sauce to reduce. Serve hot on toothpicks on serving tray. Garnish with parsley. If made ahead of time, cover with foil and keep warm in oven.

My choice of wine to accompany this dish:
CALIFORNIA CHAMPAGNE OR DRY SHERRY

Dipsy Noodles

(about 20 balls)

Mrs. Leonard Maullin, Milford Co. of California, Los Angeles

This is a "fun" hors d'oeuvre.

    1   (3 oz.) package cream cheese
    2   teaspoons anchovy paste
    2   teaspoons California Dry Sherry
        Cayenne pepper to taste
    1   cup chow-mein noodles, coarsely broken

In a small mixing bowl, blend cheese, anchovy paste, wine and cayenne. Shape mixture into small balls and refrigerate for at least 2 hours. Just before serving, roll cheese balls in noodle crumbs.

My choice of wine to accompany this dish:
CALIFORNIA APÉRITIF or DRY TABLE WINE

NOTE: These cheese and anchovy balls can also be rolled in finely chopped nuts, parsley, or chives for interesting variations.

Vintner's Cheese Spread

(9 servings)

Mrs. Andrew L. Frei, Frei Brothers Winery, Santa Rosa

Refrigerated, this will keep for several weeks.

    1   (8-1/2 oz.) box Cheddar cheese spread
    1   (9 oz.) package cream cheese
 1/2 pound blue cheese, mashed smooth
    1   teaspoon Worcestershire sauce
        Pinch of cayenne
    3   tablespoons California Sauterne or Dry Sherry

Bring all cheeses to room temperature and mash together in a bowl. Add seasoning and wine. Turn into blender and whip together. Put in bowls or mold, cover and refrigerate until well chilled. Serve with crackers.

NOTE: This hearty combination mellows nicely. California Dry Sherry, Port or Burgundy would be excellent with this spread.

Stuffed French Rolls

(40 appetizers)

Mrs. Sam Sebastiani, Samuele Sebastiani Winery, Sonoma

These rolls, after being stuffed, can be frozen for a future date. When half thawed, they will slice with ease. This is a delightful hors d'oeuvre and can be served on any occasion, alone or with something else.

    1   small (about 1-1/2 lbs.) salami, ground
    2   (5 oz.) jars sharp Cheddar cheese spread
 3/4 cup California Red Wine
    6   large French rolls

In a mixing bowl, combine salami, cheese, and wine. Hollow out rolls and fill with the salami mixture. Chill overnight to get desired consistency for slicing. When ready to serve, slice thinly with sharp knife.

My choice of wine to accompany this dish:
CALIFORNIA BARBERA

Bacon and Liver Tidbits

(8 servings)

Mrs. Harold Berg, Dept. of Viticulture and Enology,
University of California, Davis

        4   strips bacon, cut in 1 inch pieces
      1/4   cup onion, chopped
      1/4   cup green pepper, chopped
    1-1/2   pounds chicken livers
        1   cup California Burgundy
      1/2   cup parsley, chopped
             Salt and Pepper to taste

In a frying pan, sauté bacon until crisp. Remove from pan and set aside. Sauté onion and pepper in bacon drippings until soft, add chicken livers, cut in halves. When livers are lightly browned, add wine. Blend and simmer for about 10 minutes. Add bacon, parsley, salt and pepper. Serve in a chafing dish or over warmer.

NOTE: A California Medium Sherry would be a pleasant flavor partner with the livers. Guests can spear tidbits with toothpicks or livers can be served with buttered toastpoints.

PORKY PINEAPPLE is from Brother Justin, of the Christian Brothers, Napa. These wonderfully tasty things are easy to make, and can be done long before guests arrive. Simply drain 1 (14 oz.) can of pineapple chunks. Put chunks in bowl and cover with California Medium or Sweet Sherry. After marinating for at least an hour, drain and wrap each chunk in a small strip of bacon, holding bacon in place with a toothpick. Broil until bacon is lightly browned. A Medium California Sherry or Port would be a good accompaniment to these tidbits.

Easy Cocktail Franks

(6 servings)

Mrs. Douglas Richards, Weibel Champagne Vineyards,
Mission San Jose

Editor's note: Zesty flavor; quick and good.

        1   pound hot dogs, cut in bite-size
             pieces, (or cocktail franks)
      3/4   cup catsup
      1/4   cup brown sugar
      3/4   cup California Sauterne
             Dash of Worcestershire sauce
             Dash of liquid pepper sauce

In saucepan, combine ingredients and heat to boiling. Simmer for a few minutes, then remove to chafing dish. Serve with small bowl of mustard and one of hot chili sauce for dipping.

NOTE: Serve Medium or Dry California Sherry with this.

Fresno Liverwurst Spread

Mr. Scott Richert, Richert & Sons, Morgan Hill

      1/2   pound liverwurst
        1   (3 oz.) package cream cheese
      1/4   cup cream
        1   tablespoon butter, melted
        1   tablespoon Worcestershire sauce
        1   pinch of curry powder (optional)
      1/4   cup California Dry Sherry

In small mixing bowl, mash liverwurst and cheese together, then add other ingredients. Blend well, cover and refrigerate several hours to mellow and blend flavors. Serve with unsalted crackers.

NOTE: California Dry Sherry or Chablis go well with this.

Saratoga Chicken Livers

(8 servings)

Mrs. Stanford J. Wolf, Paul Masson Vineyards, Saratoga

Editor's note: Although these are simple to make they have an excellent flavor.

        4   tablespoons butter
        1   pound chicken livers cut into
             bite-size pieces
      1/2   cup California Madeira
        2   teaspoons parsley, chopped
      1/2   teaspoon salt
             Pepper

In a frying pan, melt butter and sauté livers over moderate heat. When brown, add wine, parsley, and seasoning. Simmer 10 minutes or until livers are tender. Serve hot with cocktail picks.

NOTE: Serve with California Dry Sherry or Dry Sauterne.

Anchovy Delight

(12 servings)

Mr. N. C. Mirassou, Mirassou Vineyards, San Jose

Editor's note: This appetizer has a strong taste, but it's good. The anchovies make an attractive display. Serve them on a platter with crackers or Melba toast.

        4   (2 oz.) cans anchovy fillets
      3/4   cup parsley, finely chopped
        4   small cloves of garlic, minced
             California wine vinegar

Drain anchovy fillets and arrange, one layer thick, in form of star on large platter. Cover with finely chopped parsley and garlic. Sprinkle freely with vinegar. Chill in refrigerator for 2 or 3 hours.

My choice of wine to accompany this dish:
CALIFORNIA CHAMPAGNE

Cheddar Dip

(8 to 12 servings)

Miss Mary Lester, San Jose

Simple fare is the best, and I get raves over this.

- 1 pound Cheddar cheese
- 1 teaspoon paprika
- 1/4 teaspoon salt
- 1 cup California Sauterne or Dry Sherry

In chafing dish melt and combine cheese, seasoning and half the wine. When well blended, add other half of wine. Serve warm with hot crackers for dipping.

My choice of wine to accompany this dish:
CALIFORNIA COCKTAIL SHERRY, WELL CHILLED

NOTE: Miss Lester says that this easy dip along with three or four other appetizers, such as olives, radishes, salted nuts, before a simple meal of fried chicken and green salad, would be good party fare for those who do not have much time for cooking. She suggests a California Chablis with the meal.

SHRIMP CHEESE APPETIZER. Mrs. Robert J. Weaver, Dept. of Viticulture and Enology, University of California, Davis, serves this hot hors d'oeuvre with small rounds of rye bread. Heat 1/4 cup California Sauterne with 1 (16 oz.) jar Cheddar-type cheese spread and 1/2 pound fresh shrimp, cooked, in chafing dish. Serves 10.

Cranberry Shrimp

(10 servings)

Mrs. John G. Laucci, Franzia Brothers Winery, Ripon

This is a colorful dip for Christmas or New Year's Eve.

- 1 (1 lb.) can jellied cranberry sauce
- 2 teaspoons California wine vinegar
- 1/2 teaspoon prepared mustard
- 1 fresh pineapple
  (don't cut the leaves off)
- 1/4 cup California Sherry
- 1 pound shrimp, cooked, shelled and deveined

Several hours ahead, whirl in blender (or press through a sieve) cranberry sauce, vinegar, and mustard. Refrigerate for a couple of hours until well chilled. In the meantime, split pineapple in half. Cut out pineapple meat in chunks being careful not to cut through outside skin. Combine chunks with wine and marinate 30 minutes or longer. Drain liquid into cranberry mixture. Place pineapple halves end to end on a serving dish and fill them with cranberry mixture. Arrange pineapple chunks and shrimp around filled pineapple shells.

NOTE: Serve a California Sherry or Port with this.

BOBBY'S FRANKS is the invention of Bobby Bagnani, 10, son of the late Bill Bagnani, of the Geyser Peak Winery, Geyserville. He loves to prepare appetizers. For this hors d'oeuvre, cut some frankfurters in bite-size pieces and poach in a saucepan for a few minutes with enough California white wine to cover. Spear them with toothpicks and serve on a plate with other appetizers.

NOTE: The same California white wine used in the franks would accompany this admirably.

Alaska King Crab Platter

(6 servings)

Mrs. Sam Sebastiani, Samuele Sebastiani Winery, Sonoma

This looks and tastes delicious and is usually the center of attraction at any social gathering.

- Endive
- 6 slices toast
- 1-1/2 pounds king crab meat
- 1/2 cup California Vin Rosé
- 6 tablespoons mayonnaise
- 1/2 cup parsley, chopped
- 8 stuffed olives
- 6 wedges of lemon
- 6 hard-cooked eggs
- 1 tomato, finely chopped
- 1/4 teaspoon tarragon
  Salt and pepper to taste
  Paprika
- 8 ripe olives
- 1 dozen wheat triangles
  or potato chips

Use large platter and garnish with endive. Cut toast in triangles and trim edges. Mix finely chopped crab meat, reserving all large pieces, wine and 3 tablespoons mayonnaise. Spread evenly on toast, garnish edges with parsley. Slice stuffed olives and place in center of each piece of toast. Alternate wedges of toast with lemon on edge of platter. Cut ends from hard-cooked eggs and scoop out the yolks. Add tomato, tarragon, mayonnaise, salt and pepper. Stuff egg whites with mixture, piling it high. Top with remaining mayonnaise and dust with paprika. Place on each end of platter. Place large pieces of crab meat in center of platter alternating with ripe olives. Place wheat triangles or potato chips around crab meat and serve with your favorite dip.

My choice of wine to accompany this dish:
CALIFORNIA BRUT CHAMPAGNE OR DRY SHERRY

SOUPS

"Soup of the evening, beautiful, beautiful soup," as the Mock Turtle sang in Alice in Wonderland. The soups here presented are made more beautiful by the addition of California wines, which add their warmth and tang to the first course that cheers a winter night's meal, or cools and calms a summer noontime. Everything from minestrone to a delicate bisque can be lifted to new heights of flavor by wine. Many thick soups — like vegetable soup — benefit by being made the day before serving, to allow flavor to ripen. Although Sherry is a classical accompaniment to soup, it is worthwhile to try the specific wine suggestion that follows each recipe.

Crab Bisque
(6 to 8 servings)

Mrs. Otto E. Meyer, Paul Masson Vineyards, Saratoga

1 (10-3/4 oz.) can tomato soup
1 (11-1/4 oz.) can green pea soup
2 cups milk or half milk-half cream
Meat of 1 large crab, cut in bite size pieces
1/2 cup California Dry Sherry

Heat soups and milk in double boiler. Add crabmeat and when very hot, add Sherry. Serve immediately.

NOTE: This is a different approach to canned soups and nice to begin a company dinner. If fresh crabmeat is not available, 2 (7-1/2 oz.) cans of crabmeat may be substituted with good results. The soup course could be served with the same California Dry Sherry used in preparing the bisque.

Celery-Mushroom Bisque
(4 to 6 servings)

Mrs. George Al Berry, E. & J. Gallo Winery, Modesto

I have served this dish as a light supper accompanied simply by crackers or slices of hot French bread. However, smaller servings of it could precede a full dinner.

1 carrot, shredded
2 green onions, thinly sliced
2 tablespoons butter or margarine
1 (10-1/2 oz.) can condensed cream of celery soup
1 (10-1/2 oz.) can condensed cream of mushroom soup
1-1/4 soup cans milk
1/4 cup California Sherry
1/8 teaspoon nutmeg
1/3 cup almonds, finely chopped

Lightly brown carrot and green onions in butter. Thoroughly blend in soups, milk, Sherry and nutmeg. Heat, stirring often, until bisque is hot but not boiling. Serve with sprinkling of almonds on top.

My choice of wine to accompany this dish:
CALIFORNIA GREY RIESLING, CHABLIS OR SAUTERNE

Hasty Minestrone

(4 servings)

Mrs. Joe Roullard, Petri Winery, Escalon

This recipe evolved from the nights a quick and easy meal was desired and leftover roast was on hand.

    1/2 cup California Burgundy
    2-1/2 cups water
       1 (2-5/16 oz.) envelope minestrone soup mix
    1 to 1-1/2 cups leftover roast beef, cubed
       1 small zucchini, sliced
          Parmesan cheese, grated

Bring wine and water to boil. Add soup mix and beef, simmer for 10 minutes. Add zucchini and simmer for another 5 minutes. Serve hot in soup bowls, sprinkled with cheese.

NOTE: Mrs. Roullard serves this hearty soup with crackers or hot buttered French bread, a platter of raw vegetables like carrots, cucumber and tomato slices, and winds up with apple pie and cheese. California Burgundy would go well with the meal.

Quick Onion Soup

(4 servings)

Mrs. Robert Diana, Villa Armando Winery, Pleasanton

       1 (10-1/2 oz.) can Campbell's
          condensed onion soup
       1 (13 oz.) can Habitant
          French onion soup
    1/4 cup California Burgundy
       1 large slice French bread for each
          serving, browned in butter
    1/2 cup Parmesan cheese, grated

Combine soups in saucepan, blending well over low heat. Just before thoroughly heated, add wine and bring to boiling point. Place slice browned bread in hot soup plates, ladle soup over bread and pass grated cheese.

Davis Consommé

(1 quart)

Mrs. Emil Mrak, University of California, Davis

       2 cups chicken consommé or broth
       2 cups tomato juice
       1 stalk celery, sliced very thin
       1 green onion and stalk sliced thin,
          or any other raw vegetable sliced thin
    1/2 cup Dry California Chablis

Heat consommé and tomato juice to boiling. Put everything else into hot tureen, pour soup over and serve at once.

NOTE: Simple and good. Other vegetables which could be added: carrot shavings, sliced canned water chestnuts. With the soup pour the same California Chablis.

Avocado Soup

(4 servings)

Mrs. Jack L. Davies, Schramsberg Vineyard Co., Calistoga

I have a habit of making stock from unused vegetable portions, leftover fish, poultry, game and meat bones to be used later in soup or broth. This was an accident that turned out to be a reasonable combination.

       2 cups chicken broth
       2 cups clam or shrimp broth, strained
       1 whole avocado, peeled and seeded
    1/8 teaspoon cayenne or, for variety, use
          dash of curry powder to taste
    1/4 cup California Dry Sherry

Heat liquids. Blend avocado smooth in blender with part of hot liquid. Combine all ingredients, stirring well. Heat to serving point. Float lemon slice on individual serving.

My choice of wine to accompany this dish:
CALIFORNIA BRUT CHAMPAGNE, JOHANNISBERG RIESLING, SYLVANER, CHABLIS OR CHENIN BLANC

NOTE: Mrs. Davies pleases guests by serving this as a first course for summer lunches on the veranda, followed by a chicken or game mousse, cold vegetable salad and hot rolls. Bottled clam broth may be substituted for home-simmered fish stock.

Garbanzo Soup

(8 to 10 servings)

Mrs. John Franzia, Sr., Franzia Brothers Winery, Ripon

Years ago when I was given this recipe, my mother-in-law used the Italian dry mushrooms soaked in boiling water and chopped; however I found that golden mushroom soup gives the same flavor when the dry mushrooms are not available.

       1 small onion, chopped
       3 tablespoons butter
       3 tablespoons olive oil
       1 (15-1/2 oz.) can garbanzo beans
       2 (10-1/2 oz.) cans condensed
          golden mushroom soup
    1-1/2 cups water
       1 cup California Claret
       1 teaspoon fresh salvia (sage), chopped
    1/2 teaspoon each rosemary, marjoram,
          basil, chopped
       1 teaspoon salt
       2 cloves garlic, chopped

Sauté chopped onion in butter and oil until soft. Add all other ingredients as listed. Simmer slowly for 10 minutes. Serve hot with French bread croutons; sprinkle with Parmesan cheese. This soup is better the next day when reheated.

My choice of wine to accompany this dish:
CALIFORNIA ZINFANDEL OR CLARET

NOTE: Mrs. Franzia mentions that this is a good hearty soup to serve during cold weather. After it she likes to serve pork or lamb chops, sautéed artichokes and a light dessert. For variation 1/2 cup cooked rice can be added to above ingredients and simmered for about 15 minutes. Omit croutons when serving with rice.

Onion Soup Antonette

(3 servings)

Mrs. John Franzia, Sr., Franzia Brothers Winery, Ripon

1 (1-3/8 oz.) package onion soup mix
2 cups boiling water
1 cup California Sauterne

Combine ingredients, bring to boil, lower heat and simmer 10 minutes. Serve with buttered croutons.

NOTE: The California Sauterne gives this jiffy recipe real flair and could be poured with the whole meal.

Vegetable Soup

(4 to 6 servings)

Mrs. Emil Mrak, University of California, Davis

1 onion, sliced
1 tablespoon butter
1 (10 oz.) package frozen mixed vegetables
1 cup water
2 cups chicken broth or consommé
1/4 cup California Cocktail Sherry
Salt and pepper to taste

Sauté onion in butter until barely tender. Add frozen mixed vegetables and water. Cook 5 to 8 minutes until vegetables are barely tender. Remove from stove and blend until smooth in blender. If necessary strain through sieve. Add chicken broth or consommé, Sherry, salt and pepper to taste. Reheat quickly and serve at once. Each bowl may be garnished with 1 tablespoon of sour cream, if desired.

NOTE: This speedy soup has a genuine homemade flavor and would go nicely with a glass of California Cocktail Sherry.

TWO PREPARED SOUPS are perked up with California Sherry. Mrs. Anne Matteoli, Italian Swiss Colony Winery, Asti, adds 1 ounce of California Sherry to each cup of hot beef broth or bouillon for a quick pick-me-up on a cold day. Dr. Emil Mrak, Chancellor Emeritus, University of California, Davis, suggests adding 1/4 cup California Dry Sherry to 1 (11 oz.) can black bean soup (prepared as label directs), which takes a plain soup out of the ordinary. He says this treatment is good with hot dog bean and bacon bean soups as well.

Cherry Soup

(8 servings)

Miss Nina Alexeeff, Wine Institute, San Francisco

A Canadian friend gave me this recipe. It is one of his specialties, which, I may add, is very good.

2 (16 oz.) cans pitted red cherries, packed in water
1/2 cup sugar
4 teaspoons cornstarch
1/2 teaspoon salt
1/2 teaspoon cinnamon
4 strips orange peel (optional)
1 cup orange juice
1 cup California Burgundy

Place all ingredients except Burgundy in blender. Cover and mix at high speed for 20 seconds. Pour mixture into double boiler and cook at medium heat, stirring constantly until mixture boils and thickens. Remove from heat and stir in wine.

ANOTHER CHERRY SOUP is one from Mr. Fred Cherry (appropriately), Wine Discoveries, San Anselmo. Remove stones from 1 pound of fresh sour pie cherries, add 1 cup water, small pieces of cinnamon and lemon peel. Boil 10 minutes, remove cinnamon and peel; purée cherries in blender. Bring 1 cup California Zinfandel or Cabernet to a boil, thicken with 1 teaspoon cornstarch, add sugar and almond extract to taste. Combine with puréed cherries and serve very hot with a dollop of sour cream on top. This German soup is fine served tart and hot at beginning of meal, or sweeter and chilled after the meat course. Serves 4.

Onion Soup Goorigian

(4 servings)

Mrs. Greg Goorigian, Vie-Del Company, Fresno

1 (10-1/2 oz.) can beef broth
1 (10-1/2 oz.) can condensed onion soup
1 cup water
1/3 cup California Sauterne
1/4 teaspoon Worcestershire sauce
2 tablespoons mayonnaise
2 tablespoons Parmesan cheese, grated
4 (2 inch) rounds of toasted French bread

Stir soups, water, wine, Worcestershire together in a sauce pan. Bring to simmering. Mix mayonnaise and grated cheese and spread on toast rounds. Broil slowly until mixture bubbles. Pour hot soup into bowls, top each with toast round and serve immediately.

NOTE: A glass of California Sauterne would enhance this soup.

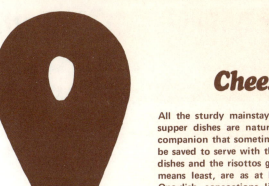

PASTA
Cheese, Eggs and Rice

All the sturdy mainstays in this category of luncheon, brunch or supper dishes are natural partners of wine. Cheese? So perfect a companion that sometimes your finest California red table wine will be saved to serve with the cheese at the end of a meal. All the pasta dishes and the risottos grew up with wine; and eggs, last but by no means least, are as at home with wine as they are with butter. One-dish concoctions like these, perfumed with herbs or garlic, bathed in wine-based, creamy sauces and powdered with cheese that turns the top gold and bubbly, have a special appeal to the appetite that cannot be ignored.

Spanish Omelet

(6 servings)

Mrs. Herbert L. Grosswendt, Brookside Vineyard Company, Guasti

This recipe, without the addition of wine or sausage, was given to me years ago by a friend from Malaga, Spain. This is a real "Spanish Omelet" — not the tomato type omelet given that name in this country.

1 pound Italian sausage, sweet or hot, depending on taste
6 potatoes, thinly sliced
6 medium onions, thinly sliced
6 eggs, beaten
1 teaspoon seasoned salt
1/8 teaspoon pepper
1/4 cup California Sauterne

Cook sausage in large omelet pan or skillet till done. Cut in bite size pieces and reserve in warm oven. Pour off all but 2 tablespoons of fat and cook raw potatoes and onions in it until just done. Beat eggs, add salt, pepper and Sauterne. Add meat to skillet and pour eggs over mixture. Cook as for omelet until done. Cut in wedge-shaped pieces and serve.

My choice of wine to accompany this dish:
CALIFORNIA RHINE OR RIESLING

Ethelwyn's Egg Delicacy

(6 servings)

Mrs. Kenneth O. Dills, Charles Krug Winery, St. Helena

I like to serve this for luncheon along with fresh broccoli and a jellied fruit salad.

4 tablespoons butter
4 tablespoons flour
2 cups milk or light cream
Salt to taste
5 tablespoons California Dry Sherry
1/2 teaspoon dry mustard
1/2 cup sharp Cheddar cheese, grated
5 tablespoons chili sauce
8 eggs, hard cooked
6 English muffins, split, toasted and buttered

Melt butter, stir in flour and cook gently for 1 minute. Slowly stir in milk or cream and cook over low heat until sauce thickens. Add Sherry and heat a minute or two longer. Add all other seasonings and keep hot but below boiling while stirring in sliced, hard-cooked eggs. Serve immediately on warm muffins.

My choice of wine to accompany this dish:
CALIFORNIA CHENIN BLANC OR ROSÉ

Rice Dressing for Turkey

(about 10 cups)

Mrs. Alvin Ehrhardt, Allied Grape Growers, Madera

Some like this stuffing better than the traditional bread mixture. The recipe was given to me by Mrs. Alpha Quilici of Murphys, California, who is noted for her sumptuous dinner parties in the Mother Lode country.

      2 pounds ground beef
  1-1/2 pounds bulk pork sausage
      2 small cloves garlic, minced fine
      2 large onions, chopped
      1 bunch parsley, chopped
  2-1/2 cups cooked rice
      6 eggs, beaten
    1/4 cup California Dry Sherry
         Salt, pepper and poultry seasoning
         to taste

Fry beef and sausage together until cooked; cool. Fry garlic and onion together until soft; cool. Add parsley and combine rice, meat and onion mixture in large bowl, add beaten eggs, Sherry and seasonings, mix and stuff bird. Allow approximately 1/2 cup of stuffing per pound.

My choice of wine to accompany this dish:
CALIFORNIA DRY WHITE TABLE WINE OR ROSÉ

NOTE: This stuffing can be baked separately in a casserole topped with grated cheese, in a 375° oven for 20 to 30 minutes, and served as an entrée in its own right.

Risotto with Pesto

(6 servings)

Mr. Dante Bagnani, Geyser Peak Winery, Geyserville

This is good with baked or barbecued lamb ribs or breast.

    1/2 cup butter or margarine
      1 (4 oz.) can pesto (basil chopped
         with garlic, available in Italian
         delicatessens)
      3 cups bouillon or chicken broth
      1 cup California Sauterne or
         other white wine
    1/2 teaspoon salt
    1/4 teaspoon pepper
  1-1/2 cups uncooked long grain rice
    1/2 cup grated Parmesan or
         Monterey Cheese

In heavy skillet or Dutch oven, combine butter, pesto, broth and wine, salt and pepper to taste. Bring to boil, add rice, stir and simmer uncovered 25 minutes or until rice is cooked and all liquid absorbed. Stir in cheese.

My choice of wine to accompany this dish:
SAME WINE USED IN RECIPE

NOTE: Mr. Bagnani points out that pesto can also be made fresh when basil is in season. Chop finely, with plenty of garlic. Preserve in refrigerator in small jars, covering herb mixture with olive oil.

Baked Rice with Shrimp

(4 servings)

Mrs. Louis J. Foppiano, L. Foppiano Wine Company, Healdsburg

    1/2 cup butter
      1 medium onion, minced
    1/2 clove garlic, crushed
  1-1/2 cups raw regular rice
  3-3/4 cups chicken stock
    1/2 cup California Dry White Wine
    1/8 teaspoon powdered saffron
      1 tablespoon boiling water
      1 pound shrimp, cooked,
         shelled and deveined
    3/4 cup Parmesan cheese, grated

Sauté onion and garlic until soft but not brown in melted butter. Add rice, stirring constantly until golden brown. Add chicken stock, wine and saffron which has been dissolved in boiling water. Bring to a rolling boil. Transfer rice mixture to a 2-1/2 quart buttered casserole. Cover tightly and bake in a 350° oven for 35 to 45 minutes until rice is tender and fluffy and all liquid has been absorbed. Stir in shrimp and 1/2 cup grated cheese. Sprinkle top with remaining cheese and return to oven to bake 10 to 15 minutes longer until browned on top.

NOTE: Toasted garlic bread and a tray of raw relishes with this dish would be pleasant to serve as a luncheon to be accompanied by a California Grey Riesling. If no homemade chicken stock is available, 3 (10-1/2 oz.) cans of chicken broth may be substituted.

Spaghetti Carbonara

(4 servings)

Mrs. Germano Colombana, Wine Advisory Board, San Francisco

Editor's note: All other preparations should be made while water comes to boil and spaghetti cooks. This is something new and different in spaghetti lore.

    1   pound spaghetti
    3   eggs, beaten
    1/3 cup Parmesan cheese, grated
    1/3 cup Romano cheese, grated
    6   slices bacon, diced fine
    2   tablespoons olive oil
    1/3 cup California Dry Sauterne
    1/2 teaspoon pepper

Cook spaghetti in salted boiling water about 8 minutes (still slightly firm when bitten). Have eggs at room temperature; beat with grated cheeses. Fry diced bacon in olive oil until crisp. Pour off all but about 4 tablespoons of fat, add wine and continue cooking until wine evaporates. Drain spaghetti, return to hot sauce pan, add cheese-egg mixture, hot bacon-oil mixture and pepper. Stir rapidly so egg mixture cooks onto hot spaghetti. Serve on hot plates, adding a lump of butter to each, if desired.

NOTE: Serve a California Chianti with this dish.

Five-Minute Spaghetti

(4 to 6 servings)

Mrs. John Franzia, Sr., Franzia Brothers Winery, Ripon

With this dish I like to serve breaded veal, green peas and wine gelatin for dessert.

    4   small cloves garlic, minced
    2   tablespoons butter
    2   tablespoons olive oil
    1   (6 oz.) can tomato paste
    1/3 cup California Burgundy
        Salt and pepper to taste
    1   (14 oz.) package long Italian
        style spaghettini
    1   cup Parmesan cheese, grated

Cook garlic slowly for three minutes in butter and olive oil. Add tomato paste, wine and simmer for 5 minutes. Meanwhile boil spaghettini in 4 quarts salted water for 10 minutes. Drain, add sauce and Parmesan cheese, toss lightly and serve immediately.

My choice of wine to accompany this dish:
CALIFORNIA BURGUNDY OR CLARET

NOTE: For a variation add 1 (7-1/2 oz.) can of minced clams to sauce, or 1 (7-1/2 oz.) can crabmeat. With these seafood variations Mrs. Franzia prefers a California Sauterne or Riesling.

Noodle-Rice Medley

(10 servings)

Mrs. V. E. Petrucci, Fresno State College, Fresno

This was given to me by a friend, Noreene Biehler, years ago, but I have altered it somewhat including the name.

    2   packages Lipton's chicken-noodle soup
    3   tablespoons butter
    1   medium size onion, chopped
    2   large celery leaves, chopped
    1   medium size green pepper, chopped
    2   tablespoons red pimiento, chopped
    1   tablespoon olive oil
    1   cup uncooked rice
    1/2 cup California Sauterne
    3-1/2 cups water
    1   cup slivered almonds

Sauté noodles from packaged soup in just enough butter to cover bottom of pan. Sauté onion, celery, pepper and pimiento in olive oil (if preferred, butter can be substituted.) Add 2 packages of soup, rice, sautéed vegetables, noodles and wine to boiling water. Mix well, add slivered almonds, dot with remaining butter and bake 1 hour at 350° covered.

My choice of wine to accompany this dish:
CALIFORNIA CHABLIS OR CABERNET

NOTE: Mrs. Petrucci says that this versatile recipe can be made into a Lenten dish by adding 1 pound small, cooked shrimp before popping into oven. In addition it can be served as a main dish by adding 1 pound cooked pork sausage before baking.

Lasagna Bahama

(12 servings)

Mrs. David R. Cofran, The Christian Brothers, Napa

This wonderful old dish is originally from Nassau in the Bahama Islands and has been in our family for years. It is an easy and delicious dish for large dinner parties.

    2   pounds chuck, ground
    4   cloves garlic, minced
    1-1/2 teaspoons salt
    1/4 teaspoon pepper
    4   (8 oz.) cans tomato sauce
    1/2 cup California Burgundy
    2   (8 oz.) packages cream cheese
    2   (1 pint) cartons sour cream
    2   (1 pint) cartons cottage cheese
    2   large onions, minced
    1   (10 oz.) package lasagne noodles

Sauté meat with garlic, salt and pepper. Add tomato sauce and wine; simmer one-half hour. Mix cream cheese, sour cream, cottage cheese and onion in separate bowl. Place layer of cooked noodles in bottom of baking dish. Cover with layer of cheese mixture. Repeat and continue until used up. Cover with meat sauce and bake in 350° oven for 45 minutes.

My choice of wine to accompany this dish:
CALIFORNIA BURGUNDY, PINOT NOIR OR GAMAY

NOTE: When boiling noodles, add salt and a little cooking oil to the water. This helps to keep the noodles from sticking together.

Imaginative Omelet

(4 servings)

Mr. D. C. Turrentine, Wine Advisory Board, San Francisco

My brother, Don, cooked this for a Sunday brunch before a hungry and interested audience at his home in Chelmsford, Mass. It was delicious.

    1   cup bacon, fried lightly
    1   apple, peeled
    1   (2 oz.) jar mushrooms
  1/2   cup green pepper
    1   small onion
  1/4   pound sharp Cheddar cheese
    4   eggs
  1/4   cup California Medium Sherry

Finely chop bacon, apple, mushrooms, green pepper and onion. Put apple, mushrooms, green pepper and onion in teflon frying pan over medium heat. Add bacon, lay on cheese carefully (enough cheese to cover). When cheese melts, turn heat slightly lower. Salt and pepper to taste. Break eggs into bowl, add wine and beat well. Pour egg mixture over bacon mixture. Cover and cook about 10 minutes. When done, place serving plate over frying pan and carefully turn pan upside-down so that omelet lands on platter unbroken, with vegetables on top. Eggs and cheese will hold all ingredients together. Garnish with maraschino cherries and fresh parsley for added eye appeal.

My choice of wine to accompany this dish:
CALIFORNIA SAUTERNE OR CHABLIS

NOTE: If an electric frying pan is used, cook vegetable mixture at 350° and when cheese melts, turn heat to 300°. Add eggs and continue to cook at 300°.

Sour Cream and Tortillas

(6 servings)

Mrs. Alvin Ehrhardt, Allied Grape Growers, Madera

This sour cream and tortilla recipe makes a big hit at patio parties with young and old alike. Its mild rich flavor is an added delight with holiday dinners. I make it often for potluck suppers.

   12   large frozen tortillas
    1   medium onion, chopped
    1   tablespoon oil
    1   (20 oz.) can solid pack tomatoes
  1/2   cup California White Table Wine
    1   teaspoon oregano
        Salt to taste
  1/2   cup Parmesan cheese, grated
  1/2   cup Monterey Jack cheese, cubed
    1   pint sour cream
    1   cup American cheese, coarsely grated

Thaw tortillas. Arrange in large casserole. Sauté onions in hot oil, add tomatoes, wine, oregano and salt. Simmer 15 minutes. Pour sauce over tortillas, add Parmesan, and cubes of Monterey Jack cheese evenly over top. Spread sour cream over all. Cover, bake at 350° for 30 minutes. Add grated American cheese and bake uncovered 5 to 10 minutes longer. Serve with tossed green salad and fruit dessert.

NOTE: This is a good year-around casserole. For a patio party serve with a California Chablis.

Paul's Pilaf

(6 servings)

Mr. Paul H. Huber, Wine Brokerage, Fresno

We use this rice dish with ham, lamb, beef, chicken and fish. Takes the place of potatoes with any menu and makes a curry more interesting, too.

  1/2   cup butter or margarine
    1   (2 oz.) package dehydrated chicken
        noodle soup
    1   onion, chopped
    1   green pepper, chopped
    1   cup raw regular rice
    2   cups California Chablis
  1/4   cup sliced almonds, toasted

Melt butter in heavy skillet. Add dehydrated soup, onion, green pepper and rice. Cook and stir until onions are soft but not browned. Add wine, bring to a boil. Cover and simmer until rice is tender, 25 to 30 minutes. Sprinkle almonds on top.

My choice of wine to accompany this dish:
CALIFORNIA CHABLIS OR RIESLING

TIRED RICE? When her family complained about the zestless taste of pre-cooked 5-minute rice, she served when hurried, Mrs. Al Nerelli, Pesenti Winery, Templeton, came up with a new, flavorsome dish. She added 1/2 cup California Dry Sauterne and when cooked, a handful of grated Cheddar cheese. "Wow! It tasted as though I had spent hours preparing it." Add a little wine and things turn out fine.

Cheese Medley

(8 servings)

Mrs. Evins R. Naman, Wine Institute, San Francisco

May be served as appetizer or dessert with any hearty meal.

- 2 envelopes unflavored gelatin
- 4 egg yolks
- 1 (10 oz.) package Camembert cheese, softened
- 1 (4 oz.) package Liederkranz cheese, softened
- 1 (2 oz.) package blue cheese, softened
- 1/4 pound butter, softened
- 1 tablespoon Dijon mustard
- 1/3 cup California Dry Sherry
- 1 cup whipping cream

Soften gelatin in 1/2 cup cold water; dissolve over hot water. Combine in large mixing bowl 4 well-beaten egg yolks, Camembert, Liederkranz and blue cheese. Whip butter until fluffy. Add whipped butter, dissolved gelatin and mustard to cheeses; beat until smooth. Stir in Sherry. Whip heavy cream; fold into cheese mixture. Spoon mixture into lightly oiled 6-cup mold; chill overnight. Unmold onto serving plate. Decorate edge of plate with small bunches of grapes, slices of apples, unsalted crackers.

NOTE: White wine can be substituted for water to dissolve gelatin. Whether Cheese Medley is served as appetizer or dessert we suggest a California Dry Sherry to accompany it.

Epicurean Risotto

(4 servings)

Mrs. Alessandro Baccari, Baccari Wine Festival, San Francisco

- 6 tablespoons butter
- 1 onion, chopped
- 1-1/4 cups uncooked rice
- 1 (1/2 oz.) package dried mushrooms, soaked in 1 cup cold water and drained
- 1/2 cup California Dry Sauterne
- 4 cups chicken broth
- 1/4 teaspoon saffron
- 1 cup Parmesan cheese, grated

Melt butter, sauté onion, rice and mushrooms until golden brown. Add wine and 3 cups chicken broth and simmer until liquid is absorbed, about 30 minutes. Five minutes before serving add saffron dissolved in remaining cup of broth, stir in cheese, cover and simmer for 5 minutes.

NOTE: An excellent risotto, good as main dish or with meats like veal or chicken, garnished with broiled tomatoes. A fine wine to accompany this dish is the California Dry Sauterne used in its preparation.

Manicotti Healdsburg

(4 servings)

Mrs. Leo Demostene, Soda Rock Winery, Healdsburg

Everyone to whom I have served this loves it. It can be made the day before, refrigerated overnight and baked the following day. Also it freezes well.

Editor's Note: Some may find half the sauce specified will suffice and may want to freeze the other half for future use.

- 1 cup chard or spinach, cooked, well drained and chopped
- 1 cup cottage cheese
- 1/2 cup Parmesan cheese, grated
- 1 egg
- 1 tablespoon basil or parsley chopped with
- 1 clove garlic
- 1/2 teaspoon salt and
- 1/16 teaspoon pepper to taste
- 1 (3-3/4 oz.) package manicotti

Mix well, stuff into uncooked manicotti and place in buttered baking dish in single layer, leaving space to allow for expansion during baking. Cover with following sauce:

SAUCE

- 1 pound ground chuck, browned
- 1/2 pound pork sausage, browned
- 1 medium onion, chopped
- 1/8 teaspoon pepper
- 1 teaspoon salt
- 1 teaspoon mixed Italian herbs
- 1/2 cup California Sauterne
- 1 (30 oz.) can solid pack tomatoes
- 1 (6 oz.) can tomato paste
- 1 (4 oz.) can sliced mushrooms, undrained

To crumbled browned meats, add onion, seasonings, wine and simmer a few minutes. Add whole tomatoes, tomato paste, mushrooms and simmer until flavors are well blended. Cover manicotti with sauce, sprinkle with cheese, cover with foil and bake 1 to 1-1/4 hours in 375° oven.

NOTE: Mrs. Demostene recommends the substitution of a meat filling of your choice for the cheese-vegetable mixture. To accompany this hearty dish we suggest a California Burgundy.

Mushrooms Benedict

(6 servings)

Mr. Evins R. Naman, Wine Institute, San Francisco

Editor's note: The author suggests serving crisp bacon and almond-paste stuffed peaches with this elegant dish to make a memorable brunch. The menu would make an equally good luncheon.

        3 tablespoons butter or margarine
    1/2 cup fresh mushrooms, coarsely chopped
    1/8 teaspoon salt
        Dash of pepper
    3/4 cup dairy sour cream
    1/8 teaspoon Worcestershire sauce
    1/4 teaspoon Dijon mustard
    3/4 cup sharp Cheddar cheese, shredded
    1/4 cup California Dry Sherry
        6 poached eggs
        3 English muffins, split,
            toasted and buttered

Melt butter in saucepan or large frying pan, add chopped mushrooms and brown slightly. Stir in salt, pepper, sour cream, Worcestershire, mustard and cheese; stir over low heat until cheese melts. Add Sherry. To prepare 6 poached eggs, place water in bottom of electric frying pan. Put 6 aluminum foil tart pans in pan, add dab of butter to each. Break egg into each tart pan, cover frying pan and cook until set, approximately 4 minutes. Egg is easy to transfer to muffin and retains a perfect shape. Cover muffins topped with eggs, which you have kept warm, with hot Benedict sauce and serve immediately.

My choice to serve before this Sunday brunch dish:
CALIFORNIA SHERRY FIZZ (See beverages, page 14)

NOTE: Another easy method for poaching eggs is to cut six rings 1/2 inch thick from large green pepper and place in skillet. Break one egg into each ring, add 1 tablespoon Sherry and 1 tablespoon water to skillet. Cover and cook until eggs are set. Eggs may be topped with fresh oregano or silver thyme if available. Cover with sauce above or your own favorite.

Fruit Curry

(6 servings)

Mrs. J. H. Elwood, Llords & Elwood Winery, Los Angeles

Nice for Sunday lunch — in Palm Springs — preceded by California Extra Dry Champagne.

        1 jar or (15 oz.) can preserved mangoes
        1 cup pineapple, diced, fresh or canned
        2 fresh peaches
        3 bananas, sliced
        2 cups sweet California Chenin Blanc
    1-1/2 cups chicken broth, or
            canned consommé
        3 tablespoons pistachio nuts, chopped
        3 tablespoons seedless raisins
        1 tablespoon arrowroot
    1 or 2 tablespoons curry powder, to taste
        4 cups cooked rice
            Shredded coconut

Gently mix well drained canned fruit with fresh fruit and pour wine over mixture. Refrigerate 2 hours, covered. Drain off wine and add to broth in saucepan. Simmer 15 minutes. Add nuts and raisins. Thicken sauce with arrowroot and add curry powder. Cook 1 minute longer. Serve rice, very hot, on individual plates, arrange cold fruits on it and pour over very hot curry sauce. Serve with shredded coconut.

My choice of wine to accompany this dish:
CALIFORNIA SWEET ROSÉ

Mushroom-Tuna Casserole

(10 servings)

Mrs. Fred Snyde, Woodbridge Vineyard Association, Lodi

This is ever so good for a large crowd, simple to prepare and can be made ahead of time.

    1-1/2 cups rice, uncooked
        1 onion, chopped
    1/2 cup celery, chopped fine
        1 (8 oz.) can water chestnuts,
            drained and sliced
        1 (4 oz.) jar pimiento, chopped
        1 cup whole blanched almonds, roasted
        1 (10-1/2 oz.) can cream of mushroom
            soup, diluted with
    1/2 cup California Sauterne
        2 (6-1/2 oz.) cans tuna
        1 (3 oz.) can Chinese crisp noodles
        2 (4 oz.) cans mushrooms
            Salt and pepper
        1 cup potato chips, crushed

Boil rice in salted water following directions on package, or your favorite method. Sauté onion and celery until golden and combine with cooked rice in large casserole. Add all other ingredients, season to taste with salt and pepper and mix well. Cover top with crushed potato chips and bake in 350° oven for 30 to 45 minutes, depending on depth of casserole.

NOTE: This recipe can be doubled successfully. Serve a California Dry Sauterne with casserole.

SAUCES

Wine, when used as a marinade, is wonderfully effective all by itself in giving tenderness and flavor to meat. Many of the sauces in this section are subtle combinations of herbs, spices and flavorings, but their soul and basis is wine. Bastes are here to barbecue the game or meat, which may inspire you to invent variations of your own. Other sauces will envelop your favorite pasta, glaze the ham, or garnish it. Wines to serve with the dishes these sauces embellish range over the whole rich variety of California table wines available everywhere.

Ham Sauce

(about 2 cups)

Mrs. Jake Rheingans, Sanger Winery Association, Sanger

- 1/2 cup brown sugar, firmly packed
- 1 tablespoon flour
- 1 tablespoon dry mustard
- 1-3/4 cups California Cream or Dry Sherry
- 1 tablespoon butter

Combine all ingredients and simmer until slightly thickened. Follow directions for preparing ham for baking, pour sauce over ham and marinate several hours or overnight. Bake in oven and baste frequently with marinade, continuing to follow directions for baked ham.

NOTE: This wine marinade could also be used for corned pork. It is a basic mixture to which could be added your own favorite spices. California Champagne is an elegant accompaniment for baked ham.

Easy Spaghetti Sauce

(about 3-2/3 cups)

Mrs. John Daddino, Guild Wine Co., Fresno

- 1 (10-1/4 oz.) can spaghetti sauce with meat
- 1 (8 oz.) can tomato sauce with mushrooms
- 1 (8 oz.) can tomato sauce with cheese
- 1 cup water
- 1/2 cup California Burgundy

Combine sauces, add water and wine. Simmer for at least an hour uncovered, or until of desired thickness. Prepare your favorite meat balls, drop uncooked into sauce and cook until done. Serve over spaghetti and sprinkle with grated Parmesan cheese.

My choice of wine to accompany this dish:
CALIFORNIA BURGUNDY

Chicken Liver Pasta Sauce

(12 servings)

Mrs. Paul J. Lunardi, Wine Institute, San Francisco

6 to 8   cloves garlic
1   stalk celery with leaves
1   small carrot
1   large bunch fresh parsley
1   large onion
1   pound chicken livers and giblets
3/4   cup olive oil
2   pounds lean ground beef
3   (15 oz.) cans tomato sauce
2   (12 oz.) cans tomato paste
1   tablespoon salt
1   tablespoon pepper
1/2   cup California Dry Sherry

Run vegetables and chicken giblets through meat grinder. Sauté greens and giblets in oil until tender but not brown. Add ground beef and fry slowly until cooked through. Add tomato sauce, tomato paste and seasoning. Cook about 1/2 hour. Before sauce is done add Sherry. This sauce can be served over macaroni, spaghetti, Indian corn meal or ravioli.

NOTE: Any California Dry Red Table Wine can accompany a pasta served with this rich sauce.

GROUND BEEF GRAVY spooned over rice or noodles makes a quick supper dish says Mrs. Leonard Berg of Mont LaSalle Vineyards, Napa. Brown 1 pound ground beef in large frying pan. Add 1 (10-1/2 oz.) can onion soup, 1/2 cup California Dry Sherry and simmer about 20 minutes. Makes about 2 cups. Garnish with chopped parsley or green onion. Serve any dry California Red Table Wine.

Orange Cranberry Sauce

(1 quart)

Mrs. Alessandro Baccari, Baccari Wine Festival, San Francisco

This sauce is a great accompaniment for turkey, chicken and other poultry dishes.

4   cups fresh cranberries
2   cups granulated sugar
1   cup California Medium Sherry
1   cup water
2-1/2   teaspoons peel, grated, of 1 thin-skinned medium-sized orange

Combine cranberries, sugar, Sherry and water. Add grated orange peel. Boil for 5 minutes, lower heat and simmer 10 to 15 minutes, uncovered. Cool and serve.

NOTE: Serve a California Rosé Wine with the poultry this sauce will garnish.

Game Sauce

(about 3-1/2 cups)

Miss Mary Lester, San Jose

This is a fantastic sauce for barbecued game. Many a person has lost a bet trying to guess just what goes into it. Of course it's to be used when the weather is nippy. It is much too heavy for warm weather.

1/8   cup California wine vinegar
3   cups California Dry Red Wine
1/2   cup olive oil
1/8   cup onions, minced
1/2   clove garlic
1-1/2   bay leaves
1/16   teaspoon each thyme, rosemary, basil, black pepper
1/2   teaspoon salt

Make sauce a day or so before barbecue. Mix all ingredients and keep in refrigerator until ready to use for basting duck or game.

My choice of wine to accompany this dish:
CALIFORNIA BURGUNDY

NOTE: For a larger quantity, Miss Lester's recipe can be doubled with ease. It is a fine marinade for beef as well as game.

Roy's Pineapple Glaze

(about 1-1/2 cups)

Mr. Don Rudolph, Cresta Blanca Wine Co., Livermore

This was given to me by a friend. We like the baked ham served with sweet potatoes and spinach dressed with lemon juice and butter.

1   (8 oz.) can crushed pineapple
1   cup brown sugar, firmly packed
1   tablespoon prepared mustard
1   teaspoon dry mustard
2   tablespoons lemon juice
  Dash of salt
1/4   cup California Port
1   (8 lb.) ham

Drain syrup from pineapple. Combine drained pineapple and remaining ingredients and mix well. Paint over ham last half hour of baking.

My choice of wine to accompany this dish:
CALIFORNIA HAUT SAUTERNE

Wild Bird Marinade

(1-2/3 cups)

Mr. John E. Swift, University of California, Berkeley

Taste this sauce carefully before using. It should be sweet and sour but with a sharp bite. It is the result of trial and error in experimenting with marinades.

> 1/3 cup tarragon flavored California
>   wine vinegar
> 1/3 cup fresh lemon juice
> 1/3 cup olive oil
> 2 teaspoons teriyaki or soy sauce
> 1 cup California Sauterne
> 1 teaspoon black pepper, coarse ground
> 2 teaspoons salt
> 2 teaspoons granulated sugar
> 1 to 2 teaspoons Worcestershire sauce
>   Pinch of oregano
> 4 to 6 drops Tabasco sauce
>   Dove or quail

Mix all ingredients thoroughly, but do not use electric beater. Put birds in marinade for 2 to 4 hours, not under refrigeration. Turn birds several times, occasionally stirring sauce so oil will not separate. Remove birds, stuff with piece of onion. Place on rack in baking pan and bake in pre-heated oven at 350°, basting frequently with marinade, making sure to squirt some into body cavities. After 1/2 hour cover breast of each bird with piece of bacon. Birds should bake about 1 hour and for final 15 minutes baste with Sauterne only.

NOTE: Mr. Swift recommends serving the birds with a combination of wild and white rice garnished with asparagus spears. A California Claret would go well with this dish.

Barbecue Sauce

(2 cups)

Mrs. C. E. Bailey, Mt. Tivy Winery, Reedley

If this sauce is made in advance, place in covered jar in refrigerator until ready to serve. It will keep up to 2 weeks.

> 1/4 cup California wine vinegar
> 1/2 cup water
> 3 tablespoons brown sugar
> 1 tablespoon prepared mustard
> 1/2 teaspoon pepper
> 1/2 teaspoon salt
> 1/4 teaspoon cayenne pepper
> 1 thick slice lemon
> 1 slice onion
> 1/4 cup margarine
> 1/2 cup catsup
> 2 tablespoons Worcestershire sauce
> 1 teaspoon liquid smoke (optional)
> 1/2 cup California Dry Sherry

Place first 10 ingredients in sauce pan. Bring to boil and simmer 20 minutes, uncovered. Add catsup and remaining ingredients; heat to boiling.

NOTE: Mrs. Bailey uses this well flavored sauce for spareribs, but it would be equally good over beef or chicken. Serve a California Burgundy with the spareribs basted with Barbecue Sauce.

Chicken Barbecue Sauce

(enough for 2 or 3 fryers)

Mr. Vincent E. Petrucci, Fresno State College, Fresno

This is best made the day before and placed in covered jar in refrigerator to ripen flavor.

> 2 to 3 rosemary sprigs, or pinch of
>   dried rosemary to taste
> 3 small cloves garlic, minced
> 1/4 cup fresh parsley, finely chopped
> 1/2 cup olive oil
> 1/2 cup California Sauterne

Wash and dry fresh rosemary sprigs if available and tie together, to be used as basting brush. Otherwise add dried rosemary along with garlic and parsley to olive oil and wine. Apply sauce to chicken which has been seasoned with salt and pepper and place on barbecue. Brush sauce on again after turning chicken when brown on one side. When chicken is done place in pan, apply sauce generously, cover and put in warm oven. Serve after 10 to 15 minutes.

NOTE: A California Zinfandel or Cabernet Sauvignon would give chicken new flavor interest, or if white wine is preferred, serve the California Sauterne used in preparing the sauce.

Clam Sauce Romano

(4 servings)

Mr. Robert Diana, Villa Armando Winery, Pleasanton

Despite its wide popularity in the United States, spaghetti is usually thought of in terms of meat or tomato sauce. The next time you have a yen for spaghetti, try it with this sauce made from clams. Sauce may look a little thin before you put it on the spaghetti, but will be quickly absorbed.

> 2 (7-1/2 oz.) cans minced clams
> 1/2 cup olive oil
> 1-1/2 teaspoons garlic powder
> 2 tablespoons parsley, minced
> 1/2 cup California Dry White Wine
> 1 teaspoon Italian red pepper (optional)
> 1 pound spaghetti
> 1/2 teaspoon salt

Drain clams, reserving juice. Place olive oil and clam juice in large skillet and heat slowly. When hot, add garlic powder, parsley and wine. At this point add red pepper also, if desired. Continue to cook slowly for about 10 minutes. Meanwhile cook spaghetti in large quantity of rapidly boiling salted water until still firm to the tooth. To sauce add salt and minced clams, stir well. While sauce is heating through, drain spaghetti and place on hot platter. Pour sauce over it, mix well and serve.

My choice of wine to accompany this dish:
CALIFORNIA SAUTERNE OR CHABLIS

SALADS

A jellied salad mold can accompany the most elegant special occasion dinner, or make a grand centerpiece for the buffet table. Because gelatin salads made with wine can be spectacular to look at as well as to taste, they are well worth constructing. Prepared gelatin powders make for ease of preparation, and the substitution of wine for water in recipes can open a whole new spectrum of flavors. Be sure to use only wine vinegar in salads and dressings, whether seafood, chicken, fruit or vegetables are ingredients. California wine vinegar makes the difference between a harsh tasting or a perfectly dressed salad.

Cleo's Christmas Salad
(12 to 16 servings)

Mrs. Don Rudolph, Cresta Blanca Wine Co., Livermore

This makes a very colorful salad but I have used it as a dessert. This was given to me by Cleo Tsapralis. I have made the salad a couple of days ahead and it lost none of its flavor.

2 (3 oz.) packages lime-flavor gelatin
2 (3 oz.) packages lemon-flavor gelatin
1 cup hot water
1 cup marshmallows
1 (20 oz.) can crushed pineapple

1 (8 oz.) package cream cheese
1 cup mayonnaise
1 cup whipping cream
2 (3 oz.) packages raspberry-flavor gelatin

Dissolve lime gelatin according to package directions, place in 10 x 12 x 2 inch pan. Chill until firm. Dissolve lemon gelatin with 1 cup hot water, add marshmallows, simmer until marshmallows melt. Mix pineapple undrained with cream cheese, beat until smooth, add to lemon gelatin. Fold in mayonnaise and stiffly beaten whipped cream. Pour over set lime gelatin layer. Dissolve raspberry gelatin according to package directions. Chill until syrupy, then pour gently over creamy lemon-pineapple layer. Result is a bright red, white and green salad to cut in squares.

My choice of wine to accompany this dish: **CALIFORNIA CHAMPAGNE, CHABLIS OR SHERRY**

NOTE: Mrs. Rudolph adds that for Valentine's Day the bottom layer can be made of red colored gelatin instead of green and for Easter the top layer can be made either yellow or orange. The red gelatin layer could have California Port added as part of liquid for added flavor.

Easy Chicken Salad

(4 to 5 servings)

Mrs. Peter Mirassou, Mirassou Vineyards, San Jose

    4 chicken breasts, boned
  1/2 cup California Sauterne
  1/3 cup French or Italian salad dressing
    1 cup seedless grapes, halved
    2 tablespoons slivered almonds
  1/2 cup mayonnaise
      Salt, to taste
  1/4 cup canned leechee nuts,
      sliced (optional)

Line a pan with foil, put in chicken breasts and add wine. Cover and bake 3/4 to 1 hour until tender in 350° oven. Cube chicken, add salad dressing and refrigerate overnight. Add grapes, almonds and mayonnaise. Season to taste and add leechee nuts, if desired.

NOTE: This exotic version of old familiar chicken salad could be served with California Sauterne or other White Table Wine.

Raspberry Gelatin Salad

(6 to 8 servings)

Mrs. W. Wallace Owen, Calgrape Wineries, Delano

    2 (10 oz.) packages frozen raspberries
    2 tablespoons currant jelly
    1 (6 oz.) package raspberry-flavor
      gelatin
    1 tablespoon lemon juice
    1 cup California Rosé

Thaw and drain berries. Add enough water to juice to make 2 cups. Turn juice combination into saucepan and bring to boil. Add jelly, stirring until melted. Add gelatin, stirring to dissolve, lemon juice and Rosé wine. Chill mixture until it begins to thicken, add berries. Turn into mold and refrigerate until firm.

NOTE: This would make a colorful centerpiece for a buffet table, surrounded with chicory. Serve with California Rosé.

Jellied Fruit Salad

(8 servings)

Mrs. Tillie Snyder, California Wine Association, Lodi

    1 (3 oz.) package peach-flavor gelatin
    1 cup boiling water
  1/2 teaspoon salt
    2 teaspoons lemon juice
  1/3 cup California Sherry
    2 tablespoons sugar
  1/4 teaspoon lemon extract
    1 (17 oz.) can fruit cocktail
  1/2 pint whipping cream
  1/2 cup roasted almonds, chopped

Dissolve gelatin in 1 cup of boiling water. Add salt, lemon juice, Sherry, sugar and lemon extract. Chill until gelatin begins to stiffen. Add well-drained fruit cocktail, fold in stiffly beaten cream and almonds. Chill until firm.

NOTE: This rich concoction would be delicious served with California Cream Sherry.

Stuffed Cherry Tomatoes

(6 servings)

Mrs. Robert H. Meyer, Italian Swiss Colony, Asti

    3 dozen cherry tomatoes
    1 cup fresh crabmeat,
      finely flaked or chopped
    1 tablespoon green onion,
      finely chopped
  1/4 teaspoon horseradish
    2 tablespoons California
      Dry White Table Wine
  1/2 teaspoon seasoned salt

Halve tomatoes and remove seeds. Mix all other ingredients and fill cavities with generous dollop of filling. Chill and serve.

NOTE: These make a pretty salad on a bed of greens. Shrimp or even drained canned tuna fish could be blended with wine and seasonings, moistened with a little mayonnaise, if necessary, and used as a substitute filling. Serve with the same California Dry White Table Wine used in the filling.

Out-of-This-World Salad

(6 servings)

Miss Margaret Shahenian, Guild Wine Co., Lodi

Serve with baked ham.

2 (11 oz.) cans mandarin orange segments
1 (14 oz.) can pineapple chunks
1 cup small marshmallows
2 tablespoons shredded coconut
1 cup dairy sour cream
2 tablespoons California Dry Sherry

Drain fruits thoroughly. Combine all ingredients and refrigerate for at least 24 hours prior to serving.

My choice of wine to accompany this dish:
CALIFORNIA CHABLIS

Under-the-Sea Salad

(6 to 8 servings)

Mrs. Earl Harrah, Wine Advisory Board, San Francisco

1 (30 oz.) can pears, diced
2 (3 oz.) packages lime-flavor gelatin
1/2 cup California Chablis
2 tablespoons California white wine vinegar
1/16 teaspoon salt
1 (8 oz.) package cream cheese
1/2 teaspoon ginger, ground

Drain pears and add enough water to syrup to make 2-1/2 cups liquid. Heat 1/2 of this mixture to boiling and pour over gelatin, stirring to dissolve. Add remaining wine, pear liquid, wine vinegar, and salt. Pour about 1-1/4 cups of this mixture into mold and chill until firm. Beat remaining gelatin mixture into softened cream cheese, add ginger and beat well. Fold in pears and pour over set layer of gelatin in mold. Chill until firm.

NOTE: Mrs. Harrah serves this zesty salad with a dressing composed of half mayonnaise, half whipped cream folded together and seasoned with California Port or other Dessert Wine.

Lime Gelatin Salad

(12 servings)

Mrs. Frank Pilone, Cucamonga

Wonderful with buffet suppers!

1 (8 oz.) can crushed pineapple
1 cup boiling water
1/2 cup California Sweet Sherry
1 (3 oz.) package lime-flavor gelatin
12 marshmallows, cut up
1 cup whipped cream
1 cup cottage cheese
1/2 cup walnuts, chopped
1/2 cup maraschino cherries

Drain pineapple syrup into pint measure. Add enough water to make 1-1/2 cups. Combine with wine and bring to boiling point. Add gelatin, stirring to dissolve. Add marshmallows, stirring until dissolved. Cool and chill. When mixture begins to thicken, beat until fluffy. Fold in stiffly whipped cream, cottage cheese, pineapple, walnuts and cherries. Turn into individual molds or 9 inch square pan.

My choice of wine to accompany this dish:
CALIFORNIA CHAMPAGNE

Ruby Cranberry Ring

(8 servings)

Mrs. Adele Brusati, Franzia Brothers Winery, Ripon

This is an excellent salad to serve with your holiday turkey, very colorful and appetizing.

1 (11 oz.) can mandarin oranges
2 cups fresh cranberries
1/4 cup sugar
1/2 teaspoon salt
1/2 teaspoon ground allspice
2 (3 oz.) packages lemon-flavor gelatin
1-1/2 cups California Port
3 tablespoons unflavored California wine vinegar
Crisp greens (optional)
Dairy sour cream

Drain oranges, saving syrup. Add water to syrup to measure 2 cups liquid. Turn into a saucepan; add cranberries, sugar, salt and allspice. Heat to boiling. Simmer about 5 minutes. Add gelatin and stir until dissolved. Remove from heat and stir in Port and vinegar. Chill until mixture thickens. Fold in drained orange segments. Turn into a 1-1/2 quart ring mold (or individual molds). Chill until firm. Unmold on serving platter. Garnish with greens, if desired.

NOTE: If greens are omitted ring can be served as a not too sweet dessert with sour cream in the center. Serve with the same California Port which flavored the gelatin.

Cranberry Salad

(8 to 10 servings)

Mrs. Peter Mirassou, Mirassou Vineyards, San Jose

I like to serve this salad with Thanksgiving dinner in place of the more traditional cranberry sauce. It complements a turkey beautifully and even the men in our family who ordinarily don't like molded salads really enjoy this.

      2 cups cranberry juice cocktail
      2 (3 oz.) packages raspberry-flavor gelatin
      1 (8-3/4 oz.) can pineapple tidbits
    1/2 cup California Port
    1/2 cup water
      1 avocado, peeled and sliced
      1 cup apple, pared and diced
    1/2 cup celery, finely chopped

Heat cranberry juice to boiling. Add gelatin, stirring until dissolved. Add pineapple tidbits undrained, wine and water. Arrange avocado slices in bottom of 5 cup ring mold. Pour enough gelatin mixture over slices to cover; chill until almost set. Chill remaining cranberry mixture until partially set; fold in apple and celery. Pour over avocado layer. Chill until firm. Unmold and garnish with fresh grapefruit sections and butter lettuce. Serve with mayonnaise thinned with juice from grapefruit.

My choice of wine to accompany this dish:
**CHILLED CALIFORNIA GEWÜRZTRAMINER
OR JOHANNISBERG RIESLING**

Gelatin Mold

(10 servings)

Mrs. Dale R. Anderson, Guimarra Vineyards, Edison

      1 (6 oz.) package cherry, or
         black cherry-flavor gelatin
  1-1/2 cups hot water
    1/2 cup California Sherry
      1 cup cold water
      1 tablespoon lemon juice
      1 cup dairy sour cream
      2 cups fresh Bing cherries,
         pitted and halved
    1/4 cup blanched almonds,
         chopped and toasted
         Cherries, pineapple chunks
         and romaine for garnish

Dissolve gelatin in hot water, add Sherry, cold water and lemon juice. Pour 1 cup of gelatin mixture into (2 qt.) mold and chill until firm. Meanwhile chill remaining gelatin in mixing bowl until partially set, whip until fluffy and fold in sour cream, cherries, almonds. Pour atop gelatin layer in mold. Chill until firm, about 5 hours, or overnight. Unmold on chilled platter. Circle with fresh Bing cherries, pineapple chunks and spears of romaine. Serve with mayonnaise mixed with sour cream to taste and sprinkled with toasted almonds.

NOTE: When fresh cherries are not available 2 (17 oz.) jars of pitted dark sweet cherries could be substituted. If this excellent salad is served at the end of a meal, or as dessert, a glass of California Port would make a suave accompaniment.

Cinnamon Gelatin

(4 servings)

Mrs. Suzanne McKethen, Wine Advisory Board, San Francisco

This dish served as a salad or dessert, would make a refreshing finish for a heavy meal.

      1 (3 oz.) package raspberry or
         strawberry-flavor gelatin
    3/4 cup boiling water
    1/4 cup California Port
      1 cup cold water
      1 (17 oz.) can fruits for salad,
         drained, or equivalent fresh fruits
    1/2 teaspoon cinnamon

Dissolve gelatin in boiling water and Port. Add cold water, chill until slightly thickened. Add fruits, cinnamon and pour into large or individual molds.

Raspberry Pear Salad

(8 servings)

Mrs. James Concannon, Concannon Vineyard, Livermore

This salad is good with many different meat and poultry menus.

      1 (17 oz.) can pears
      1 (3 oz.) package raspberry-flavor
         gelatin
    1/3 cup California Port
      2 tablespoons fresh lemon juice
      1 (9 oz.) package frozen raspberries,
         thawed
         Lettuce

Drain syrup from pears, adding water if necessary to make 3/4 cup of liquid. Heat and dissolve gelatin in it. Stir in Port and lemon juice. Cool to room temperature, blend in raspberries and their syrup. Chill until slightly thickened. Arrange pear halves in 3 or 4 cup ring mold, pour in gelatin and chill until firm. Unmold on bed of lettuce.

NOTE: Mrs. Concannon recommends choosing an accompanying wine compatible with the main dish served.

Macaroni Salad

(10 servings)

Mr. Fred Weibel, Weibel Champagne Vineyard, Mission San Jose

This recipe was developed for us by Mrs. Susan Ten Eyck of the Golden Grain Macaroni Co.

    1   pound salad macaroni
    1   tablespoon salt
  1/2   cup tangerine-flavored wine
1-1/2   cups salad dressing or mayonnaise
    1   cup dairy sour cream
    1   (13-1/4 oz.) can pineapple tidbits
  1/4   teaspoon cinnamon
  1/2   teaspoon salt
  1/2   teaspoon seasoned salt
    2   cups unpeeled apples, diced
    1   (11 oz.) can mandarin oranges, drained
  1/2   cup pecans, chopped

Cook macaroni in 4 quarts rapidly boiling water with 1 tablespoon salt for 10 minutes. Drain, rinse with cold water and drain again. Blend wine, salad dressing, sour cream, pineapple with juice, and seasonings. Combine dressing with macaroni and refrigerate at least 2 hours. Just before serving, stir in apples, oranges and nuts.

NOTE: This unusual version of the tried and true macaroni salad could be served with cold chicken for a picnic, accompanied by California White or Red Table Wine.

Red Cabbage Slaw

(6 servings)

Mrs. Alvin Ehrhardt, Allied Grape Growers, Madera

This slaw, full of robust flavor, is good as a relish or a salad.

    5   cups red cabbage, shredded
    1   tablespoon salt
  1/4   cup California Burgundy
  1/3   cup California red wine vinegar
  1/2   cup olive oil
  1/2   cup parsley, finely chopped
  1/3   cup green pepper, minced
    2   small cloves garlic, crushed
    2   teaspoons sugar

Place cabbage in mixing bowl, sprinkle with salt and let stand 20 minutes. Rub and squeeze cabbage together until juices flow. Squeeze out and discard as much juice as possible, through cheese cloth, if necessary. Mix remaining ingredients and pour over cabbage. Mix well, cover and chill several hours.

NOTE: Mrs. Ehrhardt suggests including this in a simple Smorgasbord of cold cuts and Swedish rye bread, or nestled in lettuce cups to serve as salad at a buffet.

HOMEMADE MAYONNAISE homogenized in a blender is so quick and foolproof, why not have it always on hand? Place 1 egg, 1/2 teaspoon dry mustard, 1/2 teaspoon salt, a scant 1/8 teaspoon sugar, 2 tablespoons California wine vinegar and 1/4 cup salad oil in blender. Cover and turn motor on low speed. Immediately uncover and add 3/4 cup more oil in a steady stream. Turn off motor as soon as oil is incorporated. Makes 1-1/4 cups. Season to taste with freshly ground pepper and paprika. Mayonnaise may be thinned with a dry California White Table Wine to serve with seafood, etc.

Port Pear Salad

(6 servings)

Mrs. Ben R. Goehring, Guild Wine Co., Lodi

My husband is a partner in Goehring Meat Co. After he had perfected a wine-cured ham, we had a wine and ham tasting dinner. A guest brought this delicious salad which complemented the food and wine served.

    1   (1 lb.) can pear halves
    3   ounces cream cheese
    1   tablespoon nuts, chopped
    1   cup boiling water
    1   (3 oz.) package cherry-flavor gelatin
  1/2   cup syrup from canned pears
  1/2   cup California Port

Drain pears, saving syrup. Beat cream cheese smooth, stir in nuts, shape into balls and fill each pear cavity. Arrange in 9 x 9 inch square pan. Add boiling water to gelatin, stir to dissolve. Add pear syrup and wine, cool and carefully pour around pears. Chill until firm. Cut in squares so that a pear half is the center of each serving and serve on lettuce.

NOTE: Mrs. Goehring remarks that this refreshing, light and attractive salad goes with any meal, accompanied by any California Table Wine.

Salade Niçoise

(6 servings)

Mrs. Marjorie K. Jacobs, Wine Advisory Board, San Francisco

- 3 ripe tomatoes, quartered
- 3 hard cooked eggs, sliced
- 2 (2 oz.) cans anchovy fillets, undrained
- 1 green pepper, sliced julienne
- 1 large sweet red onion, sliced in rings
- 1 cup cooked green beans
- 1 large cooked potato, diced (optional)
- 1 large head romaine, broken in pieces
  - Olive oil
  - California wine vinegar
  - Fresh ground black pepper
  - Capers
  - Black olives, pitted
  - Parsley, chopped fine

Mix first seven ingredients with romaine in large salad bowl. Add salad oil only if oil in anchovies is insufficient to coat greens. Add vinegar to taste. Grind pepper over top and garnish with capers, olives and parsley.

My choice of wine to accompany this dish:
CALIFORNIA ROSÉ

Note: This Mediterranean classic can be served as a first course or as a luncheon salad. It can be varied with other ingredients, such as good quality tuna fish, crushed garlic, other lettuces, watercress, radishes, finely sliced celery, artichoke hearts.

Black Cherry Salad

(6 servings)

Mrs. Peter Mirassou, Mirassou Vineyards, San Jose

- 1 (17 oz.) can pitted sweet black cherries
- 1 cup California Sauterne, or other dry white wine
- 1 (3 oz.) package cherry-flavor gelatin
- 1 cup walnuts, coarsely chopped
  - Fruit Dressing

Drain juice from cherries. Add water if necessary to make 1 cup. Heat juice and wine to boiling. Pour over gelatin to dissolve. Cool and chill until mixture begins to thicken. Add cherries and walnuts. Turn into ring mold or individual molds. Chill until firm. Serve with Fruit Dressing.

FRUIT DRESSING

- 1/4 cup mayonnaise
- 1/4 cup dairy sour cream
- 1 tablespoon orange juice
- 1 teaspoon lemon juice
- 1 tablespoon sugar

Blend well and serve with salad.

Varied Fruit Salad

(6 servings)

Mrs. Mary Lewis, Wine Institute, San Francisco

- 3 pears, peeled, cored and sliced
- 2 cups black and white grapes
- 4 figs, peeled and cut in quarters
- 1 tablespoon sugar
- 1 cup California Chablis
- 1 tablespoon California Brandy
- 1/2 pint whipping cream
- 2 tablespoons sugar
- 1 teaspoon vanilla extract

Place fruits in layers in serving bowl. Sprinkle with sugar and pour wine and Brandy over fruit. Place bowl over crushed ice and just before serving cover with whipped cream into which sugar and vanilla extract have been beaten.

NOTE: This would be a dainty dish to set off a cheese soufflé for a light summer luncheon. Serve with California Chablis.

DRESSING FOR FRUIT SALAD, a versatile blend to serve with any fruit salad, fresh or canned, or to accompany a molded salad, is made in a jiffy. Mrs. Suzanne McKethen, Wine Advisory Board, San Francisco, combines 1 cup dairy sour cream, 1/4 cup California Dry Sherry, 1/4 cup sugar, 2 teaspoons lemon juice, 1/2 teaspoon powdered cinnamon, and stirs to blend. This makes enough dressing for salad for 6.

Cranberry Fruit Mold

(8 to 10 servings)

Mrs. Ben R. Goehring, Guild Wine Co., Lodi

I prefer serving fruit mold with the traditional holiday turkey. This recipe has been in my family for many years and guests never fail to ask for it.

- 1 quart raw cranberries, ground
- 1-1/2 cups sugar
- 2 (3 oz.) packages cherry-flavor gelatin
- 1 cup boiling water
- 1 (13-1/2 oz.) can sour red cherries, undrained
- 1 (13-1/2 oz.) can pineapple, drained
- 1/2 cup California Port
- 1/2 cup celery, finely chopped
- 1/2 cup nuts, chopped

Combine cranberries and sugar. Let stand 1 hour. Dissolve gelatin in boiling water. Combine all ingredients and refrigerate, stirring once after mixture begins to thicken.

My choice of wine to accompany this dish:
CALIFORNIA BURGUNDY

VEGETABLES

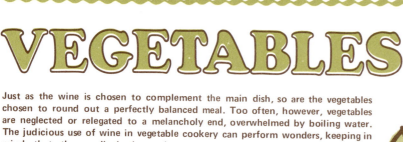

Just as the wine is chosen to complement the main dish, so are the vegetables chosen to round out a perfectly balanced meal. Too often, however, vegetables are neglected or relegated to a melancholy end, overwhelmed by boiling water. The judicious use of wine in vegetable cookery can perform wonders, keeping in mind that the cardinal sin against most garden produce is over-cooking, not under-cooking. Some of the dishes following can stand on their own as main dishes and provide a savory company to the fine California table wines you will be serving.

Baked Celery

(8 servings)

Mrs. Frank Garbini, Wente Brothers, Livermore

- 1 bunch celery
- 1 cup water
- 1/2 cup California Dry White Table Wine
- 3 tablespoons butter
- 1 tablespoon flour
- 3/4 cup canned consommé or broth made from 1 bouillon cube
- Salt and pepper
- 1/3 cup Parmesan cheese, grated
- Paprika

Separate celery into stalks, trim, rinse and cut in 2-inch lengths. Add to mixture of water and wine. Cook for 10 minutes. Drain celery and boil cooking liquid until reduced to about 1/2 cup, and reserve. Arrange celery in greased, shallow baking dish. Melt butter, blend in flour. Stir in consommé and 1/2 cup celery liquid and cook until smooth and thickened. Add seasonings and pour over celery. Sprinkle with cheese, dust with paprika and bake at 400° for 20 minutes until bubbly and lightly browned.

My choice of wine to accompany this dish:
CALIFORNIA WHITE TABLE WINE

Baked Carrots in Wine

(6 servings)

Mrs. Joseph J. Franzia, Franzia Brothers Winery, Ripon

- 1 pound young carrots, scraped
- 1 teaspoon seasoned salt
- 1 tablespoon sugar
- 1/4 cup butter
- 1 chicken bouillon cube
- 1/4 cup boiling water
- 1/3 cup California Dry Sherry

Leave small carrots whole, cut larger ones in 2-inch lengths. Arrange in shallow baking dish. Sprinkle with salt, sugar, and dot with butter. Add bouillon cube dissolved in boiling water and mixed with wine. Cover and bake until tender, about 1 hour in 350° oven.

NOTE: Depending on choice of meat for main dish, a California Red or White Table Wine could be served.

Spiced Pineapple

(1 pint)

Mrs. Myrtle Cuneo, Regina Grape Products, Etiwanda

1	(20 oz.) can pineapple chunks or spears
3/4	cup California Champagne wine vinegar
1-1/4	cups sugar
6	whole cloves
1	(3 inch) stick cinnamon
2	whole allspice
1/2	cup California Sherry
	Green or red food coloring

Drain pineapple, reserving syrup. Combine syrup, wine vinegar, sugar, spices and wine in saucepan. Bring to a boil, reduce heat, and simmer 10 minutes. Stir about 1/4 teaspoon food coloring into syrup mixture. Add pineapple and bring to a boil. Seal in sterilized jars, or store covered in refrigerator. Use as garnish for poultry or meat.

NOTE: California white wine vinegar may be used if California Champagne vinegar is not available.

Zucchini Soufflé Charlotte

(4 servings)

Mrs. Rodney Strong, Windsor Vineyards, Windsor

This is an original recipe that I created in trying to find a different way to serve zucchini.

2	large zucchini
2	tablespoons butter
2	cups white sauce
1/4	cup California Dry Sherry
4	eggs, separated
	Parmesan cheese, grated

Wash and cut zucchini in half lengthwise. Scoop out pulp without breaking outside skin. Blanch zucchini shells in boiling salted water for 2 minutes, drain. Place in baking dish. Chop pulp and brown in butter. Mix in white sauce, Sherry, beaten egg yolks. Fold in egg whites beaten until dry and standing in peaks. Fill zucchini shells with mixture, sprinkle with cheese and bake in 350° oven 1/2 hour. Serve immediately.

WHITE SAUCE

3	tablespoons butter
3	tablespoons flour
2-1/2	cups boiling milk
1/2	teaspoon salt
1/4	teaspoon pepper

Mix butter and flour, cook for 1 minute. Add hot milk, whip over low heat until thick. Add seasoning.

My choice of wine to accompany this dish:
CALIFORNIA CHENIN BLANC

NOTE: Any broiled meat goes nicely with this dish. Mrs. Strong suggests pork chops and small pickled beets. For ease and speed, canned white sauce may be substituted for homemade sauce.

Candied Sweet Potatoes

(8 servings)

Mrs. Roy W. Mineau, Roma Wine Co., Fresno

Mrs. Mineau serves this savory dish with a ham or turkey dinner.

8	large sweet potatoes or 2 (1 lb.) cans
1-1/4	cups brown sugar
1/3	cup California Sherry
1/4	cup butter or margarine
1/2	cup pecans or walnuts, chopped

Boil potatoes until tender, peel, cut in halves, or use well drained canned variety. Arrange in buttered baking dish. Mix sugar and wine, add butter and bring to a boil. Pour syrup over potatoes and bake uncovered 20 to 25 minutes, basting occasionally, in 350° oven. Sprinkle with chopped pecans or walnuts.

My choice of wine to accompany this dish:
CALIFORNIA GREY RIESLING

Burgundy Beans

(6 to 8 servings)

Mrs. Bruno Bisceglia, Bisceglia Bros. Wine Co., Madera

This would be an easy and good dish for a barbecue. 'Course I would have to omit garlic **entirely** for my family!

4	slices bacon
1	large onion, chopped
1/2	green pepper, chopped
1	clove garlic, minced (optional)
1	teaspoon dry mustard
1	tablespoon brown sugar
1	cup Dry California Red Wine
1	(8 oz.) can tomato sauce
2	(27 oz.) cans kidney beans, drained
	Salt and pepper to taste

Cut bacon into small pieces and fry until crisp. Remove bacon. Add onion, green pepper, and garlic to remaining fat and cook over low heat until vegetables are tender but not brown. Add bacon pieces and stir in remainder of ingredients. Season to taste with salt and pepper. Turn into bean pot or casserole and bake about 45 minutes at 350°.

NOTE: A California Burgundy would complement this easy and tasty dish. If time presses, the baking time can be shortened by having all ingredients hot before putting them in the casserole dish. For instance, simmering the beans and tomato sauce for a few minutes before mixing with other ingredients will give the casserole a head start.

Baked Mushrooms

(8 servings)

Mrs. Brad Webb, Freemark Abbey Winery, St. Helena

This recipe evolved through several years of effort to find an easy garnish for roasts.

    8 mushroom caps, 1-1/2 inch or
       larger in diameter
  1/3 cup butter or margarine
    2 tablespoons California Dry Sherry
  1/4 teaspoon thyme
       Salt and pepper to taste

Rinse and dry mushrooms, removing stems from caps. Place mushrooms upside down in shallow baking dish. Melt butter, add Sherry, thyme and bring to a boil. Spoon liquid into caps until full. Sprinkle with salt and pepper. Place in 325° oven, accompanying roast, and bake for 30 to 40 minutes, until tender.

My choice of wine to accompany this dish:
CALIFORNIA PINOT NOIR OR CABERNET

NOTE: Mrs. Webb points out that these mushrooms go equally well with roast beef or lamb, pan roasted potatoes and onions, and vegetables in season.

Chinese String Beans

(6 servings)

Mrs. Armand E. Bussone, Almaden Vineyards, Los Gatos

I obtained this recipe from my sister, Catherine. She is an excellent cook, always experimenting, originating new dishes. For people who have youngsters who dislike string beans, this proves to be a persuader. Also it's simple to prepare and epicurean in nature.

    1 clove garlic, minced
    2 tablespoons butter
    2 loin pork chops, cubed
    2 (1 lb.) cans cut green beans
    1 (10-1/2 oz.) can chicken
       or beef stock
  1/4 cup California Chablis
    1 bay leaf
  1/4 cup parsley, finely chopped
    1 tablespoon olive oil
    2 tablespoons soy sauce
       Salt and pepper to taste
    1 large onion, sliced in rings

Sauté garlic in butter, add cubed pork and brown. Add and mix remaining ingredients, concluding with onion rings placed on top of mixture. Cover and simmer for about 25 minutes.

NOTE: Mrs. Bussone points out that one may substitute 1/4 pound steak for pork and uncooked string beans for canned. It can accompany any meat, chicken, fish course, or oriental foods. A California Rosé could accompany almost any menu.

PICKLED ARTICHOKES may be marinated in French dressing before serving, recommends contributor Mrs. Walter S. Richert, Richert & Sons, Morgan Hill. Wash 12 artichokes, 2 to 2-1/2 inches in length. Trim stems, remove tough outer leaves and cut off top third of artichokes. Combine 2 cups water, 1/2 cup garlic-flavored California wine vinegar and 1 teaspoon salt. Add artichokes, cover and cook until tender, 15 to 25 minutes. Drain, chill. Serves 6 or more.

Zinfandel Chili Beans

(4 to 5 servings)

Mrs. John Franzia, Sr., Franzia Brothers Winery, Ripon

    1 pound ground beef
    1 teaspoon salt
    1 (1-5/8 oz.) package Lawry's
       chili seasoning mix
  1/2 cup California Zinfandel or
       Burgundy
    1 (16 oz.) can red kidney beans,
       drained
    1 (16 oz.) can tomatoes

Brown beef in skillet, add salt and Lawry's seasoning mix, stir thoroughly. Add wine, kidney beans and tomatoes. Mix thoroughly. Bring to a boil, reduce heat and simmer uncovered for 10 minutes.

NOTE: This would make a tasty, quick supper dish, served with crusty bread and the California Red Table Wine used in its sauce.

Brandied Yams

(8 servings)

Mrs. Maury Baldwin, Owens-Illinois Co., Sacramento

I always serve brandied yams with the holiday turkey. It is a favorite dish with family and friends.

    4 cups yams, cooked and mashed
    1 teaspoon salt
  1/4 teaspoon nutmeg
  1/8 teaspoon ginger, ground
       Pinch ground black pepper
    1 tablespoon sugar (optional)
    1 tablespoon heavy cream
  1/4 cup California Brandy
    3 tablespoons butter, melted
    2 teaspoons orange rind, grated

Mix all ingredients together well. If yams appear too dry, beat in an additional 1 or 2 more tablespoons cream. Turn into buttered casserole. Brush top with additional butter and sprinkle with 2 teaspoons grated orange rind. Preheat oven (375°) and bake about 30 to 40 minutes, or until heated through.

My choice of wine to accompany this dish:
CALIFORNIA DRY WHITE OR RED TABLE WINE

Potato Soufflé

(8 servings)

Mrs. Victor Repetto, California Grape Products Corp., San Francisco

This recipe was given to me by a friend who greatly improved the original with the addition of Dry Sherry.

- 1 (8 oz.) package cream cheese
- 3 cups mashed potatoes
- 1 medium onion, chopped very fine
- 3 eggs
- 3 tablespoons flour
- 1 teaspoon salt, 1/4 teaspoon pepper, to taste
- 1 (3-1/2 oz.) can French fried onions
- 6 tablespoons California Dry Sherry

Soften cream cheese to room temperature. Add potatoes, onion, eggs, flour, salt and pepper to cheese and beat thoroughly with electric mixer. Spoon into ungreased (2 qt.) casserole. Crumble French fried onions over top and sprinkle with Sherry. Cover with foil and bake 40 to 45 minutes in 300° oven. Remove foil last 5 minutes of baking to brown crust.

NOTE: Mrs. Repetto says this is good with any meat or poultry and can be served with or without gravy. When time is of the essence instant potato may be used.

Potatoes in Wine

(4 servings)

Mrs. Ed Benik, The Christian Brothers, Reedley

- 4 medium-sized potatoes
- 4 tablespoons butter
- 2 tablespoons flour
- 1-1/2 cups hot water
- 1/2 cup Dry California Vermouth, or Chablis
  Salt and pepper
- 1 clove garlic, finely minced
- 1 teaspoon fresh rosemary leaves, chopped
- 4 small onions

Wash, peel, and quarter potatoes. Melt butter in a heavy saucepan. Stir in flour and when it is lightly browned add water, wine, salt, pepper, garlic, and rosemary. Stir sauce until it is smooth. Add small peeled onions and potatoes. Cover and simmer about 1 hour, or just until vegetables are tender.

NOTE: This is a new seasoning idea for potatoes which would be excellent with any meat and either a California Chablis or Red Table Wine. Mrs. Marjorie Jacobs, Wine Advisory Board, San Francisco, makes this recipe by substituting chicken or beef broth for hot water for more intense flavor.

Baked Kidney Beans

(6 servings)

Mrs. Augusta Illich, Buena Vista Vineyards, Sonoma

- 2 (15-1/4 oz.) cans kidney beans, drained
- 1/2 cup California Red Table Wine
- 1-1/2 tablespoons soy sauce
- 1 onion, chopped fine
- 1 clove garlic, chopped fine
- 2 tablespoons brown sugar
- 1 tablespoon dry mustard

Combine all ingredients and bake in 350° oven for 45 minutes to 1 hour. Add more wine if beans become dry.

My choice of wine to accompany this dish:
**CALIFORNIA PINOT CHARDONNAY
OR CABERNET SAUVIGNON**

NOTE: These beans would make a tasty side dish to serve with cold meat and cucumbers dressed with sour cream and chives.

Zucchini Cucamonga

(4 servings)

Mrs. Frank Pilone, Cucamonga

This is my version by experimentation.

- 6 medium zucchini
- 1 pound ground lean beef
- 1 egg, beaten
- 1/2 cup soft bread crumbs
- 1/2 cup California Dry Sherry
- 1 teaspoon salt
- 1/8 teaspoon pepper
- 1 (8 oz.) can tomato sauce

Cut zucchini in half lengthwise and scoop out pulp. Blend chopped pulp with all other ingredients, except tomato sauce and stuff zucchini shells. Place in buttered baking dish, add 3 tablespoons water to bottom of dish and bake about 45 minutes in 350° oven. Spoon tomato sauce over zucchini and continue baking for about 15 minutes more.

My choice of wine to accompany this dish:
CALIFORNIA DRY SAUTERNE OR ROSÉ

LIMA BEAN CASSEROLE provides a good way to get her children to eat lima beans says Mrs. Edmund Accomazzo, Cucamonga Winery, Cucamonga. Cook 1 (10 oz.) package frozen beans according to package directions. Combine 1 (10-3/4 oz.) can cheese soup with 1/3 cup California Sauterne or other dry white table wine, season to taste with salt and pepper. Cook, stirring, until smooth. Mix well drained beans with sauce in 1-1/2 quart casserole, sprinkle top with 1/4 cup slivered almonds, and bake 20 minutes in 375° oven until bubbly. Serves 4. This would make a quick supper for a working girl to prepare, goes nicely with California Rosé.

Artichokes California

(6 to 8 servings)

Mrs. John Franzia, Sr., Franzia Brothers Winery, Ripon

My husband raises all our artichokes in our own garden; therefore we pick them fresh all the time and they are one of our favorite vegetables.

12 small fresh artichokes
1 clove garlic, chopped
2 slices bacon, chopped and sautéed
1/2 cup olive oil
1/2 cup California Dry Sherry
3/4 cup water
Salt to taste

Cut off tip and spiny point of artichokes. Cut off stems so they will sit upright when arranged in pan. Mix all other ingredients, making sure bacon is well drained, and pour over artichokes. Cover tightly, cook about 30 minutes, until tender. If necessary, add more wine during cooking.

My choice of wine to accompany this dish:
CALIFORNIA ZINFANDEL

NOTE: Mrs. Franzia adds: "With this dish I like to serve fried chicken, mashed potatoes and for dessert, strawberry shortcake."

Mushrooms Riddell

(4 servings)

Mrs. Elmer O. Murray, Owens-Illinois Co., San Francisco

Delicious! First enjoyed with Bettie and Jim Riddell at their cabin at Bass Lake. Bettie cooked the mushrooms, Jim barbecued the steaks, and we all ate everything.

1/2 pound mushrooms,
1 to 2 inches in diameter
3 tablespoons butter
3 ounces California Sherry

Select mushrooms of uniform size, wash, dry and remove stems, which may also be cooked in the same way. Melt butter in large frying pan; add mushrooms top side down. Brown well over fairly high heat. Turn mushrooms stem side down, pour Sherry over and cook over lowered heat for 3 to 4 minutes. Season to taste.

NOTE: Mrs. Murray cautions: "Do not overcook. Serve with steak or hamburger, preferably barbecued. If you happen to be out of Sherry, California Sweet Vermouth or Port may be substituted." We suggest serving a California Burgundy with this dish.

Tomato Pork Kidney Beans

(8 servings)

Mrs. August Sebastiani, Samuele Sebastiani Winery, Sonoma

My mother-in-law used this recipe as a short cut because dry beans take so long to cook. Now we like it better than the old way and enjoy it at our barbecues all summer long.

1/2 cup salt pork, diced
2 medium onions, chopped
1 clove garlic, mashed
1 (12 oz.) can solid pack tomatoes
1 (8 oz.) can hot sauce
1/2 cup California Medium Sherry
3 (27 oz.) cans red kidney beans, drained

Sauté salt pork until browned. Drain off all but 1 tablespoon fat, add onion and sauté until lightly brown. Add garlic, tomatoes, hot sauce, Sherry and simmer about 45 minutes. Add beans and bake 1/2 hour in 350° oven.

My choice of wine to accompany this dish:
CALIFORNIA DRY RED OR WHITE TABLE WINE

NOTE: Mrs. Sebastiani adds that these beans are delicious with ham, chicken, hamburgers or steak, with a tossed salad or sliced tomatoes.

Mushrooms and Artichokes

(6 servings)

Mrs. Robert W. Salles, Wine Brokerage, San Francisco

I use this as a first course, a salad, or a relish and serve it with anything that is compatible with mushrooms.

1 pound medium-size mushrooms
1 (8 oz.) package frozen artichoke hearts
1/3 cup green onions, chopped
1 (2 oz.) jar pimiento-stuffed green olives, drained, sliced
1 tablespoon pimiento, chopped
1/2 cup olive oil
1/2 cup white wine vinegar
3 tablespoons California Sherry
1/2 teaspoon salt
1/4 teaspoon each, garlic salt, oregano, coarse-ground pepper
Lettuce, romaine, or watercress

Wash and trim mushrooms, slice or cut in quarters. Cook in boiling salted water for 1 minute, drain and turn into mixing bowl. Cook artichokes as directed on package just until tender, drain and add to mushrooms. Add onions, olives and pimiento. For dressing, combine olive oil, vinegar, Sherry and seasonings. Mix until blended, pour over vegetables, cover and marinate in refrigerator for at least 4 hours or overnight, stirring several times. Arrange salad on crisp greens and serve.

My choice of wine to accompany this dish:
CALIFORNIA PINOT CHARDONNAY

Vegetables Sunnyvale

(3 to 4 servings)

Mrs. E. B. Nelson, Wine Institute, San Francisco

- 1 tablespoon chicken or beef seasoned stock base
- 1/4 cup California Chablis or Rosé
- 1 teaspoon dried chopped onion
- 1 teaspoon dried parsley or green pepper
  Salt and pepper to taste
- 2 cups cooked vegetables, string or lima beans, peas, whole kernel corn, etc.
- 1 (4 oz.) can mushrooms, drained and sliced (optional)
- 2 tablespoons butter

Blend seasoned stock base and wine. Add onion, parsley or green pepper, salt and pepper. Add vegetables, mushrooms and heat gently. Add butter just before serving.

NOTE: This is a flavorful way to make use of leftover vegetables. A California Chablis or Rosé could be served, depending on the meat chosen to accompany this dish.

Brandied Carrots

(4 servings)

Mr. Karl C. Krupp, Charles Krug Winery, St. Helena

- 3 cups carrots, cooked
- 2 tablespoons butter
- 1 tablespoon brown sugar
- 2 tablespoons California Brandy
  Salt to taste

Melt butter, add brown sugar, stirring to dissolve. Add Brandy, heat to bubbling, pour over hot carrots, sprinkle with salt and stir lightly to combine.

NOTE: This was suggested as companion to Mr. Krupp's Roast Duck au Naturel. (See page 62.)

HAPPY CARROTS make a merry meal. This recipe comes from Mrs. Geneva Shuflin, Wine Institute, San Francisco. Scrape and cut 12 carrots julienne, chop 6 green onions, add 1/2 cup butter and braise covered, very gently for 15 minutes, or until tender. Just before serving, add 4 tablespoons California Dry Sherry, 2 tablespoons finely chopped parsley, salt and pepper to taste. Serves 6.

Stewed Mushrooms

(4 servings)

Mrs. Louis J. Foppiano, L. Foppiano Wine Co., Healdsburg

- 1 pound large firm mushrooms
- 4 tablespoons butter
- 1/4 cup California Sherry
- 1/2 teaspoon salt
- 1/4 teaspoon pepper
- 1/4 teaspoon marjoram
  Hot toast, buttered

Rinse mushrooms gently in cold water; pat dry. Do not peel. Slice caps and stems. Heat butter in large pan. Add sliced mushrooms. Sauté slowly over low heat for 5 minutes. Add Sherry, salt and pepper. Sprinkle with marjoram and stir. Serve at once on hot buttered toast.

NOTE: Mrs. Foppiano warns: "Do not overcook mushrooms as this will toughen their delicate texture." We suggest serving as a first course with California Sherry.

ARTICHOKES SAUTERNE cooked in a pressure cooker, using any California White Table Wine instead of the usual amount of water, pick up a delightful flavor that adds greatly to their enjoyment, according to Mr. David Gallo, E. & J. Gallo Winery, Modesto. Trim 6 artichokes, wash, drain and place in pressure cooker. Add 1/2 cup California Sauterne, 1/4 teaspoon salt and cook in accordance with pressure cooker directions. Serve artichokes with melted butter or hollandaise sauce and a glass of California Sauterne.

Mushrooms del Bondio

(6 to 12 servings)

Mr. John Del Bondio, Beringer Brothers, St. Helena

- 12 large fresh mushrooms
- 1 tablespoon parsley, chopped fine
- 2 cloves garlic, minced
- 1 tablespoon each butter and oil
- 1/2 to 1 cup soft bread crumbs
- 1/4 cup dry Monterey cheese, grated
- 1/2 onion, chopped fine
- 3 tablespoons Dry California White Wine or Sherry

Remove stems of mushrooms and chop fine. Sauté stems, parsley and garlic in butter and oil. Cool mixture. Mix in bread crumbs, grated cheese, chopped onions and wine. Fill mushroom caps and place a little butter on top of each. Bake in moderate oven at 350º for 20 minutes.

NOTE: Mr. Del Bondio says: "Serve with steak; or if small mushrooms are used serve as a hot hors d'oeuvre." If steak is not on the menu these delicious mushrooms could dress up a hamburger dinner. We suggest a California Claret to accompany the dish.

Zucchini with Ground Beef

(8 to 10 servings)

Mrs. Leo Demostene, Soda Rock Winery, Healdsburg

This may be served as a main dish or side dish.

- 1 pound ground beef
- 1 medium onion, chopped
- 1 tablespoon fat
- 1 teaspoon seasoned or garlic salt
- 1/2 cup California Sauterne
- 1 cup long grain rice, cooked
- 1-1/2 pounds zucchini, cut in 1/4 inch rounds
- 2 cups cottage cheese
- 1 (10-1/2 oz.) can cream of mushroom soup
- 1 cup sharp Cheddar cheese, grated

Brown beef and onion together in fat. Add seasoning and wine. Add rice which has been cooked for 10 minutes in boiling salted water and drained. Place half of zucchini in bottom of (2-1/2 qt.) casserole. Cover with beef mixture and spoon on cottage cheese. Add layer of remaining zucchini and spread soup over all. Sprinkle top with grated cheese and bake 1 to 1-1/4 hours in 350° oven.

NOTE: This casserole could be assembled ahead of time and baked just before dinner. A California Dry Sauterne would be a good companion to the dish.

Zucchini Pancakes

(4 servings)

Mrs. Doris Paulsen, Wine Institute, San Francisco

- 3 medium zucchini
- 2 eggs, unbeaten
- 3 tablespoons flour
- 2 tablespoons Parmesan cheese, grated
- 1 tablespoon California Sherry
- 1 teaspoon chives, chopped
- 1/4 teaspoon parsley, chopped
  Pinch of garlic powder
- 1 teaspoon salt
- 1/8 teaspoon pepper

Wash, dry but do not peel zucchini. On a coarse grater grate zucchini into mixing bowl. Stir in all other ingredients and seasonings. If mixture appears too liquid add 1 tablespoon flour. Drop batter by spoonful on oiled, moderately hot griddle or skillet and cook as you would pancakes, until brown on both sides. Serve hot or cold.

NOTE: Mrs. Paulsen says that dried parsley and chives are satisfactory substitutes for the fresh herbs. This original recipe could furnish an interesting substitute for potato pancakes. If served with pot roast could be accompanied by a California Burgundy.

Artichoke Shrimp au Gratin

(4 servings)

Mrs. George Al Berry, E. & J. Gallo Winery, Modesto

- 1/2 pound fresh mushrooms, sliced
- 2 tablespoons butter or margarine
- 2 (6 oz.) jars marinated artichoke hearts, drained
- 2 (4 oz.) cans shrimp, or 3/4 pound fresh cooked shrimp
- 1 (10-1/2 oz.) can cream of mushroom soup
- 1/4 cup whole milk
- 1/4 cup California Dry Sherry
- 1 tablespoon Worcestershire sauce
- 1/4 teaspoon celery salt
- 1/2 cup sharp Cheddar cheese, grated

Sauté mushrooms in butter 5 or 6 minutes, set aside. Place artichoke hearts in buttered baking dish, cover with shrimp. Place mushrooms over shrimp. Combine all other ingredients except cheese and pour over mixture in baking dish. Sprinkle with grated cheese and bake 20 minutes in 375° oven.

My choice of wine to accompany this dish:
CALIFORNIA GREY RIESLING

NOTE: Says Mrs. Berry, "I serve this recipe as a luncheon dish, preceded by a cold consommé, accompanied by a molded broccoli salad and hot rolls."

Artichokes à l'Italienne

(6 servings)

Mrs. Victor Repetto, California Grape Products Corp., San Francisco

This is an unusual and delicious way of cooking artichokes.

- 6 artichokes
  Juice of 1 lemon
- 3 cups chicken broth, hot
- 2 cloves garlic, whole
- 1/2 cup butter, melted
- 1 cup Parmesan cheese, grated
- 1/2 cup California Dry White Wine
- 1 tablespoon shallot minced
- 1 tablespoon parsley, finely chopped
  Juice of 1/2 lemon

Remove outer leaves of artichokes, trim stem and cut off about 1 inch across top. Place in large bowl containing water, lemon juice, and soak 15 minutes. Drain, dry and cut in half lengthwise, from stem end through top. Put in pan, add chicken broth and garlic. Boil for about 15 minutes — they must not be soft. Drain, remove choke (hairy, inedible center) and roll each half in melted butter, then in grated cheese. Arrange in baking casserole with stem ends down. Add wine and bake in 350° oven until tops are dry, brown and beginning to curl. Just before serving pour over sauce made of remaining butter in which shallots and parsley have been slightly cooked and to which juice of 1/2 lemon has been added.

NOTE: Watch during baking and if wine is too quickly absorbed add more, as needed. A California Chablis would be good with these well flavored artichokes.

Vegetables Oriental

(4 servings)

Mrs. Jack L. Davies, Schramsberg Vineyards, Calistoga

This is an unusual dish which intrigues guests, as this combination is seldom tasted together. It complements many meat dishes and can also be served with a cold mousse for texture contrast.

- 2 cups celery, cut diagonally in 1/2 inch slices
- 1/2 cup butter or margarine
- 1/2 teaspoon salt
- 1/16 teaspoon pepper
- 1/8 teaspoon thyme
- 1 (4 oz.) can water chestnuts, drained, and sliced 1/8 inch thick
- 2 cups mushrooms, sliced 1/8 inch thick
- 1/2 teaspoon Beau Monde powder
- 1/4 teaspoon garlic salt

Sauté celery in 1/4 cup butter until crisp-tender. Season with salt, pepper, thyme and add water chestnuts. Sauté mushrooms, sliced stems included, in remaining butter until crisp-tender. Add Beau Monde powder, garlic salt, mix and serve hot.

My choice of wine to accompany this dish:
CALIFORNIA CABERNET SAUVIGNON OR ZINFANDEL

NOTE: Mrs. Davies suggests serving this original dish with game, poultry or roast beef.

Broiled Mushroom Caps

(2 servings)

Mrs. Ronald Mettler, Guild Wine Company, Lodi

This is my own original recipe, although it was initially inspired by a recipe in **Favorite Recipes of California Winemakers.** In the end mine turned out quite differently.

- 5 to 6 large mushrooms (about 2-1/2 inch diameter)
- 3 tablespoons green onions, sliced
- 1 tablespoon butter
- 1/2 pound ground chuck
- 1/2 can beef stock or 1 bouillon cube in 2/3 cup of water
- 3 tablespoons Dry California Sherry
- 1/2 teaspoon salt
- 1/8 teaspoon each oregano and thyme
- 1 tablespoon flour
- 2 tablespoons melted butter Parmesan cheese, grated
- 5 to 6 rounds toast, buttered Parsley

Wipe mushrooms with dry cloth to clean. Remove and chop stems. Slice green onions. Combine chopped stems and onions in skillet and sauté in 1 tablespoon butter until tender. Brown meat in skillet. Add beef stock, Sherry, stem and onion mix, and seasonings. Thicken sauce with flour and simmer about 3 minutes. Brush mushroom caps with melted butter. Place caps on a greased baking pan and fill with meat mixture. Sprinkle with Parmesan cheese. Broil 5 minutes at 375°. While this is cooking, cut rounds of bread, toast and butter. Serve on platter with mushrooms on toast rounds and any extra meat in center. Garnish with parsley.

My choice of wine to accompany this dish:
CALIFORNIA RUBY CABERNET OR BURGUNDY

Stuffed Zucchini Sharon

(8 servings)

Mrs. Alan Hemphill, F. Korbel & Brothers, Guerneville

An excellent way to make use of zucchini which reaches too large a size for other cooking methods. It is also delicious served cold as a leftover for luncheon.

- 2 large zucchini
- 1 onion, chopped
- 2 tablespoons oil
- 2 or 3 ripe tomatoes, peeled
- 2 eggs
- 1-1/2 teaspoons sweet basil
- 1-1/2 cups soft bread crumbs
- 1/2 cup California Dry Sherry
- 1/2 teaspoon salt
- 1/8 teaspoon pepper
- 2/3 cup Parmesan cheese, grated

Cut zucchini in half and again lengthwise. Parboil about 5 minutes, cool. Sauté onion in oil until brown; add tomatoes and cook slowly 3/4 hour. Remove pulp of zucchini, chop and mix well with all ingredients except cheese, adding salt and pepper. Refill zucchini shells with mixture, top with grated cheese and bake 45 minutes in 350° oven.

My choice of wine to accompany this dish:
CALIFORNIA GREY RIESLING

NOTE: Mrs. Hemphill says that this dish goes well with almost any entrée. Their favorite combination is with barbecued chicken and crisp green salad.

FISH

The harvest from the sea in all its profusion and variety comes to eating perfection in these dishes using California's wines, whether in the cooking liquid for poaching the fish, or in the sauce. White wine is often called for, sometimes Sherry, also red wine. Whatever the ingredients, one rule to remember is never to overcook fish. Cook only until it flakes easily when tested with a fork, preserving flavor and shape. When you want a nicely browned top, dust lightly with paprika which turns a beautiful warm brown under the broiler. Then all that is needed is a fresh vegetable or salad, plenty of good crusty bread and a glass of chilled California wine — white table wine, Rosé, or even red.

Baked Sole with Salmon

(4 servings)

Mr. Hal Cutler, E. & J. Gallo Winery, Modesto

- 8 fillets of sole
- 1/2 pound fresh salmon, or
  1 (7-3/4 oz.) can pink or red salmon
- 1/2 teaspoon salt
- 1/4 teaspoon pepper
- 1/2 cup California Chablis
- 1/4 cup heavy cream
  Paprika

Place 4 fillets in bottom of lightly oiled baking dish. Spread flaked salmon over all and season with salt and pepper. Cover with other 4 fillets. Pour wine and cream over all and cover. Bake in 350° oven about 30 minutes. Sprinkle with paprika before serving.

NOTE: Serve this fish combination with the same California Chablis that went into the sauce. Fresh new peas or string beans with dill would give nice color to the meal.

Crab Newburg

(4 servings)

Brother Timothy, The Christian Brothers, Napa

This recipe was given to the late Brother John who believed if a little is good, a lot is better. If milk was asked for, he used pure cream, a "little" butter he doubled or tripled. A tablespoon of Sherry? More likely a half bottle went in, and, as an afterthought, he would stir in a handful of mushrooms.

- 2 tablespoons butter
- 1 tablespoon olive oil
- 4 tablespoons flour
- 3 cups rich milk
- 1 teaspoon salt
- 1/4 cup California Dry Sherry
- 1 egg, slightly beaten
- 4 cups crabmeat
  Parmesan cheese, grated

Melt butter with oil. Blend in flour and cook gently 2 minutes without browning. Slowly add milk, stirring constantly until sauce is smooth and thick. Add salt and Sherry, mixing well. Stir a tablespoon of hot sauce into egg and return to sauce. Add crabmeat and heat below boiling until crab is hot through. Serve with grated cheese.

My choice of wine to accompany this dish:
CALIFORNIA PINOT CHARDONNAY

Crab Toast

(6 servings)

Mrs. Kerby T. Anderson, Guild Wine Co., San Francisco

Our daughter-in-law from Portland served this lovely crab dish on our last visit with them. She is fast becoming a gourmet cook and sings the praises of all the recipes in the now famous Wine Advisory Board cookbooks. She and her husband are proud to serve California wines at their dinners.

      5 tablespoons butter
      6 slices sourdough French bread
      1 small green pepper, chopped
      1 small bunch green onions, chopped,
        including green ends
    1/2 cup California Sherry
    1-1/2 pounds crabmeat
        Brandy (optional)

Melt 2 tablespoons butter in frying pan, brown bread slices lightly on both sides, remove to serving platter and keep warm. Add remaining butter to frying pan and sauté green pepper and onion until golden. Add Sherry and crabmeat, stirring to combine. Simmer over low heat until warmed through. Place crabmeat mixture on bread slices. If desired, pour a small amount of warm brandy on each serving and ignite just before presenting.

My choice of wine to accompany this dish:
CALIFORNIA ROSÉ

Fish Angeles

(6 servings)

Mrs. Leonard Maullin, Milford Co. of California, Los Angeles

This recipe is an example of good cooking using a convenience product.

      2 cups small fresh mushrooms
      2 tablespoons onion, chopped
      4 tablespoons butter or margarine
    1-1/2 cups California Sauterne
      2 teaspoons parsley, minced
      1 tablespoon prepared mustard
    1/4 teaspoon marjoram, crumbled
      2 (2 oz.) packages coating mix for fish
      8 fish fillets (2 to 3 lbs.)
        Salt to taste

Sauté mushrooms and onion in butter until tender but not browned. Stir in 1 cup wine, parsley, mustard, marjoram and 2 tablespoons of coating mix. Dip fillets in remaining wine, to moisten. Place remaining coating mix in bag and add fillets, shaking to coat thoroughly. Place 4 fillets in ungreased shallow baking dish and spread with mushroom mixture. Top with remaining fillets and sprinkle with salt to taste. Bake in 400º oven about 20 minutes, or until fish flakes and is golden brown.

My choice of wine to accompany this dish:
CALIFORNIA DRY OR SEMI-DRY WHITE TABLE WINE

NOTE: Mrs. Maullin says, "I suggest serving this dish with fresh fruit cocktail, well laced with California Sherry, a green salad, buttered rice or noodles, a green vegetable and a light dessert."

Crab Delight

(4 servings)

Mrs. Maury F. Baldwin, Owens-Illinois Glass Co., Sacramento

Our teen-age son was indifferent to crab dishes until he tasted this one. Now it's a great favorite with all family members.

    1/4 cup butter
    1/4 cup flour
      1 cup light cream,
      1 teaspoon salt
    1/8 teaspoon pepper
    1/3 cup California Dry Sherry
      1 pound cooked crabmeat
    3/4 cup Cheddar cheese, shredded

Pre-heat oven at 425º. Melt butter, stir in flour. Add cream, salt, pepper, Sherry and cook over low heat, stirring until thickened. Remove from heat and add crabmeat. Turn into buttered casserole, or individual dishes, sprinkle with cheese and bake until cheese melts and mixture is bubbly, about 15 minutes in 375º oven.

My choice of wine to accompany this dish:
CALIFORNIA CHABLIS

Crab Quiche

(4 servings)

Mrs. Cecil P. Kahmann, Daniel Edelman Agency, San Francisco

        Rich pastry shell, 8-inch diameter
      2 tablespoons shallots or
        green onions, minced
      3 tablespoons butter
      1 cup fresh crabmeat
    1/4 teaspoon salt
        Dash pepper
      2 tablespoons California Dry Sherry
      3 eggs
      1 cup whipping cream
    1/4 teaspoon salt
        Dash pepper
    1/4 cup Swiss cheese, grated

Make rich pastry shell, using part butter as shortening and bake in 400º oven about 5 minutes. Sauté shallots or onions in butter until limp but not brown. Add crabmeat, salt, pepper and Sherry, heating for a moment. Cool slightly, before adding eggs beaten with cream, salt and pepper. Pour into partially cooked pastry shell, sprinkle with grated cheese and bake in upper part of 375º oven about 25 or 30 minutes until knife inserted in custard comes out clean and quiche is puffed and browned.

My choice of wine to accompany this dish:
CALIFORNIA CHENIN BLANC

NOTE: Mrs. Kahmann suggests that if this excellent quiche is used as a hot hors d'oeuvre, serve with chilled California Cocktail Sherry.

Crab Casserole

(6 servings)

Mrs. Robert W. Salles, Wine Brokerage, San Francisco

This is a favorite luncheon dish. I serve small Parker House rolls and a molded fruit salad with it.

- 1-1/2 cups cooked rice
- 1 (10 oz.) package frozen chopped spinach
- 1 (6 oz.) package grated American cheese
- 2 (7-1/2 oz.) cans crabmeat, flaked
- 1 tablespoon lemon juice
- 2/3 cup dairy sour cream
- 1/2 teaspoon salt
- 1/4 teaspoon nutmeg
- 3 tablespoons California Dry Sherry
- 1 (8 oz.) can tomato sauce
- 1/4 cup Swiss cheese, coarsely grated

Preheat oven to 350°. Cook rice according to package directions. Cook spinach until barely tender, drain well and spread on bottom of buttered 1-1/2 quart casserole. Add layer of rice, grated cheese and crabmeat. Sprinkle with lemon juice. Blend sour cream, seasonings and wine. Pour over rice and crabmeat. Top with tomato sauce and bake, uncovered, 20 to 25 minutes until heated through. Before serving, sprinkle with grated Swiss cheese.

My choice of wine to accompany this dish:
CALIFORNIA JOHANNISBERG RIESLING OR CHABLIS

Milanese Crab Casserole

(6 servings)

Mrs. Nina Concannon Radisch, Concannon Vineyard, Livermore

Modern canned and frozen foods speed preparation of this fresh-tasting dish. I use it often in winter as a luncheon entrée for lady friends.

- 2 tablespoons butter or margarine
- 2 (10 oz.) packages frozen chopped spinach, thawed and drained
- 1 (10-1/2 oz.) can condensed mushroom soup
- 1 (10 oz.) can white sauce
- 1-1/4 cups Swiss Cheese, shredded (about 5 oz.)
- 1/4 cup California Dry Sherry
- 1-1/2 pounds crabmeat
- 1 (6 oz.) can water chestnuts, drained and sliced
- 3 tablespoons Parmesan cheese, grated

Melt butter in frying pan, add spinach, stirring over moderate heat until liquid is evaporated, about 2 minutes. Stir in mushroom soup. In another pan combine white sauce, cheese, Sherry and stir over low heat to melt cheese. Stir in crabmeat and water chestnuts. Butter a 2-1/2 quart casserole. Place in it a layer of half the spinach mixture, a layer of half the crabmeat. Repeat layers. Sprinkle grated cheese on top and bake, uncovered, in 300° oven about 20 minutes, until hot through and golden brown on top.

My choice of wine to accompany this dish:
CALIFORNIA MOSELLE

Mt. Tivy Crab

(3 servings)

Mrs. Ed Benik, The Christian Brothers, Reedley

- 1 medium onion, chopped
- 3 tablespoons olive oil
- 2 cups canned tomatoes
- 1/4 cup California Sauterne
- 1/2 cup celery, diced
- 1/4 cup carrots, pared and diced
- 2 tablespoons parsley, chopped
- Salt and pepper to taste
- 1 large crab, cooked (about 3/4 lb. crabmeat)

Sauté onion in olive oil until soft and golden. Add tomatoes, wine, celery, carrots, parsley and seasonings. Simmer 15 minutes. Add crab and continue to simmer just until heated through.

NOTE: Make a bed of buttered steamed rice for this dish and serve with California Dry Sauterne.

Crustacean Casserole

(8 servings)

Mrs. Arvin E. Anderson, Gallo Sales Co., San Francisco

This dish always draws raves and requests for copies of the recipe from guests. People are surprised to learn how simple it is to prepare.

- 2-1/2 pounds crabmeat or small shrimp
- 8 slices white bread, broken into pieces
- 1 pound American or Swiss cheese, cubed
- 1/2 cup butter, melted
- 1 teaspoon dry mustard
- 1 teaspoon salt
- 3 eggs, beaten
- 1 quart milk
- 1/3 cup California Dry Sherry

Arrange crabmeat or shrimp, bread and cheese in layers in buttered casserole. Over this pour melted butter. Add mustard and salt to eggs and combine with milk. Pour egg-milk mixture into casserole, cover and refrigerate a minimum of 4 hours or overnight. Before cooking add Sherry and bake in 350° oven until custard is set.

NOTE: This is a dainty luncheon or supper dish, light and puffy, and could be accompanied by a California Chenin Blanc.

Lobster Puffs

(6 servings)

Mrs. Alvin Ehrhardt, Allied Grape Growers, Madera

These are extremely rich and dressy. They are most impressive as an appetizer.

        1   (8 oz.) package cream cheese
        1   (10-1/2 oz.) can cream of chicken soup
        1   teaspoon Worcestershire sauce
        2   teaspoons California Brandy
        3   tablespoons California Sherry
        1   (7-1/2 oz.) can lobster
        6   puff pastry shells
            Paprika

Combine softened cheese, soup, Worcestershire, Brandy and Sherry. Heat thoroughly and add lobster cut in bite size pieces. Fill baked shells with mixture, add dash of paprika to top of each and serve immediately.

NOTE: Crabmeat or shrimp could be used in this party recipe as well. California Brut Champagne would make this a truly grand send-off for a dinner party.

Lobster Thermidor

(6 servings)

Mrs. Bruno Bisceglia, Bisceglia Bros. Wine Co., Madera

Lobster might be interchangeable with crabmeat or chicken in this delicious recipe.

        6   medium lobster tails,
            fresh or frozen
        1   cup California Dry Sherry
    1/3   cup butter
        1   cup onion, minced
    1/2   cup mushrooms, chopped
            Pinch each dry mustard, mace,
            thyme, nutmeg
    1/2   cup flour
        2   cups milk
    1/2   teaspoon salt
    1/8   teaspoon pepper
        3   drops yellow food coloring
            Hollandaise sauce (optional)
            Parmesan cheese, grated
            Paprika

Cook lobster tails in boiling salted water 5 minutes. Drain, remove meat, keeping shells. Dice lobster meat coarsely and put in saucepan with Sherry. Cover and simmer over very low heat 15 minutes. Meanwhile melt butter in frying pan, add onion, mushrooms and seasonings. Sauté until onions are tender but not brown. Blend in flour and gradually add milk, stirring until smooth and thickened. Add salt and pepper. Add drained lobster meat plus 1/4 cup of Sherry it simmered in. Mix well, add food coloring and spoon into clean shells. Top each with 1 tablespoon Hollandaise sauce. Sprinkle lightly with cheese and paprika. Place on cookie sheet and bake in 400° oven 15 minutes, or until bubbly and brown on top.

NOTE: This is a real company dish. If you lack time or inclination to make Hollandaise sauce, the canned variety could be substituted, or sauce could be omitted. A California Dry White Table Wine or Champagne should be poured.

Lobster Casserole

(4 servings)

Mrs. Leonard J. Berg, Mont La Salle Vineyards, Napa

        4   cups cooked lobster
        2   (10-1/2 oz.) cans cream of celery soup
    1/2   cup milk
    1/4   cup California Dry White Table Wine
        1   cup Swiss or Cheddar cheese, shredded
        2   tablespoons parsley, minced
            Bread crumbs

Combine all ingredients in casserole. Top with bread crumbs and dot with butter. Bake in 400° oven 20 minutes, until bubbly and golden brown on top.

My choice of wine to accompany this dish:
**CALIFORNIA DRY SAUVIGNON BLANC
OR JOHANNISBERG RIESLING**

NOTE: This rich-with-fish casserole could also be made with shrimp or crabmeat, and mushroom soup could be substituted for the cream of celery. An unusual finish would be to arrange thinly sliced tomatoes over top, sprinkled with buttered crumbs mixed with a teaspoon of basil.

Feathery Shrimp

(8 servings)

Mrs. Don Rudolph, Cresta Blanca Wine Co., Livermore

These shrimp may be served with tartar sauce as an appetizer or entrée.

        2   pounds raw shrimp
    1/2   cup sifted flour
    1-1/2   teaspoons seasoned salt
    1/2   teaspoon seasoned pepper
        2   eggs
    1/4   cup California Sauterne
    3 to 4   cups fine soft bread crumbs
            Oil for deep frying

Shell and devein shrimp, leaving on tails. Rinse and pat dry. Butterfly split along back curve just to tail. Combine flour, 1 teaspoon seasoned salt and 1/4 teaspoon seasoned pepper. Beat together until frothy, eggs, wine and remaining seasoned salt and pepper. Dip shrimp in flour, then in egg mixture. Very lightly coat each shrimp with bread crumbs. Avoid making a heavy, soggy coating of crumbs. Fry shrimp, a few at a time, in deep fat at 350° 2 to 3 minutes, or until golden. Bring temperature back to 350° each time, before adding more shrimp.

My choice of wine to accompany this dish:
CALIFORNIA SAUTERNE

NOTE: These crisp delicacies could also be served, Chinese style, on a bed of finely shredded lettuce, with hot mustard. Simply stir a little water and dry mustard together and let stand 10 minutes to gain strength.

Barbecue Shrimp Supreme

(6 servings)

Mrs. Edmund Accomazzo, Cucamonga Winery, Cucamonga

    1   cup California Vin Rosé
    2   tablespoons soy sauce
    1   tablespoon lime juice
    1/4 cup clear French dressing
    1/8 teaspoon rosemary or dill leaves
    2   pounds large shelled, deveined shrimp
    1/4 cup catsup or chili sauce

Combine wine, soy sauce, lime juice, French dressing and herb, mixing well. Pour over shrimp. Cover and refrigerate several hours or overnight. Drain, reserving marinade. Cook shrimp over coals or under broiler about 5 to 8 minutes. Brush with marinade during cooking. Combine remaining baste with catsup, blending well. Serve as dip for shrimp.

NOTE: The sauce could be heated and 2 or 3 tablespoons butter swirled into it. Pass crusty French bread and serve with California Vin Rosé.

Shrimp Italian Style

(4 servings)

Mrs. Al Nerelli, Pesenti Winery, Templeton

This is a delightful dish for meatless days. Serve with asparagus, French fries, and for dessert lemon meringue pie.

    1   pound fresh shrimp or
        2 (10 oz.) packages frozen
    6   tablespoons flour
    2   tablespoons Gruyère or
        Parmesan cheese, grated
    1   teaspoon salt
    1   clove garlic
    6   green peppers
    1/2 cup olive oil
    1/2 cup California Dry White Table Wine
    3/4 teaspoon salt
    1/8 teaspoon pepper

Rinse shrimp, drain, peel and remove vein. Mix flour, cheese and salt in paper bag. Add shrimp and shake well to coat. Peel and mash garlic. Remove stem and seeds from peppers; cut into strips. Heat oil in large skillet. Add shrimp and garlic. Fry about 5 minutes until shrimp are golden. Remove shrimp and set aside. Remove garlic and discard. Add green pepper to oil, cover tightly and cook over medium heat 10 to 15 minutes, or until tender. Add shrimp, wine, salt, pepper and heat gently 5 to 8 minutes.

My choice of wine to accompany this dish:
CALIFORNIA ROSÉ OR CHABLIS

Baked Pike with Herbs

(6 servings)

Mrs. Charles Rand, Wine Advisory Board, San Francisco

    5   pound pike
    2   teaspoons salt
    1/2 teaspoon black pepper, fresh-ground
    1/4 pound butter or margarine (8 tablespoons)
    1   tablespoon parsley, minced
    1/8 teaspoon each, thyme, marjoram
    2   anchovies, minced
    1   clove garlic
    1   cup California Dry White Table Wine
    2   teaspoons flour
    2   teaspoons lemon juice

Have fish split, rinse and dry. Season fish inside and out with salt and pepper. Dot inside with 5 tablespoons butter. Spread evenly with parsley, thyme, marjoram and anchovies. Close opening with skewers or toothpicks. Rub well greased baking pan with cut clove of garlic. Place fish in pan and dot with 2 tablespoons butter. Bake in 400º oven 10 minutes. Add wine, cover with foil, reduce heat to 350º and bake 40 minutes longer, or until fish flakes when fork-tested. Carefully transfer fish to hot platter and keep warm. Pour all pan juices into saucepan. Work flour and remaining tablespoon butter together and add in small pieces to pan juices over low heat, stirring until smooth and thickened. Stir in lemon juice and correct seasoning. Pour some sauce over fish to serve and pass the rest in sauce boat.

NOTE: This method could be applied to other baking fish with equally good results. Surround the fish on platter with alternating broiled tomato halves and marinated artichoke hearts. Serve with a California Grey Riesling.

Shrimp Pimiento

(4 servings)

Mrs. George Al Berry, E. & J. Gallo Winery, Modesto

    6   tablespoons butter
    1   (4 oz.) can button mushrooms, drained
    1   tablespoon flour
    2   (10-1/2 oz.) cans cream of
        mushroom soup
    1   pound cooked, shelled,
        deveined shrimp
    1   (4 oz.) jar pimientos, chopped
        Dry parsley to taste
    3/4 cup California Dry Sherry

Melt butter in skillet, add mushrooms, reserving juice, and sauté until golden. Add flour, blending thoroughly; then mushroom juice, stirring until blended, away from heat. In casserole combine soup, shrimp, pimiento, parsley and Sherry. Add mushroom mixture and stir thoroughly. Bake in 350º oven 30 minutes.

My choice of wine to accompany this dish:
CALIFORNIA CHABLIS

NOTE: This could star on a party luncheon menu, served with hot buttered cornmeal muffins and a salad composed of romaine, butter lettuce and marinated artichoke hearts, spiced with a little California wine vinegar.

Oyster Loaf

(6 to 8 servings)

Mrs. Sherwood J. Hall, Jr., Bandiera Wines, Cloverdale

This is practically a meal in itself, so we just serve a green salad.

- 1 (16 oz.) loaf milk bread
- 1 (1-1/2 to 2 lb.) eggplant
- 2 medium onions
- 4 large stalks celery
- 2 (10 oz.) jars fresh oysters
- 2 tablespoons olive oil
- 2 tablespoons butter
- 1/2 cup California Dry Sherry
- 1/2 teaspoon salt
- 1/4 teaspoon pepper
- 1/2 teaspoon sage
- 1/2 cup milk

Slice bread lengthwise about 1/3 from top to make bread boat. Remove inside of bread, being careful not to break outer wall. Save top. Preheat oven to 325° and place bread crumbs removed in oven to brown while making other preparations. Peel eggplant and dice in 1-inch cubes. Coarsely chop onions and celery. Cut oysters in halves or thirds, depending on size. Melt oil and butter in large pan. Sauté vegetables and oysters about 5 to 8 minutes. Add wine, seasonings, bread crumbs and mix well. Fill bread boat, replace top and tie lightly with string. Place on baking sheet, pour milk over top and bake in 375° oven 15 to 20 minutes. Remove string and slice at table.

NOTE: For a change serve with a California Rosé.

Shrimp in White Sauce

(8 servings)

Mrs. Anne Matteoli, Italian Swiss Colony, Asti

This is a plain recipe, easy to prepare, but very good.

- 8 frozen patty shells
- 2 (10 oz.) cans frozen cream of shrimp soup
- 1 cup milk
- 2 cups cooked shrimp, fresh, frozen or canned
- 1 (1 lb.) can peas, drained
- 2 cups sharp Cheddar cheese, grated
- 1/4 cup California Dry Sherry

Bake patty shells per package directions. Heat soup with milk, stirring until smooth. Add shrimp, peas and continue to cook slowly about 5 minutes. Stir in half the cheese and Sherry. Remove from heat. Sprinkle remaining cheese in shells and spoon in shrimp mixture.

My choice of wine to accompany this dish:
CALIFORNIA SAUTERNE

Shrimp Creole

(6 servings)

Mrs. Jack T. Matthews, Wine Institute, San Francisco

- 2 pounds fresh shrimp, or 2 (5 oz.) cans
- 1/4 cup butter or margarine
- 2 tablespoons onion, finely chopped
- 2 large tomatoes, quartered
- 1 bay leaf
- 1/2 teaspoon salt
- 1/2 teaspoon thyme
  Dash cayenne
- 1 teaspoon sugar
- 1 (10-1/2 oz.) can condensed mushroom soup
- 1/3 cup California Dry Sherry
- 2 pimientos, cut in strips

Rinse shrimp, drop in boiling water and cook about 8 minutes, or until pink. Drain and cover with cold water to cool. Shell and devein. Melt butter in large saucepan, add onion and cook until yellow. Add tomatoes, bay leaf and other seasonings. Dilute mushroom soup with wine and add to tomato mixture. Add shrimp, pimiento and cook 5 minutes longer until thoroughly heated. Serve with rice.

My choice of wine to accompany this dish:
CALIFORNIA DRY SEMILLON OR CHABLIS

Fisherman's Delight

(6 servings)

Mrs. Alessandro Baccari, Baccari Wine Festival, San Francisco

- 6 medium slices sole
- 1 large egg, beaten
  Fine dry bread crumbs
- 3 tablespoons each, butter and olive oil

Dip fish slices in egg, roll in crumbs and sauté in butter-oil mixture until golden brown on both sides. Arrange in shallow baking dish and cover with following sauce.

SAUCE

- 3 tablespoons butter
- 3 tablespoons olive oil
- 2 small cloves garlic
- 5 or 6 lemon slices
  Dash Worcestershire sauce
  Dash Tabasco sauce
- 2 tablespoons parsley, minced
- 1 cup California Dry Sherry
- 1 cup California Sauterne
- 1 teaspoon salt
- 1/8 teaspoon pepper
- 3 tablespoons parsley, minced

Combine all ingredients except final 3 tablespoons parsley and simmer for about 25 minutes. Remove garlic and add parsley. Pour sauce over fish. Garnish with cooked lemon slices. Cover with foil and bake in 250° to 300° oven for 15 minutes.

NOTE: This attractive dish would be easy to execute by making sauce ahead of time. Serve with a California Riesling or Traminer.

Tuna in Mushroom Sauce

(4 to 6 servings)

Mrs. Karl E. Droese, Sr., E. & J. Gallo Winery, Modesto

- 2 tablespoons butter
- 1-1/2 tablespoons flour
- 1/4 teaspoon salt
- 1 cup milk
- 2 cups tuna, drained and flaked
- 1 cup mushrooms, sautéed
- 1/4 cup pimiento, chopped
- 1 egg yolk, beaten
- 3 tablespoons California Dry Sherry

Melt butter, blend in flour and salt. Add milk gradually and cook over low heat, stirring until smooth and thickened. Add fish, mushrooms and pimiento. Heat 3 or 4 minutes. Mix 1 tablespoon hot mixture with egg yolk and stir this into fish mixture. Heat without boiling a minute longer. Remove from heat, add Sherry and serve immediately, poured over noodles, or on toast.

My choice of wine to accompany this dish:
CALIFORNIA VIN ROSÉ OR PINK CHABLIS

San Francisco Sole

(2 servings)

Mrs. David R. Wilcox, Wine Advisory Board, San Francisco

I received this ideal luncheon dish from a Southern friend. The original recipe called for catfish, but I substituted sole.

- 4 medium mushrooms, chopped
- 2 green onions, finely chopped
- 1 tablespoon chives, chopped (the freeze-dried chives are excellent)
- 1 teaspoon salt
- 1/4 teaspoon pepper
- 2 fillets of sole
- 1 cup California Chablis

Combine mushrooms, onions, chives, salt and pepper. Spread evenly on fish. Roll fillets and secure with toothpicks. Place in flat baking dish, pour in wine and bake in 400° oven 15 minutes, or just until fish flakes with a fork. Remove toothpicks before serving and decorate with lemon wedges and parsley.

My choice of wine to accompany this dish:
CALIFORNIA JOHANNISBERG RIESLING

NOTE: Mrs. Wilcox serves this delicate dish with saffron rice and a salad composed of lettuce, green onion and avocado lightly tossed with French dressing and a touch of dill weed.

Superb Sole

(6 servings)

Mrs. Jacqueline Gumina, Mont La Salle Vineyards, Fresno

Lemon wedges and tomato slices topped with anchovy paste are excellent garnishes for fish dishes.

- 6 pieces fillet of sole (about 2 lbs.)
- 1/4 cup oil
- 1 cup fine dry bread crumbs
- 1/4 cup butter or margarine
- 1-1/2 tablespoons garlic, finely chopped
- 2 tablespoons parsley, finely chopped
- 1/4 cup lemon juice
- 1/2 cup California Cream Sherry
- Salt and pepper to taste

Rinse fish and pat dry with paper towel. Dip each piece into oil. Coat with bread crumbs. Place in baking dish and bake in 350° oven 5 to 8 minutes. Meanwhile melt butter, add garlic, parsley and lemon juice. Cover all pieces of fish with butter mixture, add Sherry, season to taste and bake 15 minutes, or until golden brown.

My choice of wine to accompany this dish:
**CALIFORNIA JOHANNISBERG RIESLING
OR SYLVANER RIESLING**

Halibut Véronique

(6 servings)

Mrs. Leonard Maullin, Milford Co. of California, Los Angeles

I serve this with pilaf, buttered zucchini, broiled tomatoes, and citrus and avocado salad.

- 1/2 (1-5/8 oz.) package dried mushroom soup mix
- 1 cup dairy sour cream
- 1 tablespoon lemon juice
- 1/2 cup California Dry White Table Wine
- 1 teaspoon salt
- 1/4 teaspoon pepper
  Dash each, oregano, basil, thyme, marjoram
- 1/4 cup blanched almonds, slivered
- 1 cup seedless grapes, or 1 (8 oz.) can grapes, drained, rinsed and dried
- 2 tablespoons butter
- 2 pounds halibut fillets
  Salt and pepper to taste

Combine soup mix, sour cream, lemon juice, wine and seasonings. Add almonds and grapes. Melt butter in skillet arrange fillets in this and pour sauce over fish. Cover and simmer 15 minutes, or until fish flakes. Season to taste with salt and pepper.

My choice of wine to accompany this dish:
CALIFORNIA DRY WHITE TABLE WINE OR ROSÉ

CIARAVINO SOLE. Mrs. Anthony S. Ciaravino, Wine Institute, Detroit, arranges 1 pound fillets of sole in a buttered shallow casserole and combines 1/2 cup California Chablis, 1 tablespoon finely chopped parsley, 1/2 teaspoon salt and 1/4 teaspoon pepper and pours this over fillets. Fish is covered tightly and baked at 350° 20 to 25 minutes. Serves 4. Asparagus with Hollandaise sauce would complement the delicately flavored fish. Mrs. Ciaravino pours California Chablis.

Sole Marguery

(4 servings)

Mrs. Don Rudolph, Cresta Blanca Wine Co., Livermore

- 2 tablespoons green onion, chopped
- 2 tablespoons parsley, chopped
- 1-1/2 pounds fillet of sole
- 1 teaspoon seasoned salt
- 1/4 teaspoon pepper, fresh-ground
- 2 tablespoons butter
- 1/2 cup California Dry White Table Wine
- 1 (10 oz.) can frozen cream of shrimp soup
- 2 tablespoons cream
- 1 dozen cooked shrimp
- 2 tablespoons Swiss cheese, grated

Place half chopped onion and parsley in shallow baking dish. Season sole fillets on both sides with salt and pepper. Place in dish and cover with remaining onion-parsley mixture. Dot with 1 tablespoon butter, pour in wine, cover with foil and bake in 375° oven about 15 minutes, basting occasionally. Remove from oven and drain liquid off of fish into saucepan. Keep fish warm in baking dish. Boil to reduce liquid to 1/2 cup. Gradually blend in shrimp soup, stirring until smooth. When hot, stir in cream and pour over fillets. Arrange whole shrimp on top. Sprinkle on grated cheese and dot with remaining butter. Broil until top is glazed and golden brown, about 5 minutes.

NOTE: Serve a fine California Dry White Table Wine with this rich and delicately flavored fish, which is easy to prepare and provides fine cuisine.

SOLE GOLDA by Dr. Golda Joslyn, Berkeley, is deceptively simple in preparation but provides a subtle flavor. Dip 1-1/2 filets of sole per person first in cornstarch, then in beaten egg white. Fry quickly in small quantity of shortening, preferably in Teflon pan. Brown both sides, sprinkle with 1 or 2 tablespoons California Dry Sherry, turn off heat and cover for a minute. Season to taste, accompany with lemon wedges and serve with California Dry White Table Wine.

Smoked Salmon and Sole

(6 servings)

Mrs. Lorraine Wardall, Fromm & Sichel, San Francisco

Editor's note: This dish has excellent flavor. Be careful not to overcook. The court bouillon can be reduced by boiling and frozen for future use.

- 2 onions, chopped
- 4 cups California Riesling or Rhine Wine
- 15 peppercorns
- 5 cloves
- 1 herb bouquet (bouquet garni - parsley, thyme, bay leaf)
- 6 fillets of sole
- 6 thin slices smoked salmon
- 3 eggs, beaten lightly
- 1 (10 oz.) package prepared bread crumbs
- 1/2 cup butter

In large pot combine onions, wine, spices and bouquet garni. Cover and simmer 30 minutes to make court bouillon in which to poach fish. Slice fillets and salmon in two lengthwise. Lay slice of salmon on each piece of fillet. Roll up and secure with toothpick. Have court bouillon just barely simmering and lower rolls carefully into liquid. Poach fish, covered, for 10 minutes or less. Remove rolls immediately with slotted spoon, draining well. Dip in beaten eggs, then roll in bread crumbs. Place breaded rolls in shallow buttered baking dish. Preheat broiler. Dot each roll with butter, place 2 inches from heat and broil 3 to 5 minutes, until golden brown.

My choice of wine to accompany this dish:
CALIFORNIA RHINE WINE

Sole Casserole

(6 servings)

Mrs. Paul H. Huber, Wine Brokerage, Fresno

- *Paul's Pilaf
- 3 to 4 fillets of sole
- 1 (7 oz.) can shrimp, drained
- 1 (10 oz.) can frozen shrimp soup
- 2/3 cup light cream
- 2/3 cup California Dry Sherry or Chablis
  Paprika

Cover bottom of buttered baking dish 1/2 to 1 inch deep with *Paul's Pilaf (see page 30). Place fish fillets on rice bed and cover with shrimp. Combine frozen soup, cream and wine over heat, stirring until smooth. Pour over fish, dust with paprika and bake in 300° oven 1/2 hour, or until bubbly.

My choice of wine to accompany this dish:
CALIFORNIA RIESLING OR CHABLIS

NOTE: Mrs. Huber serves her casserole with two vegetables, a green and a yellow, and for dessert, she sprinkles grapefruit halves with California Brandy and brown sugar and runs them under the broiler to caramelize the sugar.

Baked Clams au Gratin

(6 to 8 servings)

Mrs. A. C. Huntsinger, Almaden Vineyards, Los Gatos

Several years ago I was looking through an old cookbook, published in 1939, and found this recipe. I have been making it ever since and it is particularly good when made with fresh clams which our son, Jim, supplies.

         2 cups clams, coarsely ground
         2 eggs
     1/2 cup Jack, Parmesan or
         Cheddar cheese, grated
         1 teaspoon salt
     1/2 teaspoon white pepper
     1/2 cup California Dry Sherry
     1/2 cup butter
         3 strips bacon, diced
     1/3 cup each, celery, green pepper,
         green onion
     1/2 cup sifted flour
         1 pint milk, scalded
         2 tablespoons cheese, grated
         Paprika

Mix together clams, eggs, 1/2 cup grated cheese, salt, pepper and wine. Set aside. In large frying pan place butter, bacon and vegetables. Braise slowly, but do not brown. Blend in flour and cook slowly for 2 minutes. Gradually add hot milk, stirring until smooth and thickened. Stir in clam mixture, transfer to buttered baking dish, sprinkle with grated cheese, dust with paprika and bake in 350° oven 10 to 15 minutes, or until nicely brown on top.

My choice of wine to accompany this dish:
CALIFORNIA DRY WHITE TABLE WINE

Sole with Wheat Germ

(4 servings)

Mrs. H. Peter Jurgens, San Francisco

4 to 6 pieces fillet of sole
     1/3 cup wheat germ
     1/2 teaspoon salt
         2 tablespoons butter
     1/3 cup California Dry Vermouth

Dredge fish with wheat germ and salt. Sauté in butter until golden on both sides. Pour in Vermouth and heat to bubbling point. Pour sauce over fish when serving.

My choice of wine to accompany this dish:
CALIFORNIA PINOT BLANC

NOTE: This dainty sole dish could be accompanied by a salad with fresh young spinach leaves among the greens, accented with crisp, garlic-flavored croutons (see page 20).

Clammer's Delight

(4 servings)

Mrs. Don Rudolph, Cresta Blanca Wine Co., Livermore

During clamming season we usually dig our share and we find this recipe a change from the chowder we all enjoy so much.

         4 green onions, chopped
     1/2 cup butter
   1-1/2 cups raw clams, chopped
     1/4 pound shrimp, shelled and deveined
     1/4 pound crabmeat
         Dash garlic powder
         Salt and pepper to taste
     1/4 cup California Dry White Table Wine

Sauté onions in butter until soft but not brown. Add remaining ingredients. Simmer until shrimp turn pink, stirring often. Serve over noodles, spaghetti or rice.

My choice of wine to accompany this dish:
CALIFORNIA CHABLIS

NOTE: A nice presentation platter would be a bed of hot noodles, a generous pat of butter in center, the clam mixture poured over all, liberally sprinkled with chopped parsley, and garnished with lemon wedges.

Fish au Vin Rouge

(4 servings)

Mrs. Maureen E. Lawless, Wine Advisory Board, San Francisco

My grandmother used to fix this dish in Ireland and it was always a great favorite. Eels are traditional, but pike, perch or haddock — any firm fleshed fish — may be used.

         2 pounds fish, cut in thick slices
         2 cups California Zinfandel
         1 carrot, pared and sliced
         1 onion, finely chopped
         2 cloves garlic, cut in halves
         1 teaspoon salt
     1/4 teapoon pepper
         Herb bouquet (1 bay leaf, 2 peppercorns,
         rosemary, oregano, thyme to taste)
         3 tablespoons California Brandy
         3 tablespoons butter
         2 level tablespoons flour
         2 tablespoons parsley, minced

Rinse fish, if necessary, and pat dry. Place in large skillet with tight fitting cover. Add next ingredients through herb bouquet and bring to boiling. Heat brandy over hot water, ignite and immediately pour over fish. When flame has died, cover pan and simmer 15 to 20 minutes, or until fish flakes when tested with fork. Remove fish to warm, deep serving dish and keep warm. Strain cooking liquid and reserve. Blend butter and flour thoroughly, cooking gently 2 minutes. Gradually stir in cooking liquid. Cook until smooth and thickened, stirring constantly. Boil 2 minutes longer. Pour sauce over fish and sprinkle with parsley.

My choice of wine to accompany this dish:
CALIFORNIA ROSÉ

Scallops Sonoma

(6 to 8 servings)

Mrs. Frank H. Bartholomew, Buena Vista Vineyards, Sonoma

       2 pounds scallops
       1 cup California Dry White Table Wine
       6 green onions, chopped fine
     1/2 pound fresh mushrooms
       4 tablespoons butter
       2 tablespoons flour
         Salt to taste
         Pinch cayenne
       2 tablespoons parsley, chopped
     1/4 cup heavy cream
         Toasted bread crumbs

Simmer scallops in wine for 5 minutes or less. (Do not overcook.) Drain, set aside, but keep broth warm. Sauté onions and mushrooms in 2 tablespoons butter 3 or 4 minutes. Remove and set aside. Add flour to remaining butter to make smooth paste (roux). Add broth and stir until thickened. Add salt, cayenne and parsley. If sea scallops, cut in half. Bay scallops are small enough. Add shellfish, mushroom-onion mixture and cream to sauce. Fill scallop shells or individual baking dishes, cover with bread crumbs and dot with butter. Place shells on cookie sheet in preheated 350° oven and bake until hot and bubbly. Just before serving run under broiler to brown.

My choice of wine to accompany this dish:
CALIFORNIA SYLVANER OR PINOT CHARDONNAY

Frog Legs Gourmet

(6 to 8 servings)

Mrs. John A. Pedroncelli, John Pedroncelli Winery, Geyserville

This recipe can be partially prepared a day or more ahead. Add wine, sour cream and cheese just before baking and serving.

       1 large red onion, chopped
       1 green pepper, chopped
       1 pound frog legs
       2 tablespoons butter
       2 cups canned or stewed tomatoes
     1/2 cup fresh mushrooms, sliced
     1/2 teaspoon salt
     1/8 teaspoon pepper
       1 (8 oz.) package noodles, cooked
     1/2 cup dairy sour cream
     1/2 cup California Chablis
       1 cup Swiss or Jack cheese, grated

Sauté onion, green pepper and frog legs in butter. Add tomatoes, mushrooms, salt and pepper. Mix into noodles in casserole. Stir in sour cream, wine, cheese and bake in 325° oven 45 minutes.

My choice of wine to accompany this dish:
CALIFORNIA GREY RIESLING

NOTE: This is a good basic casserole recipe. Most any seafood or cubed chicken breast could be substituted for frog legs, if unobtainable.

Prawns on Skewers

(6 servings)

Mrs. Maury F. Baldwin, Owens-Illinois Glass Co., Sacramento

Prawns seem to be great favorites with teen-agers. When my football-playing son has friends over, I double the recipe. Have often wondered how these would taste cold — but I've never had any left over to find out!

 3-1/2 to 4 pounds raw prawns
     1/2 cup California Dry Sherry
     1/2 cup lemon juice
     1/2 cup olive oil
     1/2 teaspoon salt (or more to taste)
       2 small cloves garlic, mashed

Peel and devein shrimp. Combine all remaining ingredients, and marinate at least 2 hours. Thread on skewers and broil until prawns turn pink, about 8 minutes. Do not overcook.

My choice of wine to accompany this dish:
CALIFORNIA GREY RIESLING

NOTE: Mrs. Baldwin points out that prawns can be charcoal, oven or rotisserie broiled, and says that sour dough French bread or rolls are a "must" with these easy-to-do delicacies.

Cod Auvergne

(6 servings)

Mrs. Yvonne Boulleray, Windsor Vineyards, Windsor

This is an original recipe. I serve it with creamed spinach and baked potato.

       5 pound cod, cleaned and oven-ready
   1-1/2 teaspoons seasoned salt
     1/4 teaspoon pepper
       2 tablespoons butter
       3 slices lemon
       1 bay leaf, crumbled

Arrange all ingredients in greased baking dish. Bake in 370° oven 1/2 hour. Pour sauce over fish and bake 1/2 hour longer.

SAUCE

       1 onion, chopped
       2 tablespoons butter
       1 (1 lb.) can solid pack tomatoes
       1 cup California Dry Sherry
     1/2 teaspoon saffron
       1 teaspoon oregano
       1 tablespoon parsley, chopped
     1/2 bay leaf, crumbled
     1/2 teaspoon thyme
       1 (4 oz.) can sliced mushrooms
       1 tablespoon cornstarch
       2 tablespoons water

Sauté onion in butter until golden. Add tomatoes, Sherry, seasonings and mushrooms. Simmer 1 hour. Dissolve cornstarch in water to thicken sauce. If prepared ahead of time, gently reheat while fish is baking first half hour.

My choice of wine to accompany this dish:
CALIFORNIA RIESLING OR CHARDONNAY

WILD GAME

Fine recipes for venison, rabbit, dove, quail, wild boar, pheasant, trout and wild duck come from the hunters among California vintners. Many of these dishes utilize marinades based on California wines and most can be adapted for use with various domestic meats from your butcher. It is also possible, of course, to obtain game from certain city markets. One general rule to apply — remove all fat from game because it is usually not palatable. Fat can be restored by larding meat, braising in butter, adding bacon and so on. A bubbling, inviting casserole, redolent of the aroma of good cooking, spiced with a breath from the wilderness, calls for a happy gastronomic union with one of the wonderful wines of California — red or white.

Quail and Vegetable Sauce

(4 servings)

Mrs. Joseph S. Concannon, Jr., Concannon Vineyard, Livermore

Quail have been scarce in the Livermore Valley. They disappear when the hunting season opens.

- 4 quail
  Seasoned salt
- 1/3 cup salad oil
- 1/4 cup green onions, chopped
- 1 carrot, chopped fine
- 1 cup fresh mushrooms, sliced
- 2 level tablespoons flour
- 1-1/2 cups chicken broth
- 1/2 cup California Dry White Table Wine

Rub whole birds with seasoned salt. Brown on all sides in deep skillet in 1/4 cup oil. Remove birds to heated casserole. Sauté vegetables in remaining oil until soft, but not brown, about 5 minutes. Blend in flour; gradually stir in broth. Cook and stir until mixture thickens and is smooth. Season with additional salt if necessary. Pour sauce over quail; add wine, cover and bake in 350° oven about 45 minutes until birds are tender.

My choice of wine to accompany this dish:
CALIFORNIA CHABLIS, SAUVIGNON BLANC OR SEMILLON

Wild Boar Barbecue

(8 or more servings)

Mr. B. C. Solari, United Vintners, San Francisco

We get the wild boar from Imperial Wild Boar Co., P. O. Box AQ, Carmel, California 94921. While it is expensive, it is a rare taste treat.

- 2 cups honey
- 1 small can dry mustard
- 1 cup California wine vinegar

- 2 cups California Zinfandel
  Salt and pepper to taste
- 16 wild boar chops, about 3/4 inch thick

Combine first five ingredients and thoroughly blend in mixer to emulsify partially. Pour over chops in large container. Allow to marinate for several hours. Remove chops and barbecue over slow fire, about 15 to 20 minutes on each side, basting often with marinade.

My choice of wine to accompany this dish: **CALIFORNIA DRY RED TABLE WINE**

NOTE: Here is Mr. Solari's recommendation for serving: "Place in center of table on a large warm platter. Provide paper napkins and eat à la Henry VIII, throwing bones into a big dish. We do this Christmas Eve *en famille* and it's all very gala." The whole loin of a 40-pound boar would yield approximately 16 chops.

Hasenpfeffer

(4 servings)

Mr. Walter E. Schmitter, The Christian Brothers, Reedley

Editor's note: Just the meatiest pieces of the rabbit are used in this recipe. The rest might be simmered in water to produce the 3 cups of stock required for the cooking liquid.

          2 legs and saddle of hare,
             cut in 2 pieces
    1-1/2 teaspoons salt
          5 tablespoons butter
          1 medium-sized onion
          4 cloves
    1-1/2 cups California Port or Zinfandel
          1 tablespoon lemon juice
        12 peppercorns
          1 herb bouquet
             (parsley, thyme, bay leaf)
          3 cups hot stock or bouillon
          1 tablespoon flour
             Red currant jelly

Rinse meat, pat dry and rub with salt. Sauté in 3 tablespoons butter until brown on all sides, about 30 minutes. Place in casserole. Add onion stuck with cloves, 3/4 cup wine, lemon juice, pepper, herb bouquet and stock. Cover and bake in 350° oven 2-1/2 to 3 hours. About 1/2 hour before serving, melt remaining butter, blend with flour and stir into hot mixture in casserole. Add remaining wine and correct seasoning. Cover casserole and cook 30 minutes. Place hare on hot platter, strain gravy over it and serve with currant jelly.

My choice of wine to accompany this dish:
**CALIFORNIA GAMAY, CABERNET SAUVIGNON
OR PINOT NOIR**

NOTE: The herb bouquet (or Bouquet Garni in French) is composed of 1/2 teaspoon thyme, a handful of parsley and a bay leaf or two, tied up in a small square of cheesecloth. Discard before thickening sauce. This little "flavoring bag" may be varied to suit your own taste.

Wild Birds over Rice

(4 to 6 servings)

Mrs. Everett Estes, Sanger Winery Association, Sanger

          6 doves or quail
             Salt and pepper to taste
             Flour
      1/2 cup butter or margarine
      1/4 cup onion, chopped
      1/2 cup mushrooms, sliced,
             fresh or canned
          1 tablespoon parsley
      1/2 cup California Sauterne
      1/2 cup heavy cream

Wash and dry birds. Rub with salt, pepper and flour. Sauté lightly in butter, remove and place in large frying pan or casserole. Lightly sauté onion, mushrooms and parsley in butter remaining in pan in which birds were sautéed. Add wine and pour over birds. Cover and cook 30 minutes on top of stove over medium heat, basting frequently. Add cream and continue cooking until thoroughly hot.

My choice of wine to accompany this dish:
CALIFORNIA CABERNET SAUVIGNON OR GREY RIESLING

NOTE: Mrs. Estes likes to serve birds over steamed rice with a spinach or squash souffle. You may also cook birds in oven with excellent results. Bake 30 minutes at 350° covered, add cream and wine, return cover and bake at 300° for 20 minutes, or until done.

Sweet and Sour Quail

(4 servings)

Mrs. Tulio D'Agostini, D'Agostini Winery, Plymouth

          8 quail
          2 teaspoons salt
      1/2 teaspoon pepper
      1/2 cup flour
          1 tablespoon mixed herbs
             (thyme, oregano, basil)
      1/4 cup olive oil

Wash quail thoroughly, pat dry, split down back and flatten. Sprinkle with salt and pepper and roll in flour herb mixture. Brown in hot oil. Drain off fat and add Sweet-Sour Sauce. Cover and simmer slowly until tender, about 1 hour.

SWEET-SOUR SAUCE

          1 cup tomato purée
          2 cups California Burgundy
          2 tablespoons capers
          3 tablespoons brown sugar
      1/2 cup olives, chopped
          1 tablespoon dry mustard

Stir all ingredients thoroughly until mixed.

My choice of wine to accompany this dish:
CALIFORNIA BURGUNDY

NOTE: This flavorsome treatment could also be applied to Cornish game hens.

Venison Chops Cumberland

(4 servings)

Mrs. Jack T. Matthews, Wine Institute, San Francisco

This recipe comes from a dear friend in Boise, Idaho who checked me out on wild game cookery when we were stationed there during World War II. As meat was rationed and wild game was plentiful, we survived nicely!

    4   venison chops
    1   teaspoon salt
    1/8 teaspoon pepper
    2   tablespoons flour
        Oil
    1   small jar currant jelly
    1/4 cup Worcestershire sauce
    1/4 pound butter
    1/2 cup California Sherry
    3   slices lemon
    3   slices orange

Dredge chops in salt, pepper and flour. Fry in heated oil in skillet over moderate heat to desired degree of doneness. Put in baking dish, cover and keep hot in warm oven. Make sauce by combining jelly, Worcestershire sauce, butter, wine and fruits and simmer, stirring, until jelly and butter melt and blend. Pour sauce over chops and serve.

My choice of wine to accompany this dish:
**CALIFORNIA SPARKLING BURGUNDY
OR DRY RED TABLE WINE**

NOTE: Mrs. Matthews serves this dish surrounded with spiced fruits, such as crab apples and pears, accompanies it with steamed rice and buttered broccoli. This same sauce would be delicious with thick loin lamb chops.

Oven-Barbecued Duck

(6 servings)

Mrs. Frank Caffarelli, Diamond International, San Francisco

    2   large wild ducks, quartered and
        brushed with lemon juice
    1/3 cup California Sauterne
    1/3 cup oil
    1   tablespoon onion, grated
    1   clove garlic, crushed
    1   tablespoon paprika
    1   teaspoon Worcestershire sauce
    1/4 teaspoon freshly ground black pepper
        Salt to taste

Arrange duck quarters in shallow baking pan. Combine remaining ingredients and brush mixture over ducks. Roast ducks in a 350° oven 1 hour, or until tender, basting frequently.

NOTE: A California Burgundy or Claret would complement these savory ducks.

Rabbit Casserole

(4 servings)

Mrs. Auguste Pirio, The Christian Brothers, St. Helena

Chicken may also be prepared this way.

    1/4 cup flour
    1   teaspoon salt
    1/8 teaspoon pepper
    1   tablespoon parsley, chopped
    1   clove garlic, minced
    1   frying rabbit,
        cut in serving pieces
    1/3 cup butter or margarine
    1/2 cup California Sauterne
    1   small bay leaf

Combine first 5 ingredients. Dredge rabbit pieces in the seasoned flour. Heat butter in skillet and brown rabbit well on all sides. Remove meat to casserole or baking pan, add wine and bay leaf and bake uncovered in 325° oven for about 1 hour.

My choice of wine to accompany this dish:
CALIFORNIA DRY RED OR WHITE TABLE WINE

Roast Duck au Naturel

(4 servings)

Mr. Karl C. Krupp, Charles Krug Winery, St. Helena

This recipe comes from the farmlands of Germany. The crisp brown skin on the breast is the best, so save a piece for yourself.

    1   4 or 5 pound duck
        Salt
    1   cup water
    1   cup California Sweet Sauterne
        Cornstarch

Thaw duck, check cavity to be sure two blood sacs at each side of spine are removed, cut off excess neck skin, rinse thoroughly and drain dry. Salt inside and outside, place breast <u>down</u> on rack in covered roasting pan, prick skin around <u>thighs</u>, add water, cover and roast in 425° oven about 1 hour, or until fat has been rendered. Remove duck, pour off all fat. Return duck, breast side <u>up</u>, on rack; add wine, cover and roast for another hour or until tender, adding water as needed to prevent burning, and basting occasionally. Cook uncovered last half hour. Remove duck, keep warm. Add water depending on quantity of gravy desired, scrape bottom and sides of roaster until all brown particles are dissolved in gravy. Thicken slightly with a little cornstarch mixed with water. Strain.

My choice of wine to accompany this dish:
CALIFORNIA GEWÜRZTRAMINER

NOTE: Mr. Krupp says, "Heat caramelizes grape sugar in Sauterne and produces a luscious, rich brown gravy. High heat will render out fat and leave skin crisp and brown like parchment." For extra flavor place 1 whole apple, 1 whole onion and 1 or 2 stalks of celery, cut up, in body cavity and discard before serving. He suggests serving with his Brandied Carrots. (See page 47.)

Pheasant Katula

(4 servings)

Mrs. Tulio D'Agostini, D'Agostini Winery, Plymouth

- 1 pheasant
- 1 small onion, chopped
- 1/4 cup olive oil
- 1 pound tomatoes, peeled
- 1-1/2 teaspoons salt
- 1/4 teaspoon pepper
- 2 cups California Burgundy
- 1/4 teaspoon rosemary, crumbled
- 1/4 teaspoon orange peel, grated
- 1/4 teaspoon sweet basil, crumbled
- 1 (2 oz.) can button mushrooms

Cut pheasant into serving pieces. Cover with cold, salted water and let stand two hours; drain well. Brown onion in olive oil in Dutch oven. Add tomatoes, salt, pepper and pheasant; cook uncovered in 375° oven until pheasant is lightly browned, about 1 hour. Add wine, seasonings, undrained mushrooms, cover tightly and continue cooking until pheasant is tender, about 1 hour more.

My choice of wine to accompany this dish:
CALIFORNIA BURGUNDY

NOTE: Mrs. D'Agostini often serves eggplant casserole, tossed green salad and fresh fruit with cheese with pheasant.

Rabbit Stew

(4 servings)

Mrs. T. E. Rogers, The Christian Brothers, Reedley

- 1 (2-1/2 to 3 lb.) rabbit
- 1 cup California red wine vinegar
- 1 cup California Red Table Wine
- 1 cup onions, sliced
- 3 bay leaves
- 2 teaspoons salt
- 1/2 teaspoon ground cloves
- 1/4 teaspoon thyme
- 3/4 teaspoon Tabasco sauce
- 1 cup flour, sifted
- 1 teaspoon salt
- 1/2 cup shortening
- 1 cup broth, or water
- 2 teaspoons sugar

Cut rabbit in serving pieces. Combine vinegar, wine, onion, bay leaves, salt, cloves, thyme and Tabasco. Marinate fresh rabbit in this marinade for 2 days, or about 5 hours if rabbit is frozen. Strain and reserve marinade. Combine flour and 1 teaspoon salt and coat rabbit pieces. Heat shortening in large skillet and sauté rabbit until brown on all sides. Drain off fat. Add strained marinade and broth. Cover and simmer about 45 minutes, stirring occasionally. Add sugar before serving.

NOTE: Mrs. Rogers serves this spicy stew with a purée of chestnuts. Any California Dry Red Table Wine would be excellent with it.

Roast Venison

(6 servings)

Mrs. Everett T. Estes, Sanger Winery Association, Sanger

For an appropriate decoration, garnish platter with clusters of grapes.

- 1 cup water
- 1 onion, sliced
- 2 carrots, sliced
- 1 teaspoon whole peppercorns
- 1 bay leaf
- 1-1/2 cups California Burgundy or Red Table Wine
- 6 to 7 pound venison roast (rump or saddle)
- 4 to 6 slices bacon or salt pork

Combine water, onion, carrots, peppercorns and bay leaf. Simmer 15 minutes, add wine and pour over meat. Cover and let stand in refrigerator overnight or up to 3 days, turning meat occasionally. Remove meat from marinade, wipe dry and lay bacon or salt pork over top. Roast in 350° oven for 1-1/2 hours. Baste with marinade, return to oven and roast about 1 hour longer, continuing to baste occasionally with marinade. Venison should be slightly rare. Serve with Cumberland Sauce.

CUMBERLAND SAUCE

- 1/2 cup marinade, strained
- 1 cup red currant jelly
- 1 tablespoon lemon juice
- 1/2 teaspoon ground ginger
- 2 tablespoons California Dry Sherry or White Table Wine

Combine all ingredients and heat, stirring, until smooth.

My choice of wine to accompany this dish:
CALIFORNIA CLARET OR BURGUNDY

BARBECUED TROUT prepared like this might cause a raised eyebrow from the purist, but it's very good anyway. Mrs. Richard W. Wilson, Vie-Del Co., Fresno, says, "To retain the delicate flavor of trout and prevent it from sticking to the grill, brush fish inside and out with 3/4 cup mayonnaise (homemade if possible) mixed with 2 tablespoons California Dry White Table Wine, seasoned to taste with salt, pepper and other desired flavoring or herb. Place trout in a greased wire chicken rack over hot coals, turning once." Mrs. Wilson suggests that any California Dry White Table Wine goes well with this dish.

Fasan Mit Ananas Kraut

(2 to 4 servings)

Mr. Walter E. Schmitter, The Christian Brothers, Reedley

    2   young pheasants, cleaned and drawn
1-1/2   teaspoons salt
        Dash pepper
    2   thin slices bacon
    2   tablespoons butter
1-1/2   pounds sauerkraut
  1/2   cup California Riesling
    1   cup fresh pineapple, diced
    1   tablespoon flour

Rinse eviscerated birds (remove heads and feet), pat dry. Season lightly inside and out with salt and pepper. Place bacon slice on breast of each bird, tie or skewer in place with toothpicks. Sauté birds in butter 15 minutes, or until lightly browned. Place in deep Dutch oven or casserole. Drain sauerkraut a little. Mix sauerkraut with wine and pineapple and surround birds. Cover and cook slowly 1 hour. When birds are done, remove from sauerkraut, remove string or skewers. Place birds on hot platter and keep warm. Stir flour into sauerkraut and cook a few minutes to thicken. Serve on platter with birds.

My choice of wine to accompany this dish:
CALIFORNIA RIESLING

Venison Casserole

(4 to 6 servings)

Mrs. John A. Pedroncelli, John Pedroncelli Winery, Geyserville

This recipe came to me from an old friend who enjoyed wild game and good wine.

    2   pounds venison, stew or steak meat
    1   (10-1/2 oz.) can mushroom soup
    1   (4 oz.) can sliced mushrooms,
        undrained
  3/4   cup California Burgundy
    1   onion, chopped

Mix all ingredients in 2-1/2 quart casserole. Cover and bake in 325° oven for 3 hours, or until meat is tender.

My choice of wine to accompany this dish:
CALIFORNIA BURGUNDY

NOTE: This is easy to prepare and good. It could be varied by using California White Table Wine for lighter color gravy; and beef stew meat could be substituted for venison.

Pheasant Provençal

(6 servings)

Mrs. Robert Diana, Villa Armando Winery, Pleasanton

  1/2   cup olive oil
    2   small cloves garlic
    2   (3 lb.) pheasants,
        cut in serving pieces
  1/2   teaspoon salt
  1/8   teaspoon pepper
    2   sprigs sage
        Pinch of rosemary
  1/4   cup dried mushrooms
        (soaked in water)
  3/4   cup California Dry Vermouth
        or Sherry

In large electric skillet at 375° heat olive oil and garlic. Add pheasant pieces and brown. Add seasonings, cover and cook until almost tender, about 1 hour. Uncover, add mushrooms, drained and 1/2 cup Vermouth or Sherry. Continue cooking until done, 15 to 20 minutes longer. Remove pheasant to heated platter. To drippings add remaining 1/4 cup Vermouth and deglaze skillet. Pour over pheasant and serve immediately.

My choice of wine to accompany this dish:
CALIFORNIA CHIANTI OR ZINFANDEL

NOTE: For those who do not like garlic with pheasant, either omit or remove from oil after heating. Mrs. Diana suggests serving with wild rice, mustard greens, sourdough bread and zabaglione for dessert.

Braised Pheasant

(2 servings)

Mrs. Irene Kershaw, Mills Winery, Sacramento

    1   tangerine
    1   pheasant
  1/2   cup oil
    8   large mushroom caps, sliced
    4   tablespoons butter
    1   small onion, chopped
    1   tablespoon flour
    2   tablespoons California Marsala
        Salt, pepper, and fennel to taste

Place peeled tangerine and liver of bird in body cavity. Lace opening shut and brown bird slowly in oil, turning frequently. Transfer bird to heavy casserole. Sauté mushrooms in oil used to brown bird. In another saucepan blend carefully butter, onion and flour and cook for 1 minute. Add wine slowly, stirring constantly. Add mushrooms and season to taste with salt, pepper and fennel, if desired. Pour sauce over pheasant in casserole, cover tightly and bake in 400° oven for 25 minutes.

My choice of wine to accompany this dish:
CALIFORNIA DRY WHITE TABLE WINE

NOTE: We suggest adding at least 1 tablespoon more wine to casserole after removing pheasant to warm platter, in order to deglaze pan and make more gravy. This recipe insures a moist, tender bird.

MEATS

There are an almost infinite number of ways that wine enhances flavor, texture and appearance in meat cookery. The many successful experiments in the kitchens of California's winemakers, presented here, prove this. Some basic guidelines might be kept in mind. Stews always improve in flavor if made the day before they are to be served. Roasts should stand in a warm place 15 or 20 minutes after cooking, so that juices will retreat back into tissue, making carving easier and taste better. Cornstarch is a lightening thickener for gravies. Wine can almost always be substituted for all or part of the water in cooking liquid. When the steaming platter is presented, fill the glasses with the California wine suggested and fall to!

Golfer's Beef Stew

(6 servings)

Mrs. Leonard P. LeBlanc, California Growers Wineries, Cutler
I find this recipe great to fix after a cool day on the golf course. It just takes minutes to prepare.

- 2 pounds beef stew, cut in chunks
- 1 (10-1/2 oz.) can cream of mushroom soup
- 1 (10-1/2 oz.) can cream of celery soup
- 1 (2-3/4 oz.) package dried onion soup
- 1 cup California Burgundy

Place meat in large casserole. Combine soups and wine, pour over beef, cover and bake in a 250° oven for 3 hours. Serve with rice or noodles.

My choice of wine to accompany this dish:
CALIFORNIA ROSÉ

Deviled Swiss Steak

(6 servings)

Mrs. Hector C. Castro, Bear Mountain Winery, Di Giorgio
Goes well with a bland vegetable like mashed potatoes or squash.

- 1/4 cup flour
- 2 teaspoons salt
- 1/4 teaspoon pepper
- 1-1/2 teaspoons dry mustard
- 1/4 cup oil
- 3 pounds round steak, cut 1-1/2 inches thick
- 1/2 cup California Dry Red Table Wine
- 1 tablespoon Worcestershire sauce
- 1 (3 oz.) can mushroom sauce

Combine first 4 ingredients. Roll steak in seasoned flour and pound into meat with mallet or edge of saucer. Brown meat in oil on both sides. Combine wine and Worcestershire; pour over meat. Stir in mushroom sauce, cover tightly and simmer 2 hours, or until meat is tender.

My choice of wine to accompany this dish:
CALIFORNIA BURGUNDY

Beef Pinot Noir

(4 servings)

Mrs. Rodney Strong, Windsor Vineyards, Windsor

Loving Boeuf Bourguignonne as I do and time always being short, I arrived at this version.

1-1/2	pounds filet of beef, sliced 1/4-inch thick
2	tablespoons butter
1	clove garlic, crushed
1	tablespoon flour
1-1/2	teaspoons salt
1/4	teaspoon pepper
1/16	teaspoon powdered thyme
1	cup California Pinot Noir
1	pound fresh mushrooms, sliced
8	small canned white onions
2	tablespoons parsley, chopped

Brown meat well in butter with garlic. Add flour and seasonings, stirring. Add wine and cook over high heat. When wine has been nearly absorbed, add mushrooms and cook again over high heat, stirring constantly. Add onions and let remain over lowered heat only until onions are heated. Sprinkle with parsley and serve immediately. This dish must not stand or it will discolor and toughen.

My choice of wine to accompany this dish:
CALIFORNIA PINOT NOIR

Dodie's Chipped Beef

(6 servings)

Mrs. Doris Paulsen, Wine Institute, San Francisco

2	tablespoons butter
1	pint dairy sour cream
1/2	cup California Dry Sauterne
1	(6 oz.) jar artichoke hearts
1	tablespoon Parmesan cheese, grated
3	(3 oz.) packages chipped beef
	Dash cayenne
1/8	teaspoon paprika

Melt butter in frying pan, add 2 tablespoons sour cream and stir to avoid curdling. Add remaining cream, stirring until smooth. Add wine, artichoke hearts, (sliced thin), cheese, beef, (cut or torn into small pieces), cayenne and paprika. Heat over very low heat until well blended.

NOTE: Mrs. Paulsen serves this easy, zesty version of chipped beef in corn muffin cups or toast cups, which can be made by placing slices of well buttered bread, crusts removed, in muffin pan cups and browning in oven. Serve with a California Dry Sauterne.

Beef Stroganoff Nerelli

(4 servings)

Mrs. Al Nerelli, Pesenti Winery, Templeton

3/4	pound fresh mushrooms, sliced
1	cup onion, sliced
1/3	cup butter
1	pound lean beef tenderloin, cut in 1/2 x 1-1/2-inch strips
1	teaspoon salt
1/8	teaspoon pepper
1	cup beef broth or bouillon
2	tablespoons tomato paste
1	tablespoon Worcestershire sauce
3	level tablespoons flour
1-1/2	cups dairy sour cream
1/2	cup California Dry Sherry

Sauté mushrooms and onion in butter until golden brown. Remove from skillet and set aside. Add meat to skillet, brown evenly and sprinkle with salt and pepper. Add beef broth, tomato paste, Worcestershire, cover and simmer until tender. Combine flour with a little water to make thin paste. Stir into meat mixture and cook until thickened. Add mushrooms, onions, stir in sour cream, wine and heat for a few minutes longer. Serve over rice or noodles.

My choice of wine to accompany this dish:
CALIFORNIA ZINFANDEL OR BURGUNDY

Steak au Poivre

(4 servings)

Mrs. Marjorie K. Jacobs, Wine Advisory Board, San Francisco

This same treatment can be applied to hamburger patties with fine results and less strain on the food budget.

4	individual steaks, 3/4 to 1 inch thick
1-1/2	tablespoons whole peppercorns
4	tablespoons butter
2	tablespoons green onions, minced
1/2	cup rich stock or canned consommé
1/3	cup California Burgundy
	Water cress

Trim excess fat off of steaks and heat in skillet to render. Crush peppercorns coarsely with mortar and pestle, or in wooden bowl. Dry steaks and press cracked pepper into both sides of meat. Cover and let stand at least 1/2 hour, preferably longer, to allow meat to absorb flavor. Add a little oil, if necessary, to beef fat and sauté steaks when pan is smoking hot, 4 minutes on each side for rare, or according to taste. Remove steaks to hot platter and keep warm. Pour off fat and add 1 tablespoon butter to skillet, add onions and sauté slowly 1 minute. Add stock, wine and boil down rapidly, stirring to deglaze pan. When reduced by half, swirl in remaining butter 1/2 tablespoon at a time, away from heat. When butter is incorporated, reheat briefly, pour over steaks, decorate platter with cress and serve.

My choice of wine to serve with this dish:
CALIFORNIA ZINFANDEL

Healdsburg Stroganoff

(3 to 4 servings)

Mrs. Robert H. Meyer, Italian Swiss Colony, Asti

This recipe utilizes leftover roast beef, which sometimes can present a problem. The dish goes well with a salad of avocado slices and grapefruit sections with French dressing that includes California wine vinegar.

      1 (3 oz.) can sliced broiled mushrooms
         Water
      2 cups roast beef, diced
    1/2 cup California Burgundy
    3/4 cup onion, finely chopped
    1/2 teaspoon paprika
    1/8 teaspoon garlic powder
      1 teaspoon salt
    1/2 cup dairy sour cream

Drain broth from mushrooms and add enough water to make 1/2 cup. Combine with all remaining ingredients except sour cream. Cover and simmer 30 minutes. Blend in sour cream, heat through but do not boil. Serve with steamed rice. Garnish, if desired, with parsley or chives.

My choice of wine to accompany this dish:
CALIFORNIA BURGUNDY

NOTE: There was an unknowing meeting of minds over the simplicity and goodness of this dish for Mrs. Frank Franzia, Sr., Franzia Brothers Winery, Ripon, sent in her version in which she used more California Burgundy (1-1/2 cups) and substituted garlic salt for powder. Both ladies serve this dish with the same garnished rice.

Burgundy Meat Rolls

(5 or 6 servings)

Mrs. D. C. Turrentine, Wine Advisory Board, San Francisco

Good with rice pilaf, green vegetable, tomato aspic, and for dessert a wine fruit compote.

  1-1/2 pounds round steak, sliced 1/2-inch
         thick by butcher
    1/2 teaspoon salt
    1/4 teaspoon white pepper
      2 cups stuffing mix
    1/4 cup flour
    1/2 teaspoon salt
    1/8 teaspoon pepper
      2 tablespoons shortening
      1 (10-3/4 oz.) can beef gravy
    1/2 cup California Burgundy
    1/2 cup dairy sour cream

Pound meat with meat hammer, or edge of saucer. Sprinkle with salt and pepper. Cut into 5 or 6 pieces, each suitable for a serving. Prepare stuffing mix according to package directions. Spoon about 1/2 cup prepared stuffing in center of each piece of steak. Roll and tie with string or skewer. Coat each roll in seasoned flour. Heat shortening in large, heavy skillet and brown rolls well. Combine beef gravy with wine, add to skillet and cook over low heat, covered, about 1 hour. Spoon gravy over meat occasionally during cooking. Remove rolls to warm platter. Stir sour cream into gravy, pour over rolls and serve.

My choice of wine to accompany this dish:
CALIFORNIA DRY RED TABLE WINE

Beef in Herb Sauce

(4 to 6 servings)

Mrs. H. Peter Jurgens, San Francisco

  3 or 4 medium onions, sliced
        2 tablespoons bacon fat
        2 pounds lean beef
           (sirloin tip preferred)
    1-1/2 tablespoons flour
        1 (10-1/2 oz.) can beef bouillon
    1-1/2 cups California Burgundy
      1/4 teaspoon each marjoram, thyme
           and oregano, finely crumbled
        1 teaspoon salt
      1/2 teaspoon pepper
      1/2 pound fresh mushrooms, sliced
      1/4 cup butter

Sauté onions in bacon fat until golden and set aside. Add meat cut in 1-1/2-inch cubes to pan, sprinkle with flour and continue cooking until meat is well browned. Add bouillon, wine, herbs and seasonings. Cover pan tightly and simmer over low heat about 2 hours. Meanwhile sauté mushrooms in butter and about 20 minutes before meat should be done, add mushrooms and onions to casserole. Cook until meat is tender.

My choice of wine to accompany this dish:
CALIFORNIA PINOT NOIR OR BURGUNDY

Swiss Steak Aguirre

(6 to 8 servings)

Mrs. Cecil Aguirre, Wente Bros., Livermore

This recipe was purely an experiment, but we enjoy it very much. I cook with the best wine available to achieve the most piquant and tantalizing flavor.

- 3/4 cup California Burgundy
- 1/4 cup water
- 2 medium cloves garlic, pressed
- 1 stalk celery, diced
  - Pinch of mixed Italian seasoning
- 1/2 pound fresh mushrooms, or 1 (4 oz.) can, sliced
- 2 tablespoons butter
- 1/3 cup flour, seasoned with 1 teaspoon salt and 1/4 teaspoon pepper
- 2 to 3 pounds round steak, 3/4 to 1 inch thick
  - Bacon fat
- 2 medium onions, chopped

Combine wine, water, garlic, celery, Italian seasoning and let stand during other preparation. Sauté mushrooms in butter until golden. If canned mushrooms are used, drain juice into wine mixture. Rub seasoned flour into tenderized round steak and fry in sufficient bacon fat to brown both sides. Remove from pan, add onions and fry slowly until lightly browned. Return meat to pan, surrounded with onions, add wine mixture and top with mushrooms. Cover tightly and simmer slowly about 1/2 hour, or until meat is tender. Add wine if more moisture is needed.

My choice of wine to accompany this dish:
CALIFORNIA BURGUNDY OR PINOT NOIR

NOTE: Mrs. Aguirre says, "I like to serve steamed carrots with mint sauce and my special potatoes with this dish. I pressure-cook whole potatoes, peel and cut in half, roll them in 2 or more tablespoons melted butter in pan, sprinkle with paprika and bake to a crisp brown in a 350° oven."

STEAK CASSEROLE. Mrs. Anne Matteoli, Italian Swiss Colony, Asti, makes this simple dish for Saturday night's dinner in winter. Cut a 1-1/2 pound slice of round steak into 6 servings and brown in 1 tablespoon of oil. Place in casserole with 1 cup California Burgundy. Cover and bake in 325° oven 1 hour. Stir in 1 (10-1/2 oz.) can cream of mushroom soup. Cover and continue to bake 50 or 60 minutes longer, until meat is tender. Season to taste. Her choice of wine to serve with this dish is CALIFORNIA BURGUNDY.

Spanish Steak

(6 to 8 servings)

Mrs. Catherine Soza, Wine Advisory Board, San Francisco

This is a recipe I learned from my mother, who originally prepared it minus the tomatoes and substituting white wine for red. It's ideal because once you've put it together you can put it in the oven and "forget it" until serving time.

- 1 cup flour
- 2 teaspoons salt
- 1-1/2 teaspoons pepper
- 1/2 teaspoon garlic powder
- 2 to 3 pounds round steak, tenderized
  - Oil
- 1 very large onion, chopped
- 1 medium green pepper, cut in strips
- 1 (1 lb. 12 oz.) can whole tomatoes, undrained
- 1 (4 oz.) can mushroom stems and pieces, undrained
- 1/2 cup California Burgundy

Combine flour, salt, pepper and garlic powder. Cut meat into serving pieces and roll pieces on all sides twice in seasoned flour. Put 1/2-inch oil in heavy large oven-proof casserole and heat. Brown meat on all sides and set aside. Drain off fat. Combine all remaining ingredients except wine, add to casserole and bring to boil. Add meat and wine and enough water to cover meat. Cover and bake in 350° oven 2 hours until meat is fork tender. Another 1/2 cup wine may be added during cooking, if desired.

My choice of wine to accompany this dish:
CALIFORNIA PINOT NOIR OR BURGUNDY

San Jose Steak

(4 to 6 servings)

Mrs. A. C. Huntsinger, Almaden Vineyards, Los Gatos

With frozen French fries, lima beans and cherry pie, this completes a good quick dinner from the freezer.

- 1 to 1-1/2 pounds frozen steak
- 1/2 to 1 cup California Burgundy or Chianti
- 1 (4 oz.) can mushrooms

Defrost steak and pan-broil until half done to taste. Pour other ingredients over steak, starting with 1/2 cup wine and increasing as needed. Simmer gently until done. Season to taste.

My choice of wine to accompany this dish:
CALIFORNIA BURGUNDY OR PINOT NOIR

Beef Berenice

(6 to 8 servings)

Mrs. Karl Kasca, Mont La Salle Vineyards, Napa

    1 to 1-1/2 cups California Burgundy
       1/2 cup butter or margarine, melted
       1/2 teaspoon lime juice
       1/2 teaspoon lemon juice
            Tabasco sauce to taste
    3 to 4 pound beef roast

Combine all liquid ingredients in bowl just large enough to contain roast, so that liquid will cover meat. Leave roast in marinade for several hours or overnight, refrigerated. Wrap meat completely with foil, overlapping folds, and place on rack in roaster. Roast according to your own method and to taste — rare, medium or well-done. The remaining marinade can be used in gravy.

NOTE: If there are sufficient drippings, make a Yorkshire pudding to serve with beef. Mix well 1/2 teaspoon salt, 1 cup sifted flour, 1 cup milk, 2 eggs, pour in roasting pan over 4 tablespoons beef drippings and bake until puffed and brown. Cut in squares. Serve a California Dry Red Table Wine with the roast, and don't forget the horseradish.

Guerneville Goulash

(4 servings)

Mr. Rudy Janci, F. Korbel & Bros., Guerneville

    1/2 pound lean beef
    1/2 pound veal
    1/2 pound pork
      1 tablespoon peanut oil
    1/4 cup California Brandy
      1 (1-3/8 oz.) package dried
         onion soup mix
    1/4 cup tomato paste
      1 (4 oz.) can button mushrooms,
         undrained
  1-3/4 cups California Red Table Wine

Cube beef, veal and pork. In large, heavy saucepan, sauté meats in oil about 10 minutes, or until nicely browned. Heat Brandy gently, pour over meats and ignite, shaking pan until flame dies out. Add all other ingredients, stir well to blend, cover pan and simmer over low heat 1 hour, or until fork tender.

NOTE: Serve over hot buttered noodles with a California Pinot Noir or Cabernet Sauvignon.

Gribelis Noodles

(6 servings)

Mrs. Gary Coleman, Wine Institute, San Francisco

This recipe has been in the family a long time and is especially liked by the male members.

      2 pounds Swiss steak
    1/4 cup flour
         Salt and pepper to taste
      1 tablespoon oil
      1 large onion, sliced
      1 teaspoon Italian seasoning
      3 cups water
      1 cup California Sauterne
      4 tablespoons melted butter
      1 cup bread crumbs
      1 pound egg noodles

Dredge meat in seasoned flour and brown in oil in Dutch oven. Add onion, Italian seasoning, water and wine. Cover and simmer 2 hours, or until meat is tender. About 1/2 hour before meat is done, place melted butter in large flat pan and cover pan with bread crumbs. Bake in 350° oven about 15 minutes or until crumbs are brown. Cook noodles in salted water according to package directions, drain well and stir into crumbs. When noodles are well coated with crumbs, return to oven and bake another 15 minutes until top is golden brown and crisp. Serve with meat.

My choice of wine to accompany this dish:
CALIFORNIA RIESLING

NOTE: Mrs. Coleman suggests French cut string beans lightly sautéed in butter and garlic, garnished with pitted olives, as a good vegetable to serve.

Barbecue Flank Steak

(4 servings)

Mrs. Douglas Richards, Weibel Champagne Vineyards, Mission San Jose

This is a recipe my sister, Mrs. W. V. Hooey, gave me.

    1/4 cup soy sauce
    1/4 cup California Dry White Table Wine
      3 tablespoons honey
      2 tablespoons California wine vinegar
  1-1/2 teaspoons garlic powder
  1-1/2 teaspoons ground ginger
      2 green onions, chopped
    3/4 cup oil
      2 flank steaks

Mix all ingredients in dish large enough to immerse steaks. Marinate at least 4 hours or overnight. Barbecue over hot coals about 5 minutes on each side. Slice diagonally in thin slices.

My choice of wine to accompany this dish:
CALIFORNIA CLARET OR CABERNET

Steak with Marinade

(6 to 8 servings)

Mrs. Robert H. Meyer, Italian Swiss Colony, Asti

In this marinade, if some of the ingredients don't happen to be on the pantry shelf, substitutions can be made without detriment to flavor.

3 to 4 pounds boneless rump, sirloin tips or top round, cut 2 inches thick
1/4 teaspoon seasoned meat tenderizer per pound
2 tablespoons salad oil
3/4 cup chili sauce
1/4 cup hot catsup
1 teaspoon garlic, minced
1 cup California Burgundy
1 tablespoon brown sugar
2 tablespoons honey
2 teaspoons dry mustard
1/2 cup water

Moisten meat with cold water, using fingers or pastry brush. Sprinkle with instant tenderizer. Use no salt. Prick meat deeply with kitchen fork or ice pick at 1/2-inch intervals. (This permits penetration of tenderizer). Choose china or glass dish large enough to accommodate steak and combine all other ingredients. Place meat in marinade for 1 hour or longer. Drain steak well and grill about 2 inches above coals, which have burned down to grey, shot with ruddy glow. Barbecue, turning several times, 25 minutes for rare, 30 minutes for medium. Carve in thin diagonal slices, across grain.

My choice of wine to accompany this dish:
CALIFORNIA DRY RED OR WHITE TABLE WINE

NOTE: Mrs. Meyer suggests that remaining marinade may be heated with beef broth or canned beef gravy for sauce. She serves hot German potato salad with the steak.

Steak in Zinfandel Sauce

(8 servings)

Mrs. Arthur J. Reese, Wine Advisory Board, San Francisco

3 pounds top round
1/2 cup flour
2 teaspoons salt
1/2 teaspoon pepper
4 tablespoons fat
3 medium onions, sliced
1 green pepper, diced
1 cup celery, diced
1-1/2 cups California Zinfandel
1 cup tomato juice

Cut round steak in chunks, dredge in flour, salt and pepper. Brown thoroughly in fat, add vegetables and half the wine, cover and bake in 400° oven 1/2 hour. Add remaining wine and tomato juice. Bake 1 hour longer, or until meat is tender.

NOTE: Ease and speed of preparation combined with moderately long cooking time produce well flavored beef bathed in good gravy. A glass of California Zinfandel is called for.

Rollatini Italia

(12 servings)

Mrs. Frank Franzia, Sr., Franzia Brothers Winery, Ripon

2 pounds beef round steak, about 1/4 inch thick
12 slices prosciutto ham
2/3 cup dry bread crumbs
1 (1-1/2 oz.) package spaghetti sauce mix
1/4 cup milk
1/2 pound Monterey Jack cheese, or Swiss
2 tablespoons olive oil
1 (8 oz.) can tomato sauce
1 cup water
1/2 cup California Dry Sherry
1/2 teaspoon salt
1 pound spaghetti
Parmesan cheese, grated

Pound meat lightly to flatten and cut into 12 squares. Place 1 slice ham on each. Combine bread crumbs with 2 teaspoons spaghetti sauce mix and milk. Top each square of meat with 1 heaping tablespoon crumb mixture. Cut cheese into 12 sticks and place one on crumbs in each square. Roll up meat being careful to enclose stuffing; tie securely with string. Brown rollatini lightly in oil, add tomato sauce, remaining spaghetti sauce mix, water, wine and salt. Cover and simmer about 1 hour until tender. Remove strings. Serve rollatini and sauce with hot spaghetti and grated cheese.

NOTE: Serve this delicious Italian specialty with any California Dry Red Table Wine.

Casserole Maddalena

(6 servings)

Mrs. Maddalena Riboli, San Antonio Winery, Los Angeles

This excellent casserole has several advantages. It will absorb leftover vegetables and diced potatoes beautifully, in addition to ingredients given.

    3   pounds top round steak
    1/2 cup flour
    2   teaspoons salt
    1/4 teaspoon pepper
    1   teaspoon paprika
    1/16 teaspoon cayenne
    1/4 cup bacon fat or oil
    1   onion, or 2 cloves garlic, chopped
    2   cups hot water
    2   cups fresh or frozen peas
    2   bunches green spring onions
    2   (4 oz.) cans button mushrooms
    1   cup chili sauce
    1/4 teaspoon marjoram, crumbled
    1   cup California Burgundy

Cut steak in 1-inch pieces and roll in mixture of flour, salt, pepper, paprika and cayenne. Brown on all sides in fat or oil, adding onion or garlic, in Dutch oven or heat-proof casserole. Add water, cover and simmer until almost tender, about 1-1/2 hours. Add peas, cook another 10 minutes. Add onions with their green ends, removing only the very coarse parts. Add mushrooms, chili sauce and marjoram. Correct seasonings. Cook until vegetables are just tender. Add wine and heat briefly.

My choice of wine to accompany this dish:
CALIFORNIA DRY RED TABLE WINE

NOTE: For a richer wine flavor 1 cup of wine may be substituted for half the water at beginning of cooking. As a change, try serving with buttered hominy grits.

Baked Chuck Roast

(6 servings)

Mrs. August Sebastiani, Samuele Sebastiani Winery, Sonoma

I have served this recipe, adding sliced mushrooms sautéed in butter. No one would believe it was a chuck roast.

2 or 3 pound chuck roast
    1   (2-3/4 oz.) package dried onion soup
    2   potatoes
2 or 3 carrots
    1   green pepper (optional)
    1   clove garlic, chopped
    1/3 cup California Burgundy or Claret

Put roast on piece of heavy duty aluminum foil large enough to wrap and seal ingredients. Rub onion soup mix into roast using whole package. Pare and quarter potatoes and carrots. Cut pepper in large strips. Add garlic and wine. Fold foil over roast, carefully sealing. Bake in shallow pan in 350⁰ oven 2-1/2 to 3 hours.

My choice of wine to accompany this dish:
CALIFORNIA DRY RED TABLE WINE

NOTE: Mrs. Sebastiani had this to add: "This roast is a meal in itself and that is what I enjoy most about it. A green salad is all that is needed to complete a balanced dinner."

Steak Lorraine

(4 servings)

Mrs. Al Nerelli, Pesenti Winery, Templeton

This recipe is wonderful for a busy homemaker because it takes so little time to prepare.

    1   tablespoon flour
    1/2 teaspoon garlic salt
    1/4 teaspoon oregano leaf
    1   green pepper
    4   cube steaks
    2   tablespoons shortening
    1/2 cup California Dry Red Table Wine
 1-1/4 cups cold water
    1   (3/4 oz.) envelope mushroom gravy mix

Blend flour with garlic salt and oregano. Remove seeds and ribs from green pepper and cut into 8 to 12 squares. Roll steaks in seasoned flour. Brown steaks on both sides in hot shortening. Reduce heat, add green pepper, wine and 1/4 cup water. Cover and cook over low heat 10 minutes. Remove steak and peppers to warm serving platter. Add remaining water and gravy mix to pan. Bring to a boil and serve over meat.

My choice of wine to accompany this dish:
**CALIFORNIA ZINFANDEL OR
OTHER DRY RED TABLE WINE**

Pot Roast Schwatzburg

(6 servings)

Mrs. Angela Danisch, Brookside Vineyard Co., Bonita

This has been a family recipe for years. I do not know its origin.

- 4 pounds top round or pot roast
- 2 tablespoons oil
- 1 carrot
- 2 stalks celery
- 8 parsley sprigs
- 2 tomatoes, peeled
  (or 1 cup tomato juice)
- 1 medium onion
- 1 bay leaf
- 1/4 teaspoon Italian seasoning
- 1 cup California Burgundy
- 1/4 cup California Brandy
- 2 tablespoons California Sherry
- 1 cup bouillon
- 2 teaspoons salt
- 1/8 teaspoon pepper
- 1 large head cabbage, quartered

Brown meat on all sides in Dutch oven. Coarsely chop carrot, celery, parsley, tomatoes and onion. Add to meat along with bay leaf and Italian seasoning. Combine wine, Brandy, Sherry and bouillon; add to meat and vegetables. Season with salt and pepper. Cover and bake 2-1/2 to 3 hours in 350° oven. Add cabbage 15 minutes before meat is done. Remove beef and cabbage to serving platter and keep warm. Strain vegetables out of liquid. To each cup of liquid add smooth paste composed of 1 tablespoon flour, 1 tablespoon water and 1 tablespoon heavy cream. Cook until thickened and pour over meat and cabbage, or serve gravy separately.

My choice of wine to accompany this dish:
CALIFORNIA PINOT NOIR, GAMAY OR BEAUJOLAIS

Beef Suzanna

(6 servings)

Mrs. Al Nerelli, Pesenti Winery, Templeton

This was given to me by my husband's mother who was an especially wonderful cook, and it's a recipe that I treasure.

- 5 pounds rump beef
- 1 small veal shank
- 3 tablespoons butter
- 3 tablespoons olive oil
- 1 teaspoon salt
- 1/4 teaspoon pepper
- 1 cup California Dry Red Table Wine
- 1 (6 oz.) can tomato paste
- 3 onions, chopped
- 3 carrots, chopped
- 1/4 teaspoon thyme
- 1/4 teaspoon rosemary
- 1 small clove garlic, minced
- 1 teaspoon parsley, chopped

Place beef and veal in hot butter and oil in Dutch oven. Brown slowly and well on all sides. Add all other ingredients except parsley, cover tightly and simmer 3 hours or until meat is tender. Serve sprinkled with fresh parsley.

My choice of wine to accompany this dish:
CALIFORNIA ZINFANDEL

Marinated Rump Roast

(8 servings)

Mrs. Frank Franzia, Sr., Franzia Brothers Winery, Ripon

A four pound rump roast, while a fine size for an average family, is also a good buy for a young couple. The leftover meat, sliced thin, is great for a cold platter, sandwiches and snacks.

- 4 pounds boneless rump roast
- 2 cups California Dry Red Table Wine
- 1/2 cup oil
- 1 large onion, cut in thin slices
- 2 teaspoons salt
- 8 peppercorns, crushed
- 1 teaspoon thyme
- 1/2 teaspoon oregano
- 1 bay leaf
- 1 clove garlic, chopped

Place roast in large bowl or non-metal casserole. Add all other ingredients, cover and marinate in refrigerator 8 to 24 hours, turning once. Remove roast from marinade, wipe dry with paper towel and place on rack in shallow roasting pan. Insert meat thermometer into thickest part of meat. Place in 450° oven for 10 minutes to sear. Reduce heat to 275° and continue roasting about 2 hours, or until thermometer reaches 130° for rare, or 140° for medium rare. Let stand on heated platter for 15 minutes before slicing very thin.

My choice of wine to accompany this dish:
CALIFORNIA BURGUNDY, CLARET OR VIN ROSÉ

NOTE: A grand result for very little effort. We suggest basting during roasting with marinade, which could also be utilized, strained, to make gravy.

Boeuf à la Mode

(6 servings)

Mrs. Armand E. Bussone, Almaden Vineyards, Los Gatos

This is one of many Italian dishes my mother-in-law brought with her from Italy. It uses a simple cut of meat, makes a delightful main course. Time is the main element necessary in this dish.

3-1/2 pounds pot roast
2 tablespoons oil
3 pieces celery, about 4 inches long
1 carrot, cut in 3 pieces
1 large onion, sliced in thirds
1 sprig rosemary, about 4 inches long
2 sprigs thyme, about 2 inches long
2 bay leaves
2 tablespoons bacon fat
1/3 cup California Burgundy
1/2 cup water
1-1/2 teaspoons salt
1/4 teaspoon pepper
1 teaspoon flour

Brown pot roast on all sides in oil in Dutch oven. In another skillet cook celery, carrot, onion, rosemary, thyme and bay leaves in bacon fat until onions turn golden brown. Add vegetables to meat. Add wine, water, salt and pepper. Cover and simmer 3 hours. One half hour before meat is done, thicken liquid with flour blended with an extra tablespoon of wine. Strain liquid, discarding vegetables.

My choice of wine to accompany this dish:
CALIFORNIA BURGUNDY

Portuguese Soup

(6 to 8 servings)

Mrs. Vincent Indelicato, Sam-Jasper Winery, Manteca

There is a tradition that during the reign of Queen Isabella of Spain she gave the people a feast of soup when there was a famine. The Portuguese people have preserved the tradition with fiestas at which everyone is invited to partake freely of this dish. They take pride in providing enough for all — no one is sent away hungry. These fiestas take place to this day in many California towns and in other parts of the country where the Portuguese have settled.

5 pounds pot roast, cut into
   6 to 8 large pieces
4 cloves garlic
12 cups cold water
1 (6 oz.) can tomato paste
3 (8 oz.) cans tomato sauce
2 large onions, chopped
5 celery stalks, chopped
   Salt and pepper to taste
3 cups California Vin Rosé
3/4 teaspoon allspice, ground
   Half head of cabbage,
   chopped (optional)
   Fresh mint leaves (essential)
   French bread

Place beef in large pot and add all ingredients except mint and bread. Bring to boil and simmer very slowly 6 to 7 hours. In large, high sided serving dish place thick slices of bread topped with mint leaves, spoon meat and soup over bread and serve immediately.

My choice of wine to accompany this dish:
CALIFORNIA VIN ROSÉ OR BURGUNDY

NOTE: Mrs. Indelicato serves the meat and soup with a platter of dill pickles, radishes, green onions, carrot sticks, olives and celery curls, and a pot of beans.

Franks and Peppers

(4 to 6 servings)

Mrs. John Daddino, Guild Wine Co., Fresno

1 medium onion, minced
2 green peppers, cut in 1-inch pieces
1 pound frankfurters
2 tablespoons oil
1/2 teaspoon salt
1/8 teaspoon pepper
1/4 teaspoon Italian seasoning
2 (8 oz.) cans tomato sauce
1 cup water
1 cup California Burgundy
1 tablespoon Parmesan cheese, grated

Brown onions, peppers and frankfurters lightly in oil. Add seasonings, tomato sauce, water and wine. Simmer uncovered in skillet for at least 1 hour. Sprinkle with grated cheese. Serve with rice.

My choice of wine to accompany this dish:
CALIFORNIA BURGUNDY

Sweet and Sour Franks

(4 to 6 servings)

Mrs. Joseph S. Concannon, Jr., Concannon Vineyard, Livermore

This is a children's special in our house — usually served when Dad is out of town. It is quick to prepare and is a one dish meal. We usually serve it with toasted French bread and ice cream sundaes for dessert. This is also an economical dish to prepare — a great budget stretcher — and the results are quite delightful.

    1   (12 oz.) package hot dogs
    1   medium size onion
    1   green pepper
    2   large ripe tomatoes
    4   tablespoons margarine
    1   (13-1/4 oz.) can pineapple chunks
        with juice
    2   tablespoons cornstarch
  1/4   cup water
  1/4   cup California Dry Sauterne or Chablis
    2   tablespoons California white wine vinegar
    2   cups cooked rice

Cut hot dogs in pieces about 1-1/2 inches long and cook in boiling, salted water for 5 to 8 minutes. Drain and set aside. Meanwhile chop onion coarsely, cut green pepper in long thin strips, cut tomatoes in chunks lengthwise. Heat margarine in a skillet, add onion and pepper and cook until limp. Add tomatoes, pineapple and pineapple juice. Mix cornstarch smoothly with water and add to skillet along with wine and vinegar. Stir in drained hot dogs. Cook slowly about 5 minutes, stirring frequently. Taste and add salt, if needed. Serve over hot rice.

My choice of wine to accompany this dish:
CALIFORNIA DRY SAUTERNE OR CHABLIS

One Dish Dinner

(4 servings)

Mrs. Helen Junker, Wine Advisory Board, San Franicsco

This dish was an old stand-by during the depression days — inexpensive, yet filling and tasty.

    1   pound ground chuck
    1   tablespoon oil
    1   small green pepper, chopped fine
    1   tablespoon onion, minced
    8   ounces noodles
    1   (17 oz.) can cream style corn
  1/2   teaspoon salt
  1/8   teaspoon pepper
    1   (10-1/2 oz.) can tomato soup
  1/2   cup California Burgundy

Brown beef in oil, adding green pepper and onion. While mixture is browning, cook noodles in boiling salted water for 5 or 6 minutes and drain. In greased baking dish place layers of noodles, meat, corn, until ingredients are used up, seasoning with salt and pepper. Mix tomato soup with wine and pour over casserole. Bake in pre-heated 350° oven for 1/2 hour. Top with grated cheese, if desired.

My choice of wine to accompany this dish:
CALIFORNIA CABERNET SAUVIGNON

Stew Rosé

(4 servings)

Mrs. Norman N. Fromm, Fromm and Sichel, San Francisco

    1   pound top round steak
    1   large potato
    1   tablespoon oil
    4   small white onions
    1   teaspoon salt
  1/2   teaspoon dry mustard
  1/4   teaspoon basil and thyme, mixed
    2   cups California Rosé

Cut meat, potato into bite-sized pieces. Brown in oil. Add onions, salt, mustard, herbs to meat and pour wine over all. Cover tightly and simmer 1 to 1-1/4 hours.

NOTE: We suggest that this simple stew be served with the same California Rosé that helps make it tender and flavorful.

Modesto Beef

(6 servings)

Mrs. Lyman Cash, E. and J. Gallo Winery, Modesto

  1-1/2   pounds lean boiling beef
          Olive oil
      1   onion, diced
      1   teaspoon Italian herbs
    1/4   teaspoon garlic powder
    1/2   teaspoon salt
    1/4   teaspoon pepper
    1/2   cup California Dry Sherry
  1 to 1-1/2   quarts water
      2   (4 oz.) packages dried vegetable soup
    3/4   cup pearl barley

Brown beef in oil. Add onion, herbs, garlic powder, salt, pepper, and Sherry. Simmer 1/2 hour. Add water, dried soup mix and barley. Cover and cook until barley is plumped, 45 to 50 minutes.

NOTE: Mrs. Cash serves this dish with dumplings. If desired, make dumpling batter according to biscuit mix package directions. Drop by spoonsful on top of hot stew and cook as directed. A California Dry Red Table Wine should accompany this hearty meal-in-a-pot.

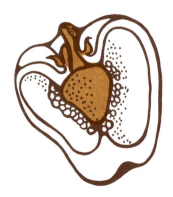

Enchilada Casserole

(8 servings)

Colonel W. A. Dunton, Jr., Golden State Winery, Fresno

I cut this recipe in half for our family of four.

- 2 pounds ground beef
- 2 small onions, diced
- 1 tablespoon oil
- 2 dozen corn tortillas
- 1 (28 oz.) can green chili sauce, or 4 (7 oz.) cans
- 1 cup ripe olive wedges
- 1-1/4 cups Cheddar cheese, grated

Sauté beef and onion in oil until lightly browned, stirring to crumble meat. Cut tortillas in 1-inch squares. Layer tortillas and beef mixture in baking dish, with sauce, olives and cheese. Bake 45 minutes in 300° oven.

NOTE: With this easy-to-prepare, good, quick company dish, serve a California Zinfandel or Rosé.

Janey's Stew

(5 or 6 servings)

Mrs. Ed Pedrizzetti, Pedrizzetti Wine Shop & Tasting Room, Morgan Hill

My daughter, Janey, "discovered" using Sweet Vermouth by accident. I told her red wine, she picked the wrong bottle. Result: a new taste treat.

- 3 tablespoons fat
- 2 pounds beef stew meat cut in bite-size pieces
- 2 tablespoons freeze dried chives
- 2 tablespoons freeze dried parsley
- 1/4 teaspoon Italian seasoning
- 1/4 teaspoon garlic salt
- 2 teaspoons salt
- 1/3 teaspoon pepper
- 1/2 cup California Sweet Vermouth
- 1 (2-3/4 oz.) package dried onion soup mix
- 2 cups boiling water
- 2 large potatoes, quartered
- 6 carrots, cut up
- 1 cup small onions

Heat fat in large pan. Brown next 7 ingredients together over high heat, stirring often. Reduce heat, add wine, onion soup mix and water. Cover and simmer 1-1/2 hours. Add vegetables and continue cooking about 1/2 hour longer, until meat is tender and vegetables are done.

My choice of wine to accompany this dish:
CALIFORNIA BARBERA

Savory Stew

(8 servings)

Mrs. Joe V. Kovacevich, Cresta Blanca Wine Co., Delano

- 3 pounds stewing meat — beef, veal or lamb
- 1/3 cup flour
- 1 teaspoon paprika
- 1 teaspoon garlic salt
- 1 teaspoon salt
- 1/4 teaspoon dried dill
- 3 tablespoons fat
- 1 cup California Dry Red Table Wine
- 2 cups boiling water
- 1 cup each carrots, turnips, celery, diced
- 1 cup whole tiny onions, or chopped large ones
- 4 cups potatoes, cubed
- 1 bay leaf
- 1/2 teaspoon thyme
- 2 tablespoons parsley, minced

Cut meat in 1-inch cubes. Roll in flour seasoned with paprika, garlic salt, salt and dill. Brown in fat in heavy casserole or skillet. Add wine and water. Simmer 1-1/2 hours, adding an additional 1/2 cup wine, if necessary. Add all vegetables and herbs except parsley. Simmer an additional 30 minutes, or until meat is tender and vegetables cooked. Garnish with parsley.

My choice of wine to accompany this dish:
CALIFORNIA BURGUNDY OR ROSÉ

Sanger Stew

(6 to 8 servings)

Mrs. Everett T. Estes, Sanger Winery Association, Sanger

Vegetables may be cooked separately and added, if desired. My family prefers this dish with a pilaf and green salad. It is excellent either for informal yard gatherings or as a cold weather menu.

- 3 pounds chuck, cut for stew
- 2 tablespoons fat
- 3 cups boiling water
- 1 cup California Dry Sherry
- 1 teaspoon Worcestershire sauce
- 1 clove garlic, crushed
- 1 medium onion, chopped
- 1 small bay leaf
- 1 tablespoon salt
- 1/2 teaspoon pepper
- 1/2 teaspoon paprika
  Dash allspice or ground cloves
- 1 teaspoon sugar
- 1 teaspoon lemon juice.

Thoroughly brown meat on all sides in hot fat. Add water, wine and all other ingredients. Cover and simmer 2 hours, or until beef is tender. Thicken gravy, if desired, with a little cornstarch blended with Sherry.

My choice of wine to accompany this dish:
CALIFORNIA CHABLIS OR VIN ROSÉ

Barbara's Beef Stew

(6 servings)

Mrs. Arvin E. Anderson, Gallo Sales Co., South San Francisco

This recipe is one we have when the cook wants a day off. I usually double the recipe and put half into the freezer for a later date. Sometimes I add a package of dehydrated vegetable soup for additional flavor.

3 pounds stewing beef
1 (3 oz.) package dehydrated mushroom soup
1 (2-3/4 oz.) package dehydrated onion soup
1 cup California Dry Red Table Wine

Combine all ingredients in Dutch oven and bake 4 hours in 250° oven. Broth may be thickened, if desired, with cornstarch mixed with cold water before serving over noodles or rice.

My choice of wine to accompany this dish:
CALIFORNIA DRY RED TABLE WINE

NOTE: A minimum of effort produces a very fine flavor. Mrs. Anderson suggests serving with French bread and a green salad with Roquefort cheese dressing, made with California wine vinegar.

Rump Roast Stew

(8 servings)

Mrs. Don Rudolph, Cresta Blanca Wine Co., Livermore

This is an uncomplicated entrée to fix for company when you are in a hurry.

4 pound rump roast
1 (10-1/2 oz.) can cream of mushroom soup
1 (2-3/4 oz.) package dried onion soup
1/2 cup California Port
1/2 teaspoon Worcestershire sauce
1/2 teaspoon Tabasco sauce
1 bay leaf

Cut meat in 1-inch cubes. Combine all remaining ingredients and add meat. Wrap securely in foil, sealing tightly, but leaving 1 or 2 inches of space for steam. Place in casserole and bake in 375° oven 1-1/2 hours.

My choice of wine to accompany this dish:
CALIFORNIA PINOT NOIR

NOTE: For an enticing vegetable Mrs. Rudolph suggests string beans, fresh or canned, combined with sliced water chestnuts sautéed in butter. This stew is a no-work dish.

Berkeley Goulash

(8 to 10 servings)

Golda F. Joslyn, M.D., Berkeley

This goes well with noodles, rice, potatoes or dumplings. For a thicker gravy, add mushrooms or sour cream.

3 large onions, coarsely chopped
4 pounds chuck, or stew beef, cubed
1 clove garlic, minced
1 tablespoon catsup
1 teaspoon caraway seeds
1 tablespoon salt
1/4 teaspoon pepper
1 teaspoon paprika
1 teaspoon dry mustard
1 whole clove
1 cup California Burgundy

Place onions in roaster or Dutch oven. Top with beef cubes, add all seasonings and pour wine over all. Bring to boil on top of stove, cover tightly and simmer 1 hour. Place in 375° oven and continue to cook, covered, another 2 hours. Add wine to moisten, if necessary.

My choice of wine to accompany this dish:
CALIFORNIA CABERNET SAUVIGNON OR PINOT NOIR

Creole Burgers

(4 servings)

Mrs. Rhonda H. Smyser, Wine Advisory Board, San Francisco

Since this is served over muffins, all that needs to go with it is a salad. Quick and easy for unexpected guests.

1 pound ground beef
1/2 cup onion, chopped
1 tablespoon oil
1 (10-1/2 oz.) can condensed chicken gumbo soup
2 tablespoons each, catsup, prepared mustard
1/4 teaspoon black pepper
1/4 cup California Burgundy

Brown beef and onion in oil in heavy skillet. Add remaining ingredients and simmer 5 minutes. Serve on toasted, buttered English muffins or toast.

My choice of wine to accompany this dish:
CALIFORNIA BURGUNDY

Zucchini Casserole

(4 servings)

Mrs. Violet McReynolds, The Christian Brothers, Napa

    3   tablespoons olive oil
    1   medium onion, thinly sliced
    1   pound ground beef
    3   (8 oz.) cans tomato sauce
    1   cup California Burgundy
    1   teaspoon mixed Italian seasoning
        Dash garlic powder
    1   teaspoon sugar
        Salt and pepper
    2   pounds zucchini, medium size
        Parmesan cheese, grated

Heat oil in large, heavy skillet, add onion and beef. Cook until meat is browned, stirring frequently. Add tomato sauce, wine and seasonings, cover and simmer gently 1 hour, stirring occasionally. While sauce is cooking, wash zucchini and trim off ends. Cook whole in boiling water about 15 minutes, or until tender. Drain. When cool, cut lengthwise in halves and arrange, cut side up, in greased shallow baking dish. Pour sauce over zucchini and bake in 350° oven about 45 minutes. Sprinkle with cheese and serve.

NOTE: Pour the same California Burgundy, used in making this fine dish, for your table beverage.

California Meat Roll

(6 servings)

Mrs. Kenneth R. Spencer, Mirassou Vineyards, San Jose

Editor's note: This is something different to do with hamburger. The roll may be shaped early, ready for baking later. A good family supper dish.

    1-1/2   pounds ground chuck
    1/2   cup California Dry Red Table Wine
    1   egg, beaten
    1/2   cup dry bread crumbs
    1/4   teaspoon each sage,
            thyme, garlic powder
    1   teaspoon salt
    2   tablespoons green pepper,
            finely chopped
    1   small onion, finely chopped
    1   cup Cheddar cheese, shredded
    1   cup fresh mushrooms, sliced

Combine meat, wine, egg, bread crumbs, seasonings, green pepper and onion, mixing thoroughly. Turn meat mixture onto 12-inch square heavy wax paper. Pat or roll mixture into 12-inch square. Sprinkle cheese and mushrooms over meat, then roll as for jelly roll, using paper to start well. Place roll, seam side down, into loaf pan. Bake at 350° 1-1/2 hours.

NOTE: The roll could be served with tomato sauce or mushroom sauce, and a California Dry Red Table Wine is guaranteed to perk up jaded appetites.

Lodi Stuffed Cabbage

(10 servings)

Mrs. Ben R. Goehring, Guild Wine Co., Lodi

This is a recipe used in my husband's family. It's very simple and economical to prepare. It is so colorful and delicious we serve it directly from the roaster — a whole meal. It can be cooked in the morning and reheated before serving.

    1   cup raw regular rice
    2   pounds ground beef
    1   unsmoked bratwurst, sliced, or
          1/2 pound pork sausage
    1   tablespoon salt
    1/2   teaspoon pepper
    1   large head cabbage
    5   potatoes
    5   carrots
    1   (46 oz.) can tomato juice
    1   cup California Sauterne
    1   large onion
    1   green pepper
    1/2   cup oil
    2   tablespoons California wine vinegar
    2   strips bacon

Cook rice in boiling salted water 10 minutes. Drain. Mix ground beef, pork sausage or bratwurst, rice, salt and pepper. Roll meat mixture up in 14 to 16 whole cabbage leaves which have been wilted in boiling water and drained. Peel and quarter potatoes, carrots, place on rack in bottom of roaster. Sprinkle with salt. Place cabbage rolls, tied with string or skewered with tooth picks, over potatoes and carrots and pour tomato juice and wine over rolls. Lay quarters of onion and wide strips of green pepper over all, pour on oil and vinegar, and top with bacon strips. Cover and bake in 250° oven until tender, about 4 hours.

My choice of wine to accompany this dish:
CALIFORNIA DRY RED OR WHITE TABLE WINE

JIFFY MEAT BALLS for those in a tearing hurry are the invention of Mrs. Charles J. Welch, Guild Wine Co., Lodi. Blend 2 tablespoons flour with 1 cup dairy sour cream in Dutch oven. Stir in 1 (6 oz.) can sliced mushrooms and liquid, 4 (15 oz.) cans meat balls in gravy, 2 tablespoons California Dry Sherry, 2 teaspoons Worcestershire sauce, 2 tablespoons chopped parsley. Season to taste with salt, pepper and garlic salt. Cover and cook over low heat 15 to 20 minutes, stirring often. Serves 8. Add California Rosé for a happy quick meal.

California Beef Patties

(3 to 4 servings)

Mrs. David R. Wilcox, Wine Advisory Board, San Francisco

A quick supper dish that is not only delicious but ideal for weight and expense watchers.

  2 medium tomatoes, quartered
  1 tablespoon parsley, chopped
1/2 onion, chopped
  1 clove garlic, chopped
1/4 cup California Burgundy
1/2 teaspoon salt
1/4 teaspoon pepper
1/4 teaspoon oregano
  1 pound ground chuck

Place tomatoes, parsley, onion and garlic in saucepan. Add wine and seasonings and allow to reduce over low heat 20 minutes. Shape meat into 3 or 4 patties. Add to tomato mixture, cover and cook about 10 minutes, or until meat is done, turning once.

My choice of wine to accompany this dish:
CALIFORNIA BURGUNDY

Copenhagen Meat Balls

(6 to 8 servings)

Mrs. Karl E. Droese, Sr., E. & J. Gallo Winery, Modesto

This dish may be prepared ahead of time and reheated before serving. I always double the recipe and freeze half in oven-proof dish. It can be popped into the oven direct from freezer and tastes even better than when first made.

  1 pound ground beef
1/2 pound ground pork sausage
3/4 cup fine dry bread crumbs
  1 egg, well beaten
1/2 cup cold water
1/4 teaspoon each nutmeg, salt, pepper
  3 tablespoons bacon fat

Combine all ingredients except fat. Shape into balls the size of large marbles. Heat bacon fat in large skillet, brown balls on all sides and remove, reserving 3 tablespoons of fat.

SAUCE

    3 tablespoons reserved fat
    3 tablespoons flour
2-1/2 cups water
    1 (1-1/2 oz.) package
      dehydrated onion soup
  1/2 cup cream, or undiluted
      evaporated milk
  1/3 cup California Dry Sherry
  1/2 teaspoon Worcestershire sauce
      Salt and pepper to taste

Blend fat and flour in large skillet, add water and cook, stirring constantly, until sauce thickens. Add remaining ingredients. Return balls to sauce, cover and simmer 1/2 hour, stirring occasionally.

My choice of wine to accompany this dish:
CALIFORNIA VIN ROSÉ

Barbarini Caliente

(6 to 8 servings)

Mrs. Kerby T. Anderson, Guild Wine Co., San Francisco

  2 pounds ground beef
  1 large onion, chopped
  1 clove garlic, chopped
  1 tablespoon olive oil
  1 (17 oz.) can whole tomatoes
  1 (17 oz.) can cream style corn
  1 (2-1/4 oz.) can sliced mushrooms
  1 (2-1/4 oz.) can ripe olives, sliced
  1 (10 oz.) package frozen chopped spinach
  2 (10 oz.) cans enchilada sauce
  2 teaspoons salt
1/4 teaspoon pepper
1/8 teaspoon garlic powder
  2 tablespoons chili powder
1/2 cup California Burgundy
      Pinch Italian seasoning herbs
 12 tortillas
  1 cup Cheddar cheese, grated

Brown beef with onion and garlic in oil. Mix all other ingredients, except tortillas and cheese, together in large casserole and heat thoroughly. Combine beef mixture with vegetables, liquid and seasonings. Cover bottom of large baking dish with film of olive oil and place 6 tortillas in it, overlapping. Cover carefully with meat and vegetable mixture, using slotted spoon so that about 1 cup sauce can be reserved. Place 6 remaining tortillas over top and cover with reserved sauce. Spread grated cheese over all. Bake in 325° oven 1 hour.

My choice of wine to accompany this dish:
CALIFORNIA DRY RED TABLE WINE

Soy-Broiled Hamburgers

(4 servings)

Mrs. Tony Marusick, Calgrape Wineries, Delano

- 1 pound ground beef
- 1/2 teaspoon salt
- 1 teaspoon Worcestershire sauce
- 1 teaspoon sugar
- 1 tablespoon parsley, minced
- 1 tablespoon onion, minced
- 4 tablespoons fine bread crumbs
- 1/4 cup California Sherry
  Soy sauce
- 1 tablespoon butter or margarine

Mix ground beef with seasonings, parsley, and onion. Add crumbs and enough wine to make mixture fairly moist. Form into patties and dip both sides in soy sauce. Arrange patties on greased shallow baking pan or broiler rack. Dot with butter. Broil about 2 inches from unit or flame until brown. Turn and brown on other side.

NOTE: For a change serve these "different" hamburgers with a California Dry White Table Wine.

Macaroni Goulash

(4 servings)

Mrs. Ferrer Filipello, Italian Swiss Colony, Asti

- 3 tablespoons oil
- 1 pound ground beef
- 1 small onion, minced
- 1 clove garlic, minced
- 1 (8 oz.) can tomato sauce
- 1/4 cup tomato catsup
- 1 tablespoon Worcestershire sauce
- 1/2 cup California Dry Red Wine
- 2 teaspoons salt
- 1 teaspoon dry mustard
- 1 teaspoon paprika
- 3-1/2 cups water
- 7 ounces macaroni (mostaccioli)

Heat oil in large skillet, add beef, onion and garlic; cook until browned, over medium heat, stirring occasionally. Combine tomato sauce, catsup, Worcestershire, wine, salt, mustard and paprika, and add to skillet, along with water. Bring to boil, cover and simmer over low heat 25 minutes. Add macaroni, cover and simmer 15 minutes longer or until macaroni is done.

NOTE: This is an inexpensive but tasty entrée with most ingredients always to be found on the pantry shelf. Serve with California Chianti.

Hawaiian Meat Balls

(4 servings)

Mrs. Vernon Singleton, University of California, Davis
Department of Viticulture and Enology

- 1 pound ground chuck
- 3 tablespoons soy sauce
- 4 tablespoons California Red Wine
- 3 tablespoons cracker crumbs, finely crushed
- 2 cloves garlic, finely minced, or pressed
- 1 tablespoon olive oil

Mix all ingredients thoroughly. Form into 1-inch balls and brown in oil. Remove from fire.

SAUCE

- Olive oil
- 2 cups water
- 2 tablespoons cornstarch
- 1 tablespoon California Red Wine
- 3 tablespoons soy sauce

Use meat drippings and add enough oil to make 2 tablespoons. Add 1-3/4 cups water to oil, using remaining 1/4 cup water to mix with cornstarch. Add wine, soy sauce and cornstarch mixture and bring to boil, stirring constantly. When thickened, add meat balls to sauce, cover skillet and simmer for about 30 minutes. Serve over buttered noodles or rice.

My choice of wine to accompany this dish:
CALIFORNIA RED TABLE WINE

NOTE: Caution! Cook noodles or rice in unsalted water because soy sauce adds sufficient salt to season whole dish.

Italian Ground Beef

(2 servings)

Miss Joan V. Ingalls, Wine Institute, San Francisco

- 1/2 pound lean ground chuck
- 1 (16 oz.) can onions, drained
- 1 large green pepper, chopped
- 1 (8 oz.) can mushrooms, or 6 large fresh ones
- 1 (8 oz.) can tomato sauce
- 1/2 cup California Burgundy
- 1/2 teaspoon salt
- 1/4 teaspoon pepper
- 1/4 teaspoon Italian herbs
  Parmesan cheese, grated

Crumble beef into ungreased, heavy skillet. Add onions, green pepper, undrained mushrooms, tomato sauce, wine and seasonings. Cover and simmer over medium heat 20 to 25 minutes, stirring occasionally. Serve with grated cheese on top.

NOTE: This recipe could be stretched by incorporating in a casserole with pasta or rice. Sprinkle with cheese, dot with butter and bake until brown on top. Serve with the California Burgundy used in preparation.

Beef Stew Filice

(5 servings)

Mrs. John M. Filice, San Martin Vineyards, San Martin

I love to prepare this dish when I am going to be away for the day. I prepare it in the morning, set my oven for Time Bake and pop it in. When I return home the rest of the meal can be prepared in 30 minutes.

    2   pounds chuck, cut in small chunks
    2   tablespoons oil
    1   (10-1/2 oz.) can golden mushroom soup
    1   (6 oz.) can V-8 juice
    1   package dried onion soup mix
    1/2 cup California Red Table Wine

Brown beef in heated oil in Dutch oven. Combine mushroom soup, vegetable juice, dried soup mix and wine. Add to beef, cover and bake 2 hours in 300° oven.

My choice of wine to accompany this dish:
CALIFORNIA PINOT NOIR OR ZINFANDEL

Bourbonnais Beef Stew

(6 servings)

Mrs. Shelton Brown, Paul Masson Vineyards, Saratoga

    1-1/2 pounds chuck, cut in 1-inch cubes
    1   tablespoon shortening
    1   clove garlic, minced
    1   medium onion, chopped
    1-1/2 teaspoons salt
    1/8 teaspoon pepper
    1   (10-1/2 oz.) can tomato soup,
        undiluted
    3/4 cup California Burgundy
    1/4 cup water
    1/4 teaspoon basil, powdered
    1/4 teaspoon thyme, powdered
    1/2 cup catsup
    3   medium carrots, cut in
        1/2-inch diagonal pieces
    1-1/2 cups celery, cut in
        1-inch diagonal pieces
    4   medium potatoes, peeled and quartered

Lightly brown beef in shortening. Add garlic and onion; sauté until transparent. Sprinkle with salt and pepper. Stir in soup, wine and water; stir in herbs and catsup. Arrange vegetables on top of meat and gravy. Cover, simmer 1-1/2 hours, or until meat and vegetables are tender. Add a little more water if necessary.

NOTE: Serve with California Burgundy.

More!!

(8 to 10 servings)

Mrs. E. B. Nelson, Wine Institute, San Francisco

This is my own version of a similar recipe. My sister-in-law once commented that it tasted like "More" and that is what it was christened.

    1/4 cup oil
    2   tablespoons Spanish seasoning
    1   teaspoon chili powder
    1   teaspoon salt
    1/4 teaspoon pepper
    1   large onion, chopped
    1   large green pepper,
        seeded and chopped
    2   small cloves garlic, minced
    1-1/2 pounds ground lean beef
    1/2 cup California Burgundy
    1   (10-1/2 oz.) can condensed tomato soup
    1   (17 oz.) can cream style corn
    1/2 pound sharp Cheddar cheese, grated
    1   (5-3/4 oz.) can pitted olives, drained
    1   pound elbow macaroni, cooked

Heat oil in Dutch oven, blend in Spanish seasoning, chili powder, salt and pepper. Sauté onion, green pepper and garlic. Add meat and brown. Blend in wine, soup, corn, cheese (saving 3/4 cup of cheese for top), olives and macaroni. Transfer to large flat pan. Bake in 325° oven 1/2 hour until bubbly. Sprinkle remaining cheese on top and bake until cheese melts.

My choice of wine to accompany this dish:
CALIFORNIA BURGUNDY OR ROSÉ

Meat Ball Stroganoff

(4 servings)

Mrs. Ferrer Filipello, Italian Swiss Colony, Asti

    1   pound ground beef
    1   egg
    3/4 cup soft bread crumbs
    1/2 teaspoon salt
        Dash black pepper
    1/4 cup Parmesan cheese, grated
        Oil
    1   (10-1/2 oz.) can cream of mushroom soup
    1/2 cup California Sauterne
    2   teaspoons tomato catsup
    1   tablespoon instant minced onion
    1   tablespoon Worcestershire sauce
    1/4 teaspoon garlic powder
    1   cup evaporated milk

Combine beef, egg, bread crumbs, salt, pepper and cheese. Form into balls about 1 inch in diameter. Brown on all sides in small amount of oil in skillet. Remove meat balls. Add all other ingredients to skillet except milk. Mix well and simmer 5 minutes. Blend in milk and add meat balls. Serve hot over noodles.

My choice of wine to accompany this dish:
CALIFORNIA ROSÉ

Savory Steak Patties

(6 servings)

Mrs. Harry H. Rose, Franzia Brothers Winery, Ripon

Delicious, zesty, simple to prepare. An ideal company dinner for a bride's first attempt and economical enough for good family eating.

- 2 pounds ground sirloin
- 1/2 cup soy sauce
- 1 cup California Burgundy
- 1 teaspoon celery seed
- 1 teaspoon garlic powder
- 1 teaspoon coarse-ground pepper
- 1 tablespoon parsley, finely chopped
- 1 tablespoon green onion, finely chopped

Make six patties and place in dish deep enough to immerse meat. Mix all other ingredients, except parsley and onions, and pour over patties. Marinate for several hours in refrigerator, turning occasionally. Place on broiler rack, spooning marinade over meat and broil at 500° 5 minutes per side for medium rare, or 8 minutes per side for medium well-done. Baste during broiling with marinade. Serve sprinkled with parsley and onion.

My choice of wine to accompany this dish:
CALIFORNIA PINK CHABLIS OR COLD DUCK

NOTE: Mrs. Rose offers the following menu: the steak patties, baked potatoes with chives, crisp cole slaw, sour dough French bread and a gelatin parfait made with California Port and embellished with whipped cream.

Five Hour Stew

(6 servings)

Mrs. Robert W. Salles, Wine Brokerage, San Francisco

This is a favorite family winter recipe.

- 2-1/2 pounds stew beef, cubed
- 1 (1 lb.) can whole tomatoes
- 1 (10 oz.) package frozen peas
- 6 slender whole carrots
- 2 medium potatoes, cubed
- 3 small onions, chopped
- 1 cup celery, chopped
- 2 slices white bread, cubed
- 3 tablespoons tapioca
- 1 tablespoon sugar
- 1 tablespoon salt
- 1/4 teaspoon each, freshly ground black pepper, thyme, marjoram, rosemary
- 1/2 cup California Zinfandel

Put all ingredients in deep casserole and cover very tightly. Bake in 250° oven for 5 hours. About 30 minutes before serving, stir well and moisten with more wine, if necessary.

NOTE: A delectable dish to accompany the stew is Pommes Anna. Butter a shallow baking dish; cut a round of brown paper to fit bottom, butter it; and add layers of thinly sliced potato sprinkled with melted butter, salt and pepper. Put in oven 2 hours ahead of serving time. Turn out upside-down on platter. The bottom should present a rich golden brown crust, but if not brown enough, simply run under broiler for 1 or 2 minutes. Serve with California Zinfandel.

Beef-Mushroom Casserole

(4 to 6 servings)

Mrs. Walter E. Kite, Guild Wine Co., San Francisco

This dish, of obscure origin, is popular with families of Italian background. It has been brought up-to-date with American additions.

- 2 tablespoons oil
- 1-1/2 pounds ground lean beef
- 1-1/2 cups onions, chopped
- 1 clove garlic, chopped
- 1 cup raw regular rice
- 1/2 cup celery, chopped (optional)
- 1 cup ripe olives, sliced
- 1 (4 oz.) can mushrooms, undrained
- 1 (30 oz.) can tomatoes
- 2 tablespoons parsley, minced
  Dash paprika
  Dash Worcestershire sauce
- 1 teaspoon sugar
  Salt and pepper to taste
- 1/2 cup California Dry Sherry
- 1 cup Cheddar cheese, grated

Heat oil in large skillet. Sauté beef until brown, crumbling it as it cooks. Add onion, garlic and brown slightly. Add rice and stir to coat with fat. Add all other ingredients except cheese, mixing well. Bring to boil, transfer, covered, to 375° oven and bake 1/2 hour. Uncover, add cheese and stir gently. Continue baking 15 minutes longer.

My choice of wine to accompany this dish:
CALIFORNIA GRENACHE ROSÉ OR RIESLING

PORK and HAM

Baked Pork Chops

(6 to 8 servings)

Mrs. Kerby T. Anderson, Guild Wine Co., San Francisco

- 8 small pork chops,
  trimmed and boned
- 1 (10-1/2 oz.) can condensed
  mushroom soup
- 1 (1-3/8 oz.) package dried
  onion soup mix
- 1/2 cup California Dry Sherry
- 1/8 teaspoon black pepper,
  fresh ground
- 1/2 teaspoon paprika
- 1 tablespoon parsley flakes

Place chops in casserole. Combine soup, dried mix, wine and seasonings. Stir until well blended and pour over chops, making sure chops are all covered with sauce. Cover and bake in 375° oven 1 hour, or until meat is tender.

My choice of wine to accompany this dish:
CALIFORNIA DRY RED TABLE WINE

Stuffed Chops au Vin

(8 servings)

Mrs. Chris S. Vetoyanis, E. & J. Gallo Winery, Modesto

I like to accompany this dish with butternut squash and tossed green salad.

- 8 center-cut pork chops,
  1-1/4 inches thick
- 3 tablespoons onion, minced
- 3 tablespoons celery, chopped
- 1/4 cup oil
- 3-1/2 cups dry, herb-seasoned croutons
- 1/3 cup butter or margarine, melted
- 3/4 cup hot water or stock
- 3 tablespoons seedless California raisins
- 3/4 cup California Sherry
- 1 cup dairy sour cream
  Spiced crab apples
  Parsley

Cut pocket in chops from outside edge to bone, or have butcher do this if possible. In large, heavy Dutch oven sauté onion and celery in oil. Reserve oil. To croutons add melted butter, hot water, raisins and sautéed onion-celery mixture. Mix well and stuff in pockets of chops. Truss with heavy thread. Brown chops in reserved oil on both sides. Pour off all excess fat. Add Sherry to chops, cover and bake in 325° oven 1 hour or until meat is fork-tender. Remove chops to platter and keep warm in oven. Stir sour cream into pan juices, stirring to incorporate browned bits. Heat gently. If desired, sauce may be thickened with a little cornstarch and cold water. Spoon over chops and garnish with spiced crab apples and parsley.

My choice of wine to accompany this dish:
CALIFORNIA ROSÉ

NOTE: Mrs. Vetoyanis adds, "I do want to stress the importance of garnishing with spiced crab apples and parsley, not only for the decorative touch, but for the tart apple flavor that goes so well with pork." For still more flavorful gravy, the sour cream may be mixed with dried French onion soup mix.

Boston Butt Roast

(6 servings)

Mrs. E. Jeff Barnette, Martini & Prati Wines, Santa Rosa

    4   pound fresh pork butt
    1   teaspoon salt
    1/4 teaspoon pepper
    1   cup apricot nectar
    1/2 cup California Sherry

Trim excess fat from pork. Sprinkle with salt and pepper. Roast uncovered in 325° oven 2-1/2 hours. Remove excess fat. Combine apricot nectar and Sherry. Continue roasting, basting meat frequently with fruit juice-wine mixture, about 1 hour more, or until liquid is reduced, and pork is done and glazed.

NOTE: If glaze should begin to thicken and burn, add 1 or 2 tablespoons water. Serve roast with California Zinfandel.

Morgan Hill Spareribs

(4 servings)

Mrs. Walter S. Richert, Richert & Sons, Morgan Hill

    1   side spareribs (about 3 lbs.)
    1   cup California Cream Sherry
    3   tablespoons soy sauce
    3   tablespoons lemon juice
    1   tablespoon parsley, chopped
    1/2 teaspoon marjoram
    1/2 teaspoon salt
    1/4 teaspoon pepper

Place side of ribs, meaty-side down, in shallow baking pan. Combine remaining ingredients and pour over meat. Bake in 300° oven 1 hour, basting occasionally. Turn meat over. Increase heat to 350° and bake 15 minutes, until well done and fork tender.

NOTE: This is an easy and quick treatment and could be accompanied by garlic bread, heated to crustiness in the same oven, and a California Zinfandel.

Sausages and Cabbage

(5 servings)

Mrs. Leo Demostene, Soda Rock Winery, Healdsburg

Very good dish to serve in the winter.

    1   medium head cabbage
    1/4 cup California wine vinegar
    1/4 cup California Sauterne
    1   pound Italian sausages, or
         dinner franks
         Salt and pepper to taste

Trim core and shred cabbage into skillet. Add vinegar and wine; cook over low heat until crisp-tender. Add sausages which have been parboiled 15 to 30 minutes, depending on variety. Salt and pepper to taste and continue cooking 20 to 30 minutes more.

NOTE: Mashed potatoes would be a natural companion to this dish, and serve the California Sauterne used in making it.

Ham in Champagne

(4 servings)

Mr. J. H. "Mike" Elwood, Llords & Elwood Winery, Los Angeles

         Center cut ham slice 2 inches thick
    2-1/2 cups California Champagne
    8   pineapple fingers, canned or fresh
    2   tablespoons honey
    1/8   teaspoon each ground cloves,
           nutmeg, cinnamon
    1   tablespoon arrowroot

Trim fat from ham and place in shallow baking dish. Pour 1-1/2 cups Champagne over ham and marinate 3 or 4 hours. At the same time, marinate pineapple in 1/2 cup pineapple juice and 1 cup Champagne. Place ham in 400° oven and after wine begins to simmer, bake for 30 minutes, or until ham is tender. Remove from oven, spread with honey and sprinkle with cloves, nutmeg and cinnamon. While ham cooks, drain liquid from pineapple into saucepan, bring to boil and thicken with arrowroot. Add pineapple and when ham is ready to go under broiler, arrange pineapple fingers around it and pour sauce over all to mingle with pan juices. Broil long enough to glaze ham.

NOTE: For contrast serve this luscious dish with California Rosé.

Pork Chops and Apples

(4 servings)

Mrs. Frank Franzia, Jr., Franzia Brothers Winery, Ripon

We were served this dish by close friends a few years ago. I've been serving it ever since — with the addition of California wine.

    8   medium pork chops
    1/2 tablespoon oil
    1/2 teaspoon salt
    1/8 teaspoon pepper
    1/4 teaspoon garlic powder
    1/4 cup California Sauterne
    1/4 cup water
    6   apples, pared and cored

Brown chops well in oil and pour off any excess fat. Return to low heat, add seasonings and liquids. Simmer 1/2 hour, covered. Add apples sliced 1/8-inch thick, arranged on top of chops. Cover again and simmer about 10 minutes, or until apples are cooked through.

My choice of wine to accompany this dish:
CALIFORNIA RHINE WINE

NOTE: Wine flavor could be intensified by using all wine, no water. Mrs. Franzia serves it with tiny buttered carrots, rice, lettuce wedges dressed with oil and wine vinegar, and zabaglione for dessert.

Spareribs in B.B.Q. Sauce

(6 to 8 servings)

Miss Gyl Rheingans, Sanger Winery Association, Sanger

    1 cup golden molasses
    1/2 cup California Sherry
    2 tablespoons soy sauce
    1/2 cup hot chili sauce
    1/4 cup tomato catsup
    1 tablespoon prepared mustard
    1/4 teaspoon each garlic salt, onion salt
    2 sides meaty spareribs

Combine first 8 ingredients and pour over spareribs. Marinate several hours or overnight. Barbecue over charcoal 1 hour, brushing on sauce throughout cooking.

My choice of wine to accompany this dish:
CALIFORNIA GREY RIESLING

NOTE: The ribs could also be oven-barbecued. For those who find the molasses flavor a little too insistent, 1/2 cup brown sugar could be substituted for half the molasses.

Pork Chops St. Helena

(4 servings)

Mrs. William Bonetti, Charles Krug Winery, St. Helena

    8 thin sliced loin pork chops
    1 tablespoon oil
    1/4 teaspoon salt
    1/16 teaspoon pepper
      Few leaves of sage
    1 clove garlic
    1/2 cup California Port
    2 tablespoons parsley, finely chopped

Brown meat in oil. Add salt and pepper, sage and garlic. Add Port and turn meat to absorb wine on both sides. Simmer until tender, about 45 minutes. Add parsley. If more moisture is required, add water or beef bouillon made with 1 cube and 3/4 cup boiling water.

My choice of wine to accompany this dish:
CALIFORNIA CHABLIS

GERMAN SAUSAGE BURGUNDY. Mrs. Richard Norton, Fresno State College, says, "We had always enjoyed the flavor of this style sausage, which we pan fried. Our butcher suggested baking it, with a little water. We said if water will work, wine will enhance, and tried the following method. We love it and it is so simple." Mettwurst or Kielbasa (Polish sausage) rings, or frankfurters may be used. Place ring, or 6 franks, in a baking dish and pour over it about one cup of California Burgundy. Place in oven uncovered and bake at about 275° for an an hour to an hour and a half, 4 servings. My choice of wine to accompany this dish: CALIFORNIA CABERNET SAUVIGNON.

Sausage Vermouth

(4 servings)

Mrs. Anthony S. Ciaravino, Wine Institute, Detroit

    1/4 cup vegetable oil
    1 pound Italian sausage
    1/2 cup California Sweet Vermouth

Heat oil in skillet to 380°. Add Italian sausage. Cook on each side for approximately 10 to 12 minutes. When nicely browned and done through, drain off all oil and add Vermouth. Cover and let sausage simmer for approximately 5 to 6 minutes. Serve immediately.

My choice of wine to accompany this dish:
CALIFORNIA PINOT NOIR

Pork Chops Supreme

(4 servings)

Mrs. Clement Viano, Conrad Viano Winery, Martinez

My family always demanded catsup with their pork chops, so I used my imagination and came up with something they enjoy more than catsup.

    6 pork chops
    1/4 cup flour
    1/2 teaspoon salt
    1/16 teaspoon pepper
    1/8 teaspoon nutmeg
    1/2 tablespoon oil
    1/4 cup tomato sauce
    1/2 cup California Zinfandel
    1/4 cup light molasses

Trim excess fat from chops. Combine flour, salt, pepper and nutmeg, rub chops in mixture and brown in oil on both sides. Combine tomato sauce, wine and molasses. Pour over chops, cover and simmer 30 to 40 minutes, turning occasionally, until tender.

My choice of wine to accompany this dish:
CALIFORNIA ZINFANDEL OR BURGUNDY

Chinese Spareribs

(4 servings)

Mrs. Frank Franzia, Sr., Franzia Brothers Winery, Ripon

- 1 side lean spareribs, cut
- 2 tablespoons catsup
- 1/4 cup California Dry Sherry or Chablis
- 1/4 cup soy sauce
- 1/2 teaspoon ground cinnamon
- 1/2 teaspoon garlic powder

Place ribs in shallow baking pan. Combine all other ingredients, pour over ribs and marinate several hours or overnight. Bake in 350⁰ oven 1 to 1-1/2 hours, or until tender and cooked through.

NOTE: Serve with steamed rice and a California Rosé.

Greek Spareribs

(4 servings)

Mrs. Phyllis Huntsman, The Christian Brothers, St. Helena

- 2-1/2 to 3 pounds spareribs
- 1 (14 oz.) bottle catsup
- 1 cup sweet pickle relish
- 6 drops liquid smoke
- 3 small onions, finely chopped
- 1 (8-1/2 oz.) can pineapple chunks
- 1/4 cup California Dry Vermouth

Bake spareribs in shallow pan in 325⁰ oven 1 hour. Drain off all fat. Combine remaining ingredients and pour over ribs. Cover and continue baking until tender and well done about 1 to 1-1/2 hours longer.

My choice of wine to accompany this dish:
CALIFORNIA DRY RED TABLE WINE

French Sauerkraut

(6 servings)

Mrs. Florence I. Eriksen, Wine Advisory Board, San Francisco

- 6 thick slices bacon, parboiled
- 1 quart sauerkraut, rinsed slightly and drained, or 2 (1 lb.) cans
- 6 pork chops, 3/4-inch thick
- 1 medium onion, sliced
- 12 whole black peppercorns
- 2 cups bouillon
- 1 cup California Chablis

Arrange bacon in bottom of large saucepan. Top with sauerkraut and pork chops. Combine remaining ingredients and pour over chops. Cover and simmer 1 hour.

NOTE: For more flavor, smoked pork chops may be substituted for the fresh meat, and sausage added to dish. Serve with California Chablis.

Tart Ham Chablis

(4 to 6 servings)

Mrs. Daniel Mirassou, Mirassou Vineyards, San Jose

This is a wonderful recipe for last minute guests. It's quick, easy, looks like you've slaved for hours!

- 8 slices pre-cooked ham
- 1 (8 oz.) can unsweetened grapefruit sections
- 1 (11 oz.) can mandarin orange sections
- 1 (20 oz.) can pineapple chunks
- 1 cup unsweetened grapefruit juice
- 1 cup California Chablis

Arrange ham slices in baking dish and cover with drained fruit. Pour grapefruit juice and Chablis over all and bake in 350⁰ oven about 30 to 40 minutes. Do not overcook fruit.

My choice of wine to accompany this dish:
CALIFORNIA CHABLIS OR JOHANNISBERG RIESLING

NOTE: Here is Mrs. Mirassou's menu for the whole dinner: oranges stuffed with sweet potatoes; green beans with almonds and mushrooms; fried cornbread; summer salad (tomatoes, red onion slices, cucumber, celery, dressed with oil, wine vinegar and a little mayonnaise); fresh pineapple flambé!

Ham Mardi Gras

(12 to 16 servings)

Mrs. Alessandro Baccari, Baccari Wine Festival, San Francisco

- 8 to 10 pound canned ham
  Cloves
- 1-1/2 cups brown sugar, firmly packed
- 1 (4/5 qt.) bottle California Burgundy
- 1 (16 oz.) can pineapple juice
- 1/3 cup honey
- 1 cup marmalade
- 1 (20 oz.) can crushed pineapple
  Small jar maraschino cherries

Score ham fat. Stud top and sides with whole cloves. Pat 1 cup brown sugar over top and sides. Place ham in large crock or stainless steel pot. Pour wine and pineapple juice over ham. Let stand 24 hours, turning 5 or 6 times. Put in baking pan, saving marinade for basting. Warm honey, brush over ham. Spread marmalade and crushed pineapple over ham. Add remaining brown sugar to form a crust on top. Garnish with maraschino cherries. Bake in 350⁰ oven 1 hour, basting with marinade.

NOTE: A festive ham for a festive occasion deserves a California Brut Champagne.

VEAL

Veal Provolone

(4 servings)

Mrs. Angela Danisch, Brookside Vineyard Co., Bonita

I received this recipe from an esteemed patron.

        4 veal steaks, fresh or frozen
        2 tablespoons flour
      1/2 teaspoon salt
      1/8 teaspoon pepper
        2 tablespoons butter
        4 slices boiled ham
        4 slices domestic Provolone cheese
        3 teaspoons butter
      3/4 pound mushrooms
        1 chicken bouillon cube
      1/4 cup water
      1/2 cup California Dry Sherry
      1/4 teaspoon oregano

Dredge steaks in seasoned flour and sauté lightly in butter. Place steaks in buttered baking dish in one layer. Sauté ham slices on one side and place on steaks. Place slices of cheese on top of ham. Add 3 teaspoons butter to pan meat was browned in, add sliced mushrooms and sauté until golden brown. Arrange mushrooms on cheese. Into same frying pan place bouillon cube, add water, stirring to melt cube and deglaze pan. Add wine and oregano and pour over assembled veal steaks. Bake in 375° oven 15 to 20 minutes.

My choice of wine to accompany this dish:
CALIFORNIA VIN ROSÉ

Veal Stew

(4 servings)

Mrs. Greg Goorigian, Vie-Del Co., Fresno

    1-1/2 pounds veal stew
        2 tablespoons oil
      1/2 teaspoon paprika
        1 tablespoon dried onion flakes
        1 teaspoon salt
      1/4 teaspoon pepper
      1/2 cup California Sauterne

Brown cubed veal slowly in oil. Add seasonings and wine; stir to blend ingredients. Cover tightly and simmer about 45 minutes, or until veal is tender. Add to cheese sauce and serve immediately.

CHEESE SAUCE

        2 tablespoons butter
        2 level tablespoons flour
        1 cup milk
      1/2 teaspoon salt
      1/3 cup Parmesan cheese, grated
      1/4 cup California Sauterne

Melt butter, blend in flour and cook slowly for 1 or 2 minutes. Stir in milk and salt; continue cooking over low heat, stirring constantly until sauce thickens. Stir in cheese and wine. Heat through.

My choice of wine to accompany this dish:
CALIFORNIA RIESLING

NOTE: With this different and tasty dish Mrs. Goorigian suggests serving buttered oven-baked frozen shoestring potatoes and a salad composed of chopped lettuce, 1 grated carrot, a diced avocado, quartered fresh tomatoes, dressed with oil, California wine vinegar, a little mayonnaise and seasoning to taste.

Pan Roasted Veal

(4 to 6 servings)

Mrs. Paul H. Huber, Wine Brokerage, Fresno

- 3 pound veal roast, rolled
- 2 teaspoons salt
- 1/2 teaspoon fresh ground black pepper
- 1/2 teaspoon rosemary, finely crumbled
- 3 tablespoons butter
- 1/4 cup California Dry Sherry
- 1/4 cup milk
- 2 tablespoons parsley, minced

Rub meat with mixture of salt, pepper and rosemary. Melt butter in Dutch oven. Brown meat on all sides, being careful not to prick it. Add Sherry, cover, and cook over low heat 1-1/2 hours or until tender. Add milk after first hour of cooking. Skim and discard any fat from pan juices; add parsley. Serve over thinly sliced veal.

NOTE: We suggest adding 1 tablespoon California Brandy to pan juices after skimming off fat. Serve a California Chenin Blanc with this delicately flavored veal.

Veal Scallopini Zucchini

(6 servings)

Mrs. Sherwood J. Hall, Jr., Bandiera Wines, Cloverdale

While on a visit to Mexico, we found this recipe and since our family is so fond of zucchini, any new way to prepare it is a treat. The Spanish title is Escalopes de Ternera Con Calabacines.

- 1 tablespoon flour
- 1/2 teaspoon salt
- 12 thin slices of veal, for scallopini
- 2 tablespoons milk
- 1 egg, well beaten
- 2 tablespoons fine dry bread crumbs
- 2 tablespoons butter
- 1 tablespoon olive oil
- 2 zucchini squash, sliced
  Juice 1/2 lemon
- 2 to 3 tablespoons very dry California Sherry

Pound flour and salt into veal slices with mallet or edge of plate, making veal as flat as possible. Dip in milk blended with egg, then in crumbs. Heat butter and oil until butter is melted. Sauté veal in oil-butter over moderate heat until golden on both sides. Remove veal to hot platter and keep warm in oven. In same pan, cook squash until almost tender and slightly browned. Arrange zucchini around veal; sprinkle lemon juice over all. Add Sherry to pan in which veal and squash cooked, increase heat, cook and stir until browned bits have been loosened and pan deglazed, making a thin, brown bubbling sauce. Pour over veal and zucchini.

My choice of wine to accompany this dish:
CALIFORNIA CHABLIS

Meat Birds San Rafael

(4 servings)

Mrs. D. C. Turrentine, Wine Advisory Board, San Francisco

I developed this recipe by improving one I found in a magazine many years ago. It never fails to make a hit with family and friends.

- 1 pound veal or pork steak
  Flour, salt and white pepper
- 1 medium onion, chopped fine
- 1 clove garlic, minced
- 4 tablespoons shortening
- 3 tablespoons parsley, chopped
- 3 cups rye bread crumbs
- 1 egg, slightly beaten
- 3/4 cup California Sauterne
- 1/2 cup canned beef consommé
- 1/2 teaspoon caraway seeds

Have your butcher pound meat thin as for scallopini. Cut into 8 uniform pieces. Coat meat with flour and sprinkle with salt and pepper. Brown onion and garlic lightly in 2 tablespoons shortening. Remove and mix with parsley, bread crumbs and egg. Mix wine and consommé and add 1/2 cup to stuffing. Add caraway seeds and mix well. Spoon a heaping tablespoonful of stuffing onto each piece of meat. Roll meat up over stuffing and secure with tooth pick and tie with string. Heat remaining shortening in skillet used for browning onion and in it brown meat on all sides. Pour remaining wine mixture over meat. Cover and cook over low heat about 30 minutes, until tender.

My choice of wine to accompany this dish:
CALIFORNIA DRY SAUTERNE

German Chow Mein

(4 to 6 servings)

Mr. Karl C. Krupp, Charles Krug Winery, St. Helena

Depending on amount of leftover meat and gravy, this can be stretched to serve more people by increasing vegetables.

- 1 or 2 cups leftover roast veal or pork, diced
  Leftover gravy
- 1 small bunch celery, diced
- 1 or 2 tablespoons oil or fat
- 1 (1 lb.) can bean sprouts, drained
- 1 (4 oz.) can sliced mushrooms, undrained
- 1/2 cup California Sweet Sauterne
  Salt
- 1 large onion, chopped (optional)
  Garlic salt, to taste (optional)
- 1 (3 oz.) can Chinese noodles

Place meat and gravy in saucepan. Sauté celery in oil until tender and slightly brown. Add to meat, along with bean sprouts, mushrooms, wine and salt to taste. Sautéed onion and garlic salt may be added at this time, if desired. Heat thoroughly and serve over noodles.

My choice of wine to accompany this dish:
CALIFORNIA CHENIN BLANC OR VIN ROSÉ

NOTE: If you have no leftover gravy, 1/2 cup beef bouillon thickened with 1 teaspoon cornstarch may be substituted.

Breaded Roast Veal

(6 servings)

Mrs. Catherine L. Menth, California Wine Association, Burlingame

    3-1/2 pound veal roast, boned and rolled
      1/2 cup soft bread crumbs
        1 teaspoon rubbed sage
        2 tablespoons parsley, finely chopped
      1/2 teaspoon garlic, minced, or 1/4 teaspoon
           dried garlic flakes
        1 teaspoon seasoned salt
      1/4 teaspoon pepper
        1 egg, beaten
        1 large onion, cut in 1/8ths
        1 bay leaf
        1 cup California Chablis
        3 tablespoons tomato sauce

Preheat oven to 400°. Untie roast and unroll on flat surface. Combine bread crumbs, sage, parsley, garlic, half of seasonings and egg, mixing well. Spread mixture over veal. Roll up and re-tie securely. Sprinkle with remaining salt and pepper and place seam side down in roasting pan. Arrange onion and bay leaf around roast. Bake uncovered 30 minutes, turn roast seam side up and bake 30 minutes longer. Turn seam side down and pour wine mixed with tomato sauce over meat and continue baking 1 hour and 15 minutes, basting frequently. If roast browns too fast cover with aluminum foil.

My choice of wine to accompany this dish:
CALIFORNIA RED OR WHITE TABLE WINE

Mock Partridges

(6 servings)

Mrs. J. C. Russell, Almaden Vineyards, San Francisco

       12 very thin slices veal, about 2 oz. each
       12 very thin slices cured ham
       12 very thin slices salami
           Flour for dusting meat
           Salt and pepper to taste
        3 teaspoons olive oil
        1 teaspoon mixed Italian herbs,
           or to taste
        1 large clove garlic, crushed
      1/2 cup California Dry White Table Wine

Flatten veal with mallet or edge of saucer. Put 1 slice ham and salami on each piece of veal. Roll up firmly, tucking in loose ends. Tie with thread. Dust in flour, salt and pepper and brown well in oil in flat pan large enough to hold all 12 rolls without crowding. Add herbs, garlic and wine. Cover and cook slowly 1-1/2 to 1-3/4 hours. During cooking add small quantities of water as sauce thickens. Correct seasoning, remove threads and serve birds in sauce, which should be fairly thick.

My choice of wine to accompany this dish:
CALIFORNIA GRENACHE ROSÉ

NOTE: This is a Basque dish invented to console the hunter when partridges were not obtainable.

Spanish Veal Roast

(8 servings)

Mrs. Roy H. Richardson, Paul Masson Vineyards, Saratoga

This is a favorite "company" dish for me as I can make it the day before and then reheat it.

    3 to 4 pound boned leg of veal
        2 tablespoons oil
      1/3 teaspoon thyme
        1 bay leaf
      1/2 teaspoon cinnamon
      1/4 teaspoon coarse ground pepper
        1 carrot, peeled and sliced
        2 small tomatoes, quartered
        1 clove garlic, peeled
      1/4 cup California Brandy
      3/4 cup California Sauterne
        1 cup chicken broth or beef bouillon
        1 tablespoon butter
        1 tablespoon flour
        1 (10 oz.) package frozen peas,
           cooked and drained

Brown veal in large pot in heated oil, on all sides. Add next ingredients, from thyme through broth, to veal; cover and simmer 2 hours, turning meat occasionally. Remove meat and strain sauce. Blend butter, flour and brown over low heat. Add strained liquid and cook until thickened. Return meat to sauce, whole or sliced, add peas and heat thoroughly before serving.

My choice of wine to accompany this dish:
**CALIFORNIA EMERALD RIESLING
OR CABERNET SAUVIGNON**

Veal Roast Moutarde

(6 to 8 servings)

Mrs. Francis Gould, Charles Krug Winery, St. Helena

This is originally a French recipe. In Switzerland where veal is abundant and excellent I used this recipe very often, and it was always enjoyed and appreciated by my guests.

- 5 pound boneless veal roast, rolled and tied
- 1 teaspoon salt
- 1/2 teaspoon pepper
- 1/4 cup prepared mustard
- 1-1/2 cups cream or half-and-half
- 1 bay leaf
- 1 onion stuck with 2 or 3 cloves
- 1 carrot, quartered
- 2 cups California Dry White Table Wine
- 1 (4 oz.) can mushroom stems and pieces (optional)

Salt and pepper roast all over, cover with a thick coating of mustard and place in earthenware or glass vessel in which it fits fairly snug. Cover carefully with cream so as not to disturb mustard coating and refrigerate 24 hours or longer. Drain off cream and reserve, again being careful to preserve mustard coating. Place roast in casserole with bay leaf, onion and carrot. Roast in 350° oven about 2-1/2 hours until tender, basting frequently with wine. Fifteen minutes before roast is done, remove bay leaf, onion and carrot. Add mushrooms and cream used in marinade. Baste a few times; cream will take on a nice brown color. Serve with rice or noodles.

My choice of wine to accompany this dish:
CALIFORNIA DRY WHITE TABLE WINE OR VIN ROSÉ

Veal Elegant

(6 to 8 servings)

Mrs. Robert H. Meyer, Italian Swiss Colony, Asti

This is a real "quickie" — excellent for a last-minute emergency. All it requires is a tart tossed salad and a colorful vegetable.

- 2 tablespoons butter or margarine
- 2 tablespoons salad oil
- 2 pounds veal cutlets, cut into 1-inch pieces
- 1 (8 oz.) can sliced mushrooms, drained
- 1 clove garlic, minced
- 2 tablespoons flour
- 1 (1-3/8 oz.) envelope onion soup mix
- 2 cups water
- 1/4 cup California Zinfandel
- 2 tablespoons parsley, chopped

In large skillet, heat butter and oil. Lightly brown veal, mushrooms and garlic. Remove from skillet. Into remaining fat stir flour, onion soup mix, water and wine. Cover and simmer 10 minutes, stirring occasionally. Add meat, mushrooms and parsley. Heat through and serve over noodles, sprinkled with poppy seed.

My choice of wine to accompany this dish:
CALIFORNIA GAMAY

Veal, Ham and Eggplant

(4 servings)

Mrs. D. C. Turrentine, Wine Advisory Board, San Francisco

I have been preparing this dish many years. It always succeeds.

- 2 medium onions, chopped fine
  - Oil
- 1/2 pound ground veal
- 1/2 pound ground smoked ham
- 1/2 cup California Dry Sherry or White Table Wine
- 1/4 cup parsley, chopped
- 1 medium eggplant (about 1-1/4 lbs.)
- 1/4 cup fine dry bread crumbs
- 1/4 cup Parmesan cheese, grated
- 1 (10-1/2 oz.) can white sauce
- 1 egg yolk, lightly beaten

Sauté onion in 1 tablespoon oil. Add veal and ham and brown lightly. Add 1/4 cup wine and parsley. Simmer about 15 minutes. Meanwhile cut eggplant in 1/2-inch slices. Sauté in oil until almost tender. Place layer of eggplant in buttered 2-quart casserole. Top with layer of meat mixture, sprinkle with half the crumbs and cheese and repeat layers. Heat white sauce with remaining wine. Stir hot sauce into egg yolk. Pour over casserole and bake in 300° oven 40 to 45 minutes.

My choice of wine to accompany this dish:
CALIFORNIA TRAMINER

NOTE: Mrs. Turrentine continues, "We love this for a picnic. Wrap covered casserole in newspaper, then a blanket. It gets an especially enthusiastic response when accompanied by cold slices of cantaloupe and banana or nut bread. Bring an ice bucket and a cold bottle of wine."

San Mateo Casserole

(6 servings)

Mrs. Jack T. Matthews, Wine Institute, San Francisco

Serve with wine-marinated artichoke heart salad, Russian rye bread. For dessert have brandied fresh fruit.

    3 tablespoons salad oil
    1 pound ground veal
    1 pound ground pork
    1 onion, sliced
    2 tablespoons flour
    2 (8 oz.) cans tomato sauce
  1/2 cup California Burgundy or Claret
       Salt, garlic salt, pepper to taste
       Pinch each sweet basil and rosemary
    2 teaspoons steak sauce
  1/2 teaspoon sugar
  1/2 cup grated Parmesan cheese
    2 cups cooked white rice
    1 cup pitted ripe olives

Heat oil in large, heavy skillet, add ground veal, pork, and sliced onion. Cook and stir until meat is no longer pink. Sprinkle flour over meat and onion, blend well. Add tomato sauce and wine. Cook, stirring until mixture thickens. Add seasonings and cheese, stir over low heat until melted. Combine rice, olives and meat mixture. Turn into greased casserole. Sprinkle extra grated cheese over top. Cover and bake in 350⁰ oven for 30 minutes, uncover and bake 15 minutes longer to brown.

My choice of wine to accompany this dish:
CALIFORNIA GAMAY

Joaquin Veal Parmigiana

(6 servings)

Mrs. E. A. Humphrey, Guild Wine Co., Lodi

This being a very rich dish, only a light soup, green salad and a light dessert would be necessary to complement it.

    2 pounds veal steak
    2 eggs, beaten
    1 teaspoon salt
       Dash pepper
  3/4 cup dry bread crumbs
  1/2 cup olive oil
    2 (8 oz.) cans tomato sauce
  3/4 cup California Dry White Table Wine
  1/4 teaspoon basil
  1/4 teaspoon Worcestershire sauce
  1/8 teaspoon garlic salt
    1 tablespoon butter
  1/4 cup Parmesan cheese, grated
  1/2 pound Mozzarella cheese, sliced

Divide veal into 6 portions, dip into egg beaten with salt and pepper, and coat with bread crumbs. Brown meat in hot oil on both sides. Transfer to flat baking dish in one layer. Heat tomato sauce, wine, seasoning and butter 10 minutes. Pour over veal, sprinkle with Parmesan cheese, cover with foil and bake in 350⁰ oven about 1/2 hour. Arrange slices of Mozzarella on veal pieces and continue baking, uncovered another 10 minutes, until cheese melts.

My choice of wine to accompany this dish:
CALIFORNIA CABERNET

Veal Chops Geneva

(4 servings)

Mrs. Geneva Shuflin, Wine Institute, San Francisco

The gravy is really luscious. Truly a party dish — not inexpensive, but worth the cost.

    3 tablespoons bacon drippings
       or other fat
    4 thick veal rib chops
    3 tablespoons flour
    1 (10-3/4 oz.) can beef gravy
  1/3 cup California Sherry
    1 tablespoon tomato paste
    1 (4 oz.) can mushroom stems and
       pieces undrained
       Dash each thyme and marjoram
       Garlic salt, salt and pepper to taste

Heat bacon drippings in large, heavy skillet; brown chops slowly on both sides. Remove chops. Add flour to drippings and blend well. Add beef gravy and wine; cook, stirring, until mixture boils and thickens. Blend in tomato paste; add mushrooms and seasonings. Return chops to skillet. Cover and bake in 350⁰ oven 1 hour, until chops are tender, turning and basting chops several times.

My choice of wine to accompany this dish:
CALIFORNIA GRENACHE ROSÉ

NOTE: A suggested menu to accompany the chops, buttered noodles sprinkled with poppy seed, fresh broccoli with lemon-butter and fresh melon balls in California Port for dessert.

LAMB

Lamb with Lima Beans

(4 servings)

Mrs. Greg Goorigian, Vie-Del Company, Fresno

- 4 pounds lamb riblets
- 1/8 teaspoon pepper
- 1 teaspoon onion powder
- 1/2 teaspoon salt
- 1/2 cup California Burgundy
- 2 tablespoons tomato catsup
- 1/2 cup tomato sauce
- 1 onion, sliced
- 1/4 cup green pepper, diced
- 1 teaspoon Worcestershire sauce
- 1-1/2 cups large dry lima beans
- 5 cups water
- 1/2 teaspoon salt

Arrange riblets in baking dish or broiler, sprinkle with pepper, onion powder and salt. Brown in hot oven or under broiler on both sides. Pour off excess fat and arrange riblets in large casserole. Combine rest of ingredients except limas in saucepan and bring to boil. Pour hot mixture over lamb, cover and bake in 350º oven 3/4 hour. Meanwhile, simmer limas 1/2 hour in salted water. Place limas in casserole with riblets on top. Cover and bake 1-1/2 hours until most of liquid is absorbed. If desired, cover can be left off last few minutes of cooking to crisp riblets.

NOTE: A hearty casserole to serve with California Burgundy. To save time, canned lima beans could be substituted for dried ones, adding them to casserole for last 20 minutes of cooking.

Leg of Lamb Saratoga

(6 servings)

Mrs. Dave Weinberg, Paul Masson Vineyards, Saratoga

This good recipe, given to me by a friend, has become a favorite of mine.

- 1 (5 lb.) leg of lamb
- 1/4 cup dry mustard
- 1/4 teaspoon each salt and pepper
- 1/2 teaspoon garlic salt
- 4 teaspoons caraway seeds
- 1 (10-1/2 oz.) can tomato soup
- 1 cup water
- 1/2 cup California Sauterne

Pat dry mustard into entire surface of meat. Sprinkle other seasonings over all and place in roasting pan. Combine soup, water, wine, and add to pan. Roast, uncovered, in 325º oven, basting often, about 2 hours, or until meat is done to taste. As liquid evaporates, add additional wine.

My choice of wine to accompany this dish:
CALIFORNIA EMERALD RIESLING OR VIN ROSÉ

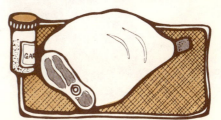

Simple Lamb Stew

(6 servings)

Mrs. Joseph A. Pfeiffer, Sr., San Juan Bautista

One of my daughters gave me this lovely recipe. My husband says it is the best stew he ever ate.

- 2 pounds lamb stew meat
- 1 (10-1/2 oz.) can mushroom soup
- 1/2 cup California Dry Sherry
- 1 (1-3/8 oz.) envelope onion soup mix

Place meat in casserole. Combine remaining ingredients and pour over lamb. Cover tightly and bake in 300⁰ oven about 2 hours, or until done.

NOTE: Mrs. Pfeiffer, a graduate of our Wine Study Course and a user of our cookbooks, warns against adding any salt or pepper, for condensed soups and dried soup mixes are very well seasoned. Serve this stew with a California Zinfandel.

Lamb Shanks in Red Sauce

(6 servings)

Professor Edward Rousek, Fresno State College, Fresno

- 6 lamb shanks
- 2 tablespoons oil
- 1 (11 oz.) can tomato soup
- 1/4 cup California Red Table Wine
- 2 tablespoons soy sauce
- 1 tablespoon Worcestershire sauce
- 1 small bay leaf
- 1/4 teaspoon each dried marjoram, thyme and garlic salt
- 1/2 teaspoon salt

Brown meat in oil in heavy saucepan. Combine rest of ingredients and pour over shanks. Cover tightly and bake in 300⁰ oven about 2 hours, or until tender. Serve with rice.

NOTE: Professor of Viticulture, Vincent Petrucci, at Fresno State College, sent us Professor Rousek's excellent recipe, which he distributes each year to students. The California Red Table Wine used in the sauce should be served with the dish.

Lamb Fricassee

(6 servings)

Mr. Joe Dodd, Sam-Jasper Winery, Manteca

- 3 pounds lamb shoulder or breast, cut into 1-inch squares
- 1/2 cup California Dry Sherry
- 1/4 cup flour
- 1/2 teaspoon turmeric
- 1 teaspoon dry mustard
- 2 teaspoons salt
- 1 teaspoon freshly ground black pepper
- 1/4 teaspoon cayenne
- 1/8 teaspoon fenugreek (optional)
- 2 tablespoons olive oil
- 2 tablespoons butter
- 2 cloves garlic
- 1 large leek
- 1 medium green pepper
- 2 stalks celery
- 2 medium potatoes
- 3 carrots
- 1 cup frozen or fresh peas

Place lamb in bowl just large enough to contain it (so that liquid rises over meat) and add Sherry. Let stand 15 minutes, turning occasionally. Combine flour and seasonings. Drain Sherry from meat and reserve. Coat lamb with seasoned flour, brown lightly in oil and butter and remove to Dutch oven. Add garlic, leek, green pepper and celery, all thinly sliced, to fat and cook over high heat, stirring constantly. Add to lamb along with the Sherry and enough water to cover. Bring to boil and lower to simmer. Cook until meat is tender, about 1-1/2 hours. Half hour before meat is done, add cubed potatoes, carrots and peas. Thicken liquid, if desired, with a little cornstarch blended with dry Sherry.

NOTE: Serve this exotically herbed lamb with a California Claret.

Gourmet Lamb Chops

(6 servings)

Mrs. D. C. Turrentine, Wine Advisory Board, San Francisco

This is an excellent dish for company dinner.

12 rib lamb chops, 1-1/4 inches thick
1 (3 oz.) can liver pâté
1 (3 oz.) can broiled mushrooms,
   drained and chopped fine
1 tablespoon onion, chopped fine
1 tablespoon parsley, chopped fine
   Garlic salt and pepper to taste
1 cup California Dry Red Table Wine
3 to 4 tablespoons butter
   Parsley, chopped, for garnish, if desired

Slit each chop all the way through from fat side to bone to make stuffing pocket, or have butcher do it. Mix paté, mushrooms, onions, parsley and seasonings. Stuff each pocket. Brown chops under broiler on both sides. Reduce heat to 350º and bake in oven, uncovered, 10 to 15 minutes, until done as you prefer. Remove chops to platter and keep warm. Pour off all fat from pan. Add wine, stirring over low heat to deglaze pan. Stir in butter and parsley. When butter is incorporated, pour over chops and serve immediately.

My choice of wine to accompany this dish:
CALIFORNIA DRY WHITE TABLE WINE

NOTE: Mrs. Turrentine serves these elegant chops with baked potatoes, sweet and sour red cabbage, green salad, and for dessert 3 different sherbets — a scoop of each.

Lamb Goulash

(6 servings)

Mrs. Walter A. Raich, Sr., Paul Masson Vineyards, Saratoga

I found this recipe in an old Serbian cookbook which belonged to my husband's mother. Cookbooks of that era did not go into detail as to measurements, so we had to do some experimenting to adapt it to our tastes. Guests seem to enjoy this sample of Balkan old world cookery as much as we do.

2 pounds lamb for stew
1/4 cup fat or oil
4 medium onions, chopped
2 teaspoons salt
1/2 teaspoon freshly ground pepper
1-1/2 cups chicken broth
1/2 cup California Dry Vermouth
4 medium potatoes, peeled and cubed
2 large carrots, pared and
   thickly sliced

Brown lamb on all sides in fat. Add onions and continue cooking until they are soft and golden. Drain off excess fat. Add salt and pepper, chicken broth and wine. Cover and simmer 1 hour or until meat is tender. Add vegetables and simmer 1/2 hour longer, or until tender.

My choice of wine to accompany this dish:
CALIFORNIA RIESLING OR CHABLIS

NOTE: Mrs. Raich's menu — buttered broad noodles, wilted cucumbers in sour cream dressing, sour dough rolls, and assorted cheeses and fruits for dessert.

Braised Lamb Chops

(4 servings)

Mrs. Ronald Mettler, Guild Wine Co., Lodi

When I was a child, my favorite meat was lamb, so my mother tried many recipes, and this became a family favorite.

4 shoulder lamb chops
1 clove garlic, cut
3 tablespoons butter or margarine
1 onion, thinly sliced
1/4 pound fresh mushrooms, sliced, or
   1 (4 oz.) can
2 tablespoons flour
1 teaspoon tomato paste, or catsup
3/4 cup stock or water
1/2 cup California White Table Wine
   Salt and coarse ground black pepper
   to taste

Rub chops with cut clove of garlic. Heat 1 tablespoon butter in heavy skillet and brown chops on both sides. Melt remaining butter in another pan, add onion and mushrooms and sauté until golden brown. Remove from heat, blend in flour and tomato paste. Add stock and wine. Return to heat, add salt and pepper to taste. Stir mixture until it starts to boil. Drain all fat from browned chops and add sauce. Simmer, covered, 40 minutes, or until tender.

NOTE: Serve a well-chilled California Chablis with these chops for added enjoyment.

VARIETY MEATS

New Baked Liver

(4 servings)

Mrs. Earle M. Cobb, California Growers Wineries, Cutler

- 1 pound beef liver, sliced
- 4 slices bacon
- 1 small onion, minced
- 1 teaspoon Worcestershire sauce
- 4 tablespoons catsup
- 1 tablespoon green pepper, chopped
- 1/4 teaspoon salt
- 1 cup California Rosé

Trim membrane from liver and arrange slices in lightly greased casserole. Cover with bacon slices. Combine remaining ingredients and add to casserole. Cover and bake in 300° oven 1-1/4 hours. Remove cover last 15 minutes to brown bacon.

My choice of wine to accompany this dish:
CALIFORNIA VIN ROSÉ

NOTE: Serve this original dish as Mrs. Cobb suggests with lima beans, sliced tomatoes and, for dessert, mandarin orange sections.

Pickled Tongue

(6 to 8 servings)

Mrs. Clifton Chappell, Thomas Vineyards, Cucamonga

- 1 large beef tongue, fresh or smoked
- 1 (4/5 qt.) bottle California Sauterne
- 1-1/2 teaspoons salt
- Water
- 2/3 cup California wine vinegar
- 2/3 cup salad oil
- 1/3 cup water
- 1 tablespoon parsley, minced
- 2 cloves garlic, mashed

Place tongue in large kettle, add wine, salt and enough water to cover. Bring to boil, lower heat and simmer until tender to fork. Cool in liquid. Drain, skin and slice into thin slices. Blend vinegar, oil, water, parsley and garlic in large bowl. Add tongue slices and marinate at least 3 hours. Serve with crackers as hors d'oeuvre, or use in sandwiches.

My choice of wine to accompany this dish:
CALIFORNIA SAUTERNE OR CHABLIS

Sautéed Veal Kidneys

(1 serving)

Mrs. Yvonne Boulleray, Windsor Vineyards, Windsor

- 2 veal kidneys
- 2 tablespoons butter
- 1 tablespoon California Brandy
- 1 tablespoon flour
- 1/2 cup California Dry White Table Wine
  Salt and freshly ground pepper
  to taste
- 1 tablespoon parsley, finely chopped

Cut kidneys in slices, removing fat. Sauté rapidly in hot butter. When nicely browned pour warm Brandy over them and ignite. Shake pan until flame dies. Blend in flour, add wine and cook 1 or 2 minutes longer. Season to taste, sprinkle with parsley and serve with hot, buttered toast points. Garnish with lemon wedge.

My choice of wine to accompany this dish:
CALIFORNIA ROSÉ

NOTE: This dish, when served with creamy scrambled eggs, makes a sumptuous brunch or luncheon entrée.

Liver and Mushrooms

(4 servings)

Mrs. J. W. Fleming, Lockeford Winery, Lockeford

- 1/4 cup butter
- 2 large onions, thickly sliced
- 1/3 cup flour
- 1 teaspoon salt
- 1/2 teaspoon pepper
- 1/4 teaspoon Italian seasoning
- 1 pound baby beef liver, thinly sliced or cubed
- 1/2 pound fresh mushrooms
- 1 cup California Red Table Wine

Melt butter, if using electric skillet, at 300°, add onions and sauté until golden. Meanwhile shake flour, seasonings and liver in paper bag to coat slices well. Remove onions and reserve, leaving butter in pan. Brown liver quickly over high heat (375° to 400°). Wash and slice mushrooms and add to liver. Lower heat and add wine and onions. Simmer until wine is reduced by 2/3 and serve immediately.

NOTE: We suggest this dish be served with the same California Dry Red Table Wine that went into its savory sauce.

Grand Mixed Grill

(4 servings)

Mrs. Robert Diana, Villa Armando Winery, Pleasanton

- 8 pork sausage links
- 8 lamb kidneys
- 16 mushrooms
- 16 pieces green pepper
- 16 pieces red pepper
- 8 cherry tomatoes

Parboil sausages 3 minutes. Drain and dry. Marinate kidneys and sausages 1 hour. Arrange meats and vegetables, alternating, on skewers. Brush well with marinade and grill until browned, continuing to baste with marinade.

MARINADE

- 1/2 cup California Dry Vermouth
- 1 cup olive oil
- 1 teaspoon lemon juice
- 1 medium onion, finely chopped
- 1 clove garlic, minced
- 1 teaspoon fresh basil, chopped
- 1 teaspoon salt
- 2 peppercorns, crushed

Combine all ingredients and pour over meats.

My choice of wine to accompany this dish:
CALIFORNIA BURGUNDY OR CHIANTI

Kidneys and Heart in Wine

(6 servings)

Mr. John Del Bondio, Beringer Brothers, St. Helena

- 2 beef or veal kidneys
- 1 veal heart
- 1 medium onion, chopped fine
- 3 cloves garlic, chopped fine
- 3 leaves sage, chopped fine, or
  1/4 teaspoon dried
- 1/8 teaspoon rosemary
- 3 tablespoons butter or bacon fat
- 1/2 teaspoon ground cloves
- 1 teaspoon salt
- 1/8 teaspoon pepper
- 2 to 3 cups California Dry Red Table Wine

Cube kidneys and soak in salt water 1 hour. Change water and parboil 2 or 3 minutes. Cube heart. Brown onion, garlic, herbs and meats all together in fat. Add cloves, salt, pepper and wine. Cover and simmer 1 hour or until tender.

My choice of wine to accompany this dish:
CALIFORNIA DRY RED TABLE WINE

NOTE: Mr. Del Bondio says to serve this unusual dish with polenta or rice and your favorite tossed salad.

Liver and Macaroni Shells

(6 servings)

Mrs. William B. Hewitt, University of California, Davis

The trick to this recipe is: Do it fast.

- 1/2 pound calf's liver
- 2 cups macaroni shells
- 1 tablespoon oil
- 2 tablespoons dried onion soup mix
- 1/4 cup California Dry Sherry
- 2 tomatoes, quartered
- 1 large green pepper, cut in eighths
- 1-1/2 cups Parmesan cheese, grated

Cut liver into small squares. Cook macaroni in boiling salted water with a little oil added for 8 minutes. Drain. Fry liver pieces quickly in oil 2 to 3 minutes. Sprinkle onion soup mix over pieces and turn once. Add Sherry, cover and shake pan over heat briefly. Place good lump of butter in hot platter, pour hot shells into platter and place liver pieces on top. Garnish with pieces of fresh tomato and green pepper. Serve with big bowl of grated cheese.

NOTE: This makes a pretty platter. Even people who are dubious about liver are likely to enjoy this. Serve with California Rosé.

Liver Santa Rosa

(6 servings)

Mrs. E. B. Nelson, Wine Institute, San Francisco

- 3 tablespoons oil
- 1 large onion, chopped
- 2 pounds beef or calf's liver
- 3 level tablespoons flour
- 1/2 teaspoon salt
- 1/4 teaspoon pepper
- 1/2 cup California Rosé
  Water to cover

Heat oil in large skillet or Dutch oven. Sauté onion until golden. Drain and set aside, reserving fat. Remove membrane from liver and dredge in seasoned flour. Brown in remaining oil on both sides. Return onion to pan. Add wine and just enough water to cover. Cover and simmer just until gravy thickens. Serve with noodles, rice or mashed potatoes.

NOTE: Serve with the California Rosé that enriched the sauce.

Stewed Kidneys

(3 servings)

Mr. Arthur J. Reese, Wine Advisory Board, San Francisco

- 6 lamb kidneys
- 1 teaspoon salt
- 1/4 teaspoon pepper
- 1-1/2 tablespoons oil or butter
- 1 tablespoon parsley, chopped
- 1 bay leaf, crumbled
- 1/4 teaspoon thyme
- 1 cup California Dry Sherry
- 1 teaspoon California wine vinegar

Rinse kidneys, pat dry, and slice thin. Season with salt and pepper. Sauté quickly in fat with herbs until tender and lightly browned. Add wine and vinegar, heat to boiling and serve at once.

NOTE: These go nicely with small whole new potatoes sautéed golden brown in butter. California Rosé complements the meal.

Tripe Burgundian

(8 to 10 servings)

Mr. E. A. Mirassou, Mirassou Vineyards, San Jose

This is an excellent hors d'oeuvre, when dunked with sour dough French bread, or it can be used as a sauce over spaghetti or polenta.

- 3 pounds honeycomb tripe
- 1/2 cup olive oil
- 2 large Spanish or Bermuda onions
- 1 large clove garlic, pressed
- 1 (20 oz.) can tomatoes
- 1 cup California Burgundy
  Salt and pepper to taste
- 1/4 teaspoon oregano
- 1/4 teaspoon basil
  Tabasco sauce to taste
- 1/3 cup parsley, chopped

Simmer tripe in salted water 1-1/2 hours, or until tender. (If desired, 1 bay leaf adds to flavor.) Meanwhile prepare Burgundy sauce. Heat oil in large frying pan and sauté onions and garlic until golden. Add tomatoes, wine and all remaining ingredients. Simmer until blended. Drain and slice tripe 1/2 inch wide and 3 inches long. Add to sauce and simmer about 1/2 hour.

My choice of wine to accompany this dish:
CALIFORNIA ZINFANDEL

POULTRY

Is it any wonder that chicken is a favorite on American dinner tables? It is delicious, inexpensive, quickly and easily cooked and lends itself to endless variety. While there are enticing recipes here for other poultry, the fryer is king. When combined with other flavors, and bonded together by the California wines, you have chicken fit for a king as well. White wine is most often suggested as the beverage accompaniment for chicken, because the mild flavor of white meat is usually more compatible with its delicate taste, but some of the more robust dishes, cooked in red wine or pungently seasoned, will go with red table wines. Either way will provide a taste revelation!

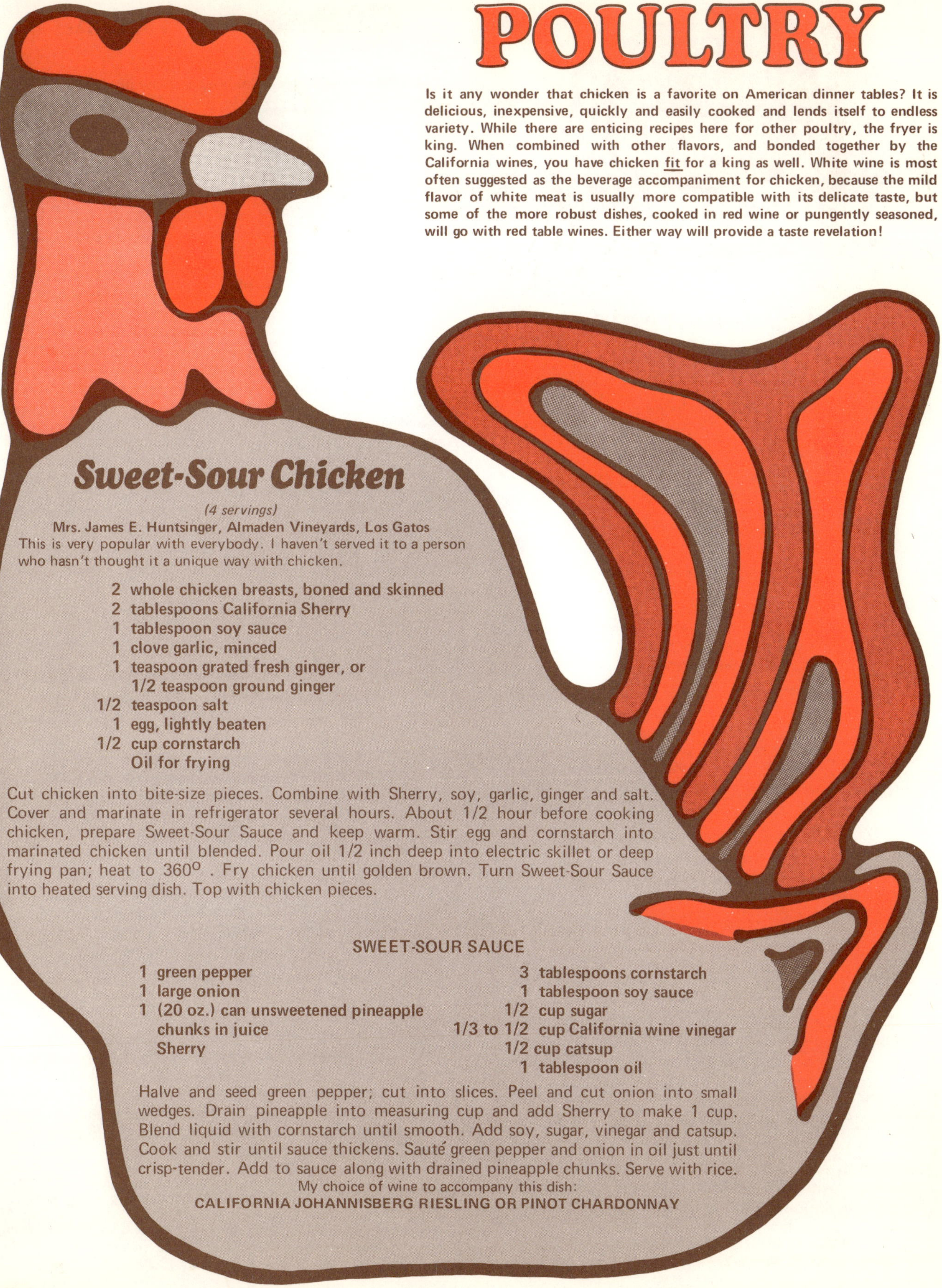

Sweet-Sour Chicken

(4 servings)

Mrs. James E. Huntsinger, Almaden Vineyards, Los Gatos

This is very popular with everybody. I haven't served it to a person who hasn't thought it a unique way with chicken.

- 2 whole chicken breasts, boned and skinned
- 2 tablespoons California Sherry
- 1 tablespoon soy sauce
- 1 clove garlic, minced
- 1 teaspoon grated fresh ginger, or
- 1/2 teaspoon ground ginger
- 1/2 teaspoon salt
- 1 egg, lightly beaten
- 1/2 cup cornstarch
- Oil for frying

Cut chicken into bite-size pieces. Combine with Sherry, soy, garlic, ginger and salt. Cover and marinate in refrigerator several hours. About 1/2 hour before cooking chicken, prepare Sweet-Sour Sauce and keep warm. Stir egg and cornstarch into marinated chicken until blended. Pour oil 1/2 inch deep into electric skillet or deep frying pan; heat to 360°. Fry chicken until golden brown. Turn Sweet-Sour Sauce into heated serving dish. Top with chicken pieces.

SWEET-SOUR SAUCE

- 1 green pepper
- 1 large onion
- 1 (20 oz.) can unsweetened pineapple chunks in juice
- Sherry
- 3 tablespoons cornstarch
- 1 tablespoon soy sauce
- 1/2 cup sugar
- 1/3 to 1/2 cup California wine vinegar
- 1/2 cup catsup
- 1 tablespoon oil

Halve and seed green pepper; cut into slices. Peel and cut onion into small wedges. Drain pineapple into measuring cup and add Sherry to make 1 cup. Blend liquid with cornstarch until smooth. Add soy, sugar, vinegar and catsup. Cook and stir until sauce thickens. Sauté green pepper and onion in oil just until crisp-tender. Add to sauce along with drained pineapple chunks. Serve with rice.

My choice of wine to accompany this dish:

CALIFORNIA JOHANNISBERG RIESLING OR PINOT CHARDONNAY

Pollo Supreme

(8 servings)

Mrs. V. E. Petrucci, Fresno State College, Fresno

Our niece, Jane Troiani of Tulare, served us this "luscious" chicken and this is my interpretation of her recipe.

- 2 to 3 fryers, cut in pieces
- 1/2 cup flour
- 2 teaspoons salt
- 1/2 teaspoon pepper
- 1 clove garlic
- 1/2 to 1 cup olive oil
- 2 tablespoons margarine
- 1 cup fresh mushrooms, sliced
- 1/2 cup onions, sliced
- 1 (4 oz.) can green chilies, diced
- 1 (4 oz.) can pimientos, diced
- 1/2 cup California Sauterne

Coat chicken pieces in flour seasoned with salt and pepper. Fry garlic in olive oil until brown and discard. Add chicken to hot oil and sauté until golden brown all over. Transfer chicken to electric skillet or casserole. Heat margarine in another pan and sauté mushrooms and onions until soft. Add chilies, pimientos and wine. Heat through and pour over chicken. Bake covered at 300° 1 hour. Serve with pilaf or scalloped potatoes.

My choice of wine to accompany this dish:
CALIFORNIA JOHANNISBERG RIESLING OR GAMAY ROSÉ

BROILERS CALIFORNIA are the inspiration of Mrs. Dale R. Anderson, Guimarra Vineyards, Edison. Season 2 or 3 split broiler-fryers to taste with salt and pepper. Place over hot coals and brush with melted butter and broil 15 to 20 minutes. Combine 3/4 cup California Sherry, 1/4 cup melted butter, 1/4 cup currant jelly and 1 teaspoon salt and simmer 10 minutes. Turn chicken and brush with wine baste. Continue broiling another 15 to 20 minutes, basting frequently with wine mixture. Mrs. Anderson serves this dish with California Rosé and includes lima beans, sliced tomatoes and cucumbers and parsley bread in her menu.

Chicken and Wild Rice

(4 servings)

Mrs. Angela Danisch, Brookside Vineyard Co., Bonita

So very simple, and so good.

- 1 cup wild rice
- 3/4 cup California Sauterne
- 1-1/2 cups water
- 2 whole chicken breasts, halved
- 1 (2-3/4 oz.) package dry onion soup mix
- 1 (10-1/2 oz.) can cream of mushroom or cream of chicken soup

Put rice in bottom of casserole. Cover with wine and water. Arrange chicken pieces on top. Over this sprinkle onion soup mix. Cover with creamed soup, spreading evenly. Bake, uncovered, in 350° oven 1/2 hour. Cover and bake 1/2 hour more.

NOTE: In her version of this dish, called Los Gatos Chicken, Mrs. J. C. Russell, Almaden Vineyards, Los Gatos, uses the same ingredients, eliminating water and using both cream of celery and chicken soups. She mixes undiluted soups, 1-1/4 cups California White Table Wine, onion soup mix and 1 cup wild rice and lets stand several hours. She arranges 3 chicken breasts, split in two, on top and bakes, covered 1 hour in 350° oven; stirs, turns breasts over and bakes another hour. Both dishes would be delicious served with a California Rhine Wine.

Chicken Napa

(8 servings)

Mr. John Del Bondio, Beringer Brothers, St. Helena

- 2 frying chickens, cut in pieces
- 1-1/2 teaspoons salt
- 1 teaspoon paprika
- 1/2 teaspoon pepper
- 2 tablespoons each, butter and olive oil
- 1/8 teaspoon dried rosemary, crumbled
- 1/2 pound fresh mushrooms, or 1 (4 oz.) can button mushrooms
- 3/4 cup California Sherry
- 1/4 cup California Dry White Table Wine
- 6 baby artichokes, cooked and halved, or 1 (11 oz.) can artichoke hearts, water packed
- 2 tablespoons parsley, chopped

Season chicken with salt, paprika and pepper. Brown chicken in butter and oil on all sides. Sprinkle with rosemary, cover and cook over medium heat 20 to 25 minutes, or until tender. Remove chicken to platter and keep warm. Quarter mushrooms and add to pan chicken was cooked in. Add Sherry and white wine, let cook 2 or 3 minutes stirring to deglaze pan. Add artichokes in juices and heat through. Arrange artichokes around chicken. Cook down sauce over high heat until smooth and thick. Pour over chicken and sprinkle with parsley.

My choice of wine to accompany this dish:
ANY CALIFORNIA DRY WHITE TABLE WINE

NOTE: Mr. Del Bondio says: "This recipe may be changed by using 3/4 cup California Dry White Table Wine, 2 tablespoons Sherry and the juice of 1 lemon, if a more tart flavor is desired."

Alice's Chicken Casserole

(6 to 8 servings)

Mrs. Alice Reiner, Fromm & Sichel, San Francisco

- 5 medium onions, finely chopped
- 2 (3 lb.) fryers, cut in pieces
- 2 teaspoons salt
- 1/4 teaspoon pepper
- 1 teaspoon paprika
- 3/4 cup California Chablis
- 1/4 cup water

Grease shallow baking dish lightly. Spread chopped onions over bottom. Arrange chicken, skin side down on onions. Sprinkle seasonings over chicken. Combine wine, water and pour over meat. Bake in 375° oven 20 minutes. Turn chicken pieces over and bake 15 to 20 minutes longer, until nicely browned and tender, basting occasionally with pan drippings.

NOTE: A simple recipe resulting in superior flavored chicken. It would go well with any California Dry White Table Wine.

Thyme Flavored Chicken

(4 servings)

Mrs. Leon Peters, Valley Foundry & Machine Works, Fresno

This casserole should come right to the table from the oven. I prepare it in the morning, for it is one chicken recipe that is just as good reheated. A pilaf can be baked at the same time, to be savored with plenty of the good gravy.

- 1 fryer, cut in pieces
- 1/2 cup flour
- 1/2 teaspoon salt
- 1/4 teaspoon pepper
- Oil
- 1 onion, chopped
- 1/3 cup California Sauterne
- 1/3 cup water
- 1/4 teaspoon thyme, crumbled
- 1 tablespoon parsley, chopped
- 1/2 cup sliced mushrooms

Dredge chicken in seasoned flour and sauté in oil until lightly browned. Remove chicken to casserole. Add onion to oil in pan, sauté until soft. Add wine and water, bring to boil and pour over chicken. Sprinkle with thyme and parsley. Cover and bake in 300° oven 1 hour. Last 10 minutes add mushrooms.

My choice of wine to accompany this dish:
CALIFORNIA PINOT CHARDONNAY OR PINOT BLANC

Amandine Chicken

(6 servings)

Mrs. Louis P. Martini, Louis M. Martini Winery, St. Helena

This was given to me as a bride. With certain modifications, it has turned out to be my husband's favorite recipe. I garnish it with glazed oranges and parsley.

- 1/2 cup flour
- 1 teaspoon salt
- 1/4 teaspoon pepper
- 2 fryers, cut in pieces
- 1/2 cup oil
- 1-1/2 cups clear chicken broth
- 2 tablespoons butter
- 1/4 cup onion, finely chopped
- 1 clove garlic, sliced fine
- 1/4 cup celery, finely chopped
- 1/2 pound fresh mushrooms, sliced
- 1/2 cup California Dry White Table Wine
- 1 cup apple cider
- 3 tablespoons soy sauce
- 1 cup blanched almonds, chopped

Combine flour, salt and pepper. Coat chicken pieces carefully with seasoned flour and brown in oil. Drain and place in large serving and baking casserole. Pour off oil, add chicken broth and heat, stirring to incorporate brown bits in pan. Pour over chicken. Wipe pan dry and melt butter. Add onion, garlic and celery. When nearly soft, add mushrooms and cook 2 or 3 minutes longer. Add wine, cider and simmer 5 minutes. Add soy sauce. Pour over chicken and move pieces around to blend liquids. Refrigerate 24 hours. One hour before serving time place in 325° oven, uncovered. About 10 minutes before removing, scatter almonds over top. Serve with rice.

My choice of wine to accompany this dish:
CALIFORNIA TRAMINER

Delano Chicken

(6 servings)

Mrs. Fred Perelli-Minetti, A. Perelli-Minetti & Sons, Delano

    3 whole chicken breasts, halved
    1/2 cup butter
    2 teaspoons seasoned salt
    1/4 teaspoon pepper
    2 (10-1/2 oz.) cans cream of celery soup
    2 (5 oz.) cans water chestnuts, drained
    1/2 cup California Dry White Table Wine

Brown chicken in butter on both sides. Season and place in baking pan. Add soup to butter in browning pan and blend. Add thinly sliced water chestnuts and wine. Stir well and pour over chicken. Bake in 375° oven 50 minutes, moistening with more wine, if necessary.

My choice of wine to accompany this dish:
CALIFORNIA SAUVIGNON BLANC

NOTE: In the Perelli-Minetti household this dish goes with steamed rice, snow peas and as dessert, lime sherbet with fortune cookies.

MEAT PIE ELEGANT is a quick, easy method of producing something special with a frozen meat pie. Mrs. Charles J. Welch, Guild Wine Co., Lodi, says, "Use individual chicken or meat pies. Bake until crust is warm. Remove from oven, cut gently around edge of top crust, lift crust up and turn back. Add 2 tablespoons leftover vegetables and 1 tablespoon California Sherry or Red or White Wine, as desired. Replace crust, reshaping gently. Continue baking as package directs until done and brown."

Vermouth Baked Chicken

(6 to 8 servings)

Mrs. Jane Murphy, Wine Institute, San Francisco

    3 fryers, cut in pieces
      Oil
    2 (4 oz.) cans mushrooms, undrained
    7 small potatoes, cut in eighths
    1 (6 oz.) can pitted ripe olives
    1 large onion, chopped
    1-1/2 teaspoons salt
    1/2 teaspoon pepper
    1/2 cup California Dry Vermouth

Brown chicken pieces well in a little oil. As chicken browns, remove to roasting pan. Add undrained mushrooms, potatoes, olives and onion. Season with salt and pepper. Add Vermouth, cover and bake in 325° oven 30 to 40 minutes, until tender. Remove cover during last 15 minutes of cooking.

My choice of wine to accompany this dish:
CALIFORNIA RIESLING

Barbecue Basted Chicken

(4 servings)

Mrs. T. E. Rogers, The Christian Brothers, Reedley

    1 large fryer, cut in pieces
    1/2 cup olive oil
    1 cup California Dry White Table Wine
    1 tablespoon dried parsley
    1 teaspoon salt
    1/4 teaspoon pepper
    2 cloves garlic, chopped

Arrange chicken in baking dish. Combine all remaining ingredients and pour over chicken. Marinate several hours, turning pieces occasionally. Broil chicken over glowing coals 45 to 50 minutes, turning and basting often with marinade.

NOTE: This barbecue dish could be accompanied by roasting ears of corn wrapped in foil done on the same grill, and served with melted butter. A glass of California Rhine Wine would complement the menu.

Herbed Chicken

(4 servings)

Mrs. Don Rudolph, Cresta Blanca Wine Co., Livermore

Sometimes for a change I flavor one batch of chicken with curry, another with oregano and a third with tarragon, instead of the rosemary/thyme mixture.

    1/3 cup flour
    1-1/2 teaspoons salt
    1/4 teaspoon pepper
    1 teaspoon paprika
    1 large fryer, cut in pieces
    1/2 cup shortening
    1 cup mushrooms, sliced, or
      (4 oz.) can
    1 cup celery, chopped
    1 clove garlic, crushed
    1 bay leaf
    1/2 teaspoon rosemary or thyme
    1 teaspoon salt
      Pinch of pepper
    1/2 cup California Sauterne

Combine flour, salt, pepper and paprika in bag and place chicken pieces in it, a few at a time. Shake to coat evenly. Brown quickly in heated fat. Place individual servings on double thick squares of aluminum foil. Combine all remaining ingredients and spoon this mixture over chicken. Fold corners of foil up over chicken and seal. Place packets in shallow roasting pan and bake in 350° oven 1 hour.

My choice of wine to accompany this dish:
CALIFORNIA SAUTERNE OR CHABLIS

Festive Cornish Hens

(6 servings)

Mrs. Fred J. Leitz, Paul Masson Vineyards, Saratoga

This is a wonderful Christmas season dinner party dish. The colorful hens are served with wild rice. For salad I use a cranberry-orange mold.

- 6 Rock Cornish Game Hens
  Salt and pepper
- 1/2 cup butter or margarine, melted
- 1 (1 lb. 4 oz.) can dark sweet pitted cherries
- 2/3 cup California Brandy
- 2 tablespoons lemon juice
- 3/4 (13-3/4 oz.) can chicken broth
- 2 teaspoons cornstarch
- 3 tablespoons cherry syrup

Heat oven to 425°. Sprinkle hens inside and out with salt and pepper. Brush hens with butter and place on sides. Roast 10 minutes. Turn hens on other side, brush with butter and roast 10 or more minutes. Turn hens breast side up, again brush with butter and roast 25 to 40 minutes, until brown, basting often. Remove hens to platter and keep warm. Drain cherries, reserving syrup. Pour off excess fat in roaster, place over medium heat, add Brandy and cook 1 minute, stirring. Add all but 3 tablespoons of cherry juice, lemon juice and chicken broth. Simmer 3 to 4 minutes. Add cherries. Mix cornstarch with 3 tablespoons cherry syrup, stir into sauce. Bring to boil, stirring constantly. Correct seasoning. Pour sauce over hens on platter.

NOTE: Serve with a California Burgundy and have a successful dinner party!

Joella Chicken

(8 servings)

Mrs. George Al Berry, E. & J. Gallo Winery, Modesto

With this dish I usually serve parsleyed carrots, or buttered peas and a salad of marinated cucumbers.

- 1 (2-1/2 oz.) jar chipped beef
- 4 whole chicken breasts, halved
- 1 (10-1/2 oz.) can cream of mushroom soup
- 1 cup dairy sour cream
- 1 (4 oz.) can sliced mushrooms, undrained
- 1/2 cup California Dry Sherry
  Paprika

Place chipped beef (which may be rinsed in water first, if too salty) in bottom of shallow casserole. Arrange chicken breasts on top. Cover with mixture of soup, sour cream, mushrooms and liquid and Sherry. Dust with paprika. Bake, uncovered, in 350° oven 1-1/2 hours.

My choice of wine to accompany this dish:
CALIFORNIA GREY RIESLING OR CHABLIS

Budget Bake

(4 servings)

Mrs. Roy W. Mineau, Roma Wine Co., Fresno

- 1/2 cup soy sauce
- 1/2 cup brown sugar, firmly packed
- 1/3 cup California Sherry
- 3 green onions, chopped
- 12 chicken wings

Heat soy sauce with sugar until sugar is dissolved. Add wine and green onions. Arrange wings in single layer in baking pan. Pour over sauce mixture. Bake in 350° oven about 1 hour, turning wings during cooking.

My choice of wine to accompany this dish:
CALIFORNIA SAUTERNE

NOTE: These might be served with creamed potatoes topped with cheese, scalloped potatoes, or macaroni and cheese.

Poulet Avec Raisins Blancs

(4 servings)

Mrs. Fendel Whaley, Guild Wine Co., Lodi

This prize-winning recipe was given to me by Mrs. Thomas J. O'Connor and we have served it many times with great enjoyment.

- 1/4 pound uncooked ham, diced
- 2 whole chicken breasts, halved
- 1 teaspoon salt
- 1/4 teaspoon pepper
- 3 tablespoons butter
- 1 tablespoon oil
- 1 (1 lb.) can new potatoes, drained
- 2 tablespoons flour
- 2 cups cream
- 1 cup California White Table Wine
- 1/4 pound fresh mushrooms, sliced
- 1 cup seedless white grapes

Simmer ham in a little water 15 minutes. Season chicken breasts with salt and pepper and sauté in 1 tablespoon each butter and oil. Remove to a casserole. Brown potatoes well in fat remaining in pan and add to casserole. Melt remaining butter, blend in flour, cook 1 minute and add cream and wine. Stir until smooth and thickened. Add drained ham and mushrooms to casserole and correct seasoning. Pour cream-wine sauce over all and bake in 350° oven 1/2 hour. Add white grapes and bake 10 minutes more.

My choice of wine to accompany this dish:
CALIFORNIA SAUTERNE OR CHAMPAGNE

Lazy Sunday Chicken

(4 servings)

Mrs. James P. Gray, Beaulieu Vineyard, Rutherford

This is for people on a low cholesterol diet.

          1 frying chicken, cut into pieces, or
            8 single breasts
          1 cup water
          2 tablespoons minced onion, or
            dried onion flakes
            Dash garlic powder
          1 teaspoon salt
        1/4 teaspoon pepper
            Lawry's seasoning salt to taste
        1/2 cup California Dry Sherry or Sauterne
          6 small carrots
          1 (4 oz.) can mushrooms, undrained
   3 or 4 medium potatoes, quartered
          1 cup frozen peas

Preheat electric skillet to 350° and place in it chicken pieces. Add water, seasonings and cook down until chicken is brown on one side. Turn and add wine. Cook covered 45 minutes to 1 hour, adding small amounts of wine, as necessary. About 1/2 hour before meat is done, lay carrots on top, mushrooms, undrained and potatoes, peeled and quartered. During last 5 minutes, add frozen peas.

My choice of wine to accompany this dish:
CALIFORNIA RIESLING OR RED TABLE WINE

NOTE: Mrs. Gray suggests a fruit ice and a slice of angel food cake to complete this diet meal.

QUICK CHICKEN is a slightly different version of Lazy Sunday Chicken above, by Mrs. Earl Harrah, Wine Advisory Board, San Francisco. She sets the electric skillet at 350°, places chicken pieces skin side down in it and sprinkles over meat 1/2 cup each chopped onion and celery. Season with salt and pepper and add 1/4 cup each California White Table Wine and chicken broth. Cover leaving steam vent open and cook 15 or 20 minutes until liquid has evaporated and chicken has browned. Turn chicken over, add 1/2 cup more onion and celery, season, and add 1/4 cup each broth and wine. Cook, covered 10 to 15 minutes or until chicken is done. Make gravy by mixing 2 tablespoons flour with stock, mix into pan juices, adding more broth and wine to taste, and cook, stirring until thickened and smooth. This should be served with the California White Table Wine used in the cooking. Serves 4.

Coq au Vin

(8 to 10 servings)

Mrs. Ben R. Goehring, Guild Wine Co., Lodi

This dish is a San Francisco version of the classic French dish. It is very attractive served on a large platter, surrounded by the onions.

         24 chicken pieces (3 fryers)
          1 cup flour
          1 tablespoon salt
          1 teaspoon pepper
          1 cup oil
          1 pound bacon, diced
          4 tablespoons butter
          2 cups fresh mushrooms, sliced
         10 green onions, chopped
     1-1/2 teaspoons garlic powder
          5 cups California Burgundy
          3 bay leaves
          2 (1 lb. 1 oz.) cans small whole onions

Roll chicken in seasoned flour and brown all over in oil. Remove and place in deep casserole. Drain off oil and fry bacon until crisp. Drain off bacon fat, reserving 4 tablespoons. Add 4 tablespoons butter and sauté sliced mushrooms, green onions and garlic powder in this mixture of fats until brown. Arrange over chicken, add cooked bacon, wine and bay leaves. Cover and bake in 325° oven 1/2 hour. Reduce heat to 250° and continue baking 2 hours. Add small onions 45 minutes before dish is cooked, using onion liquid to thin gravy if necessary.

My choice of wine to accompany this dish:
CALIFORNIA BURGUNDY OR VIN ROSÉ

Chicken à la King

(4 servings)

Mrs. Arthur Caputi, Jr., E. & J. Gallo Winery, Modesto

This is a fast easy dish to serve to unexpected company, if you have some leftover chicken or turkey in the refrigerator.

          2 tablespoons butter
          1 green pepper, finely chopped
          1 cup sliced mushrooms
          2 tablespoons flour
        3/4 cup chicken broth or stock
        1/4 cup California Dry Sherry
          2 cups cooked chicken meat, diced
          1 cup evaporated milk
          2 egg yolks
          1 pimiento, diced
            Salt and pepper to taste

Melt butter, add green pepper and mushrooms. Sauté until tender and remove from pan. Stir in flour and cook 1 minute. Add broth and wine, stirring until thickened. Add chicken and vegetables and heat thoroughly. Combine milk and lightly beaten egg yolks and stir into hot mixture. Keep warm over hot water, but do not allow to boil. Add remaining ingredients, stirring to blend. Serve over toast or rice.

My choice of wine to accompany this dish:
CALIFORNIA RIESLING OR CHABLIS

California Chicken

(6 servings)

Mrs. Kenneth O. Dills, Charles Krug Winery, St. Helena

  3 chicken breasts, halved and boned
  2 cups dairy sour cream
  1 (10-1/2 oz.) can mushroom soup, undiluted
1/2 cup California Traminer
  2 cups (8 oz. solid) Cheddar cheese, grated
  1 (3-1/2 oz.) can French fried onion rings

Place chicken breasts, skin side up in buttered baking dish. Mix together sour cream, mushroom soup and wine. Spread over chicken pieces. Sprinkle on grated cheese. Top with onion rings. Bake in 325º oven 1 hour.

NOTE: This easy and succulent dish would go well with herb-flavored rice and the California Traminer used in its preparation.

Pollo Fiorentino

(4 servings)

Mrs. Alessandro Baccari, Baccari Wine Festival, San Francisco

1/4 cup olive oil
3 to 3-1/2 pound fryer, cut in 4 quarters
1 to 2 teaspoons dried sage (not powdered)
1 to 2 teaspoons dried oregano
  Pepper and salt
1/4 large onion (red or white)
  2 cloves garlic
1/2 cup California Dry Sauterne
1/2 cup California Dry Sherry

Put thin film of oil in bottom of baking pan. Rinse and dry chicken thoroughly. Place in pan skin side down. Sprinkle herbs over chicken generously; add pepper and salt to taste. Cut onion in 4 pieces and place in different parts of pan. Pour remaining olive oil over chicken. Dot chicken with crushed garlic. Place on middle rack and bake in 350º oven. After about 3/4 hour, move to lower rack when chicken commences to brown and bake 20 minutes longer. Pour wines over chicken, cook 5 minutes more at 350º. Cover with foil, lower oven to 225º and bake 15 minutes longer.

NOTE: Serve this savory chicken from Florence with California Sauterne.

Rosemary Chicken

(8 servings)

Brother Justin, The Christian Brothers, Napa

1/3 cup butter
  4 whole chicken breasts, halved
1/2 cup flour
1/2 teaspoon salt
1/2 teaspoon paprika
  1 cup chicken broth
1/2 teaspoon rosemary
1/2 teaspoon salt
1/8 teaspoon fresh ground pepper
  1 cup California Dry White Table Wine

Heat butter to bubbling. Coat chicken breasts with flour seasoned with salt and paprika. Sauté until a rich golden brown. Remove chicken and keep warm. Add broth to skillet. Stir to remove brown bits over medium heat. Add crushed rosemary, salt, pepper and wine. Replace breasts in sauce and simmer, covered, 10 minutes, or until tender.

NOTE: This simple recipe results in a fine-flavored chicken. It would be delicious with cucumbers, sliced lengthwise, simmered in heavy cream, just until tender, and any California Dry White Table Wine.

Chopped Chicken Casserole

(6 to 8 servings)

Mrs. Kenneth R. Spencer, Mirassou Vineyards, San Jose

  1 cup soft bread crumbs
  2 eggs, slightly beaten
  1 teaspoon salt
  Dash of pepper
  1 onion, minced (optional)
  1 cup chicken stock
  1 (10-1/2 oz.) can mushroom soup
  1 cup California White Table Wine
  5 cups cooked chicken, diced

Add bread crumbs to eggs along with salt, pepper, onion and stock. Mix mushroom soup with wine and stir into crumb mixture. Fold in diced chicken. Place in baking dish and bake in 375º oven 50 to 60 minutes.

My choice of wine to accompany this dish:
CALIFORNIA PINOT BLANC

NOTE: For a different flavor, add 1 cup California White Wine to water in which chicken is boiled, along with salt and seasonings of your choice. Egg sauce or Sauce Mornay (1 cup white sauce to which is added 1/3 cup heavy cream and 1 cup grated Gruyère or Cheddar cheese) would go well with this casserole.

Hurried Broiled Chicken

(6 servings)

Mrs. Greg Goorigian, Vie-Del Company, Fresno

3 to 4 pounds broiling chickens
1/2 cup soy sauce
3/4 cup sugar
1/4 teaspoon pepper
1/2 teaspoon onion powder
1/2 cup California Dry Sherry or Sauterne

Split broilers in halves. Combine all other ingredients in shallow baking dish large enough to accommodate chicken. Bring to boil. Add chicken, cover and simmer 15 minutes. Turn chicken pieces over and simmer 10 minutes more. Transfer chicken to broiler pan and broil about 5 minutes, turning once. Keep sauce hot to serve over chicken.

My choice of wine to accompany this dish:
CALIFORNIA CHENIN BLANC OR SWEET SEMILLON

NOTE: Mr. Goorigian recommends serving this unusually prepared chicken with a rice pilaf, green peas with water chestnuts, and sliced tomatoes. For dessert a quick ambrosia made with canned mandarin orange sections sprinkled with dried coconut.

Quick Cacciatore

(6 servings)

Mrs. Hubert Mettler, Guild Wine Co., Lodi

1 package spaghetti sauce mix
1 (8 oz.) can tomato sauce
1/2 cup California Dry White Table Wine
1/2 teaspoon Italian herbs
6 large pieces frying chicken
2 (4 oz.) cans mushrooms, undrained
Salt and pepper to taste

Combine sauce mix, tomato sauce, wine and herbs. Dip each piece of chicken in mixture and arrange on large piece of heavy duty foil in baking pan in one layer. Pour remaining sauce over chicken. Add mushrooms and season to taste. Fold foil over meat, making tight seal. Bake in 350° oven 1 to 1-1/2 hours, until tender.

My choice of wine to accompany this dish:
CALIFORNIA SAUTERNE

Roast Halves of Chicken

(4 servings)

Mrs. Earl Hoff, Mont La Salle Vineyards, Napa

2 small fryers, cut in half
1/2 cup California Dry White Table Wine
1/4 cup butter
3 tablespoons olive oil
1 onion, finely chopped
1 tablespoon parsley, chopped
1/8 teaspoon garlic powder, if desired
1/2 teaspoon salt
1 teaspoon oregano
1 (4 oz.) can mushrooms

Place chicken in baking dish and pour over wine. Allow to marinate at least 1 hour, turning occasionally. Combine remaining ingredients, except mushrooms, in saucepan, bring to boil and pour over chicken. Start in 500° oven. Reduce heat to 350° after chicken begins to brown. Continue baking 45 minutes, basting occasionally. Add 1 (4 oz.) can mushrooms, adding liquid to pan if needed, just a few minutes before chicken is done.

My choice of wine to accompany this dish:
CALIFORNIA CHABLIS

Chicken Atherton

(6 servings)

Mrs. Arvin E. Anderson, Gallo Sales Co., San Francisco

12 pieces frying chicken
(breasts, legs, thighs)
1/4 cup each butter and oil
1 pound fresh mushrooms, sliced
1 (1-5/8 oz.) package dried mushroom soup
Salt and pepper to taste
1/2 cup California Sherry or Sweet Vermouth

Brown chicken pieces on all sides in butter and oil. Remove to casserole. Sauté mushrooms in remaining fat until golden brown. Sprinkle soup mix over chicken. Season to taste. Arrange drained mushrooms on top, cover and refrigerate overnight. Remove from refrigerator at least 2 hours before dinner is to be served. Add Sherry or Vermouth, cover and bake in 350° oven 1-1/2 hours. Serve with rice.

My choice of wine to accompany this dish:
CALIFORNIA DRY WHITE TABLE WINE

NOTE: Mrs. Anderson serves this do-ahead dish along with a fresh fruit salad with a tart California wine vinegar flavored dressing. For dessert she suggests a chocolate mousse.

Pilaf and Chicken

(4 to 5 servings)

Mrs. Peter Mirassou, Mirassou Vineyards, San Jose

This is good for an informal company dinner. It can all be put together very quickly, and it holds well in the oven.

        1-1/3 cups packaged pre-cooked rice
          1/2 (2-3/4 oz.) envelope dry onion soup mix
            1 (10-1/2 oz.) can condensed cream of
                 mushroom soup
      1/2 to 3/4 cup boiling water
          1/4 cup Dry California Sherry
            1 pound chicken breasts
            3 tablespoons melted butter
                 Salt, pepper, paprika to taste

In a 1-1/2 quart casserole, combine rice, onion soup mix, cream of mushroom soup, water and wine. Brush chicken with butter; season with salt, pepper and paprika. Place on top of rice. Cover. Bake in 375° oven 1 hour or until chicken is tender.

My choice of wine to accompany this dish:
CALIFORNIA PINOT BLANC OR PINOT CHARDONNAY

Mexican Chicken

(4 servings)

Mrs. Joe Carrari, Paul Masson Vineyards, Saratoga

      2-1/2 pound frying chicken
        1/4 cup flour
          1 teaspoon salt
        1/4 teaspoon pepper
          2 tablespoons oil
          1 cup California Chablis
          1 (2 oz.) can sliced mushrooms
        1/4 teaspoon garlic powder
          4 green onions, sliced
          2 tablespoons parsley, chopped

Have chicken cut into pieces and coat with flour seasoned with salt and pepper. Sauté in oil until golden brown on all sides. Pour off excess fat. Add wine, liquid from mushrooms, garlic powder and onions. Cover and simmer 15 minutes. Turn chicken pieces. Sprinkle with parsley and sliced mushrooms. Cover and simmer 15 minutes longer, or until done.

My choice of wine to accompany this dish:
CALIFORNIA RIESLING OR CHABLIS

Sanger Fryers

(6 to 8 servings)

Mrs. Everett T. Estes, Sanger Winery Association, Sanger

          1 cup flour
          2 teaspoons salt
        1/4 teaspoon pepper
          2 fryers cut up, or 1 fryer and 4 breasts
        1/4 cup butter
          2 (10-1/2 oz.) cans cream of
                 mushroom soup
          1 (4 oz.) can sliced mushrooms
        1/2 cup California Dry Sherry
        1/2 cup California Sauterne

In paper bag mix flour, salt and pepper, add each chicken piece and shake well to coat evenly with flour. Fry chicken in butter until golden brown and place in casserole. Mix mushroom soup, undrained mushroom slices and wines. Pour over chicken and bake in 350° oven 1-1/2 hours. Cover and bake 15 minutes more.

NOTE: This excellent dish may be prepared ahead and baked in time for serving. It also reheats well. Serve with a California Dry White Table Wine.

Chicken Tarragon

(4 servings)

Mr. Rudy Janci, F. Korbel and Bros., Guerneville

          4 small whole chicken breasts, halved
        1/4 cup butter, melted
        1/2 teaspoon paprika
        1/2 teaspoon dried tarragon
          1 (10 oz.) package frozen broccoli,
                 partially thawed
        3/4 cup California Riesling
        1/2 teaspoon seasoned salt
          1 small onion, finely chopped
        3/4 cup fresh mushrooms, sliced

Place chicken skin side up in greased, shallow casserole. Pour butter over chicken and sprinkle with paprika. Bake in 400° oven 15 minutes. Arrange all other ingredients over and around chicken. Cover and bake 40 minutes longer.

My choice of wine to accompany this dish:
CALIFORNIA BRUT CHAMPAGNE

NOTE: Mr. Janci's advice: "Serve with wild rice and a salad of orange and grapefruit sections and slices of avocado on lettuce doused with clear French dressing. Pass crescent rolls. Of course, Champagne before, during and after dinner."

Chicken Livers and Bacon

(4 servings)

Mrs. Joseph S. Concannon, Jr., Concannon Vineyard, Livermore

Our children were introduced to chicken livers last summer and asked me to make some more. I combined ideas from several recipes, added a favorite ingredient — mushrooms — and this is the result.

- 4 strips bacon
- 1 pound chicken livers
- 1/3 cup flour
- 1 teaspoon salt
- 1/4 teaspoon pepper
- 1/4 cup green onions, chopped
- 1/2 pound fresh mushrooms, sliced
- 1/2 cup chicken broth, or 1 bouillon cube dissolved in 1/2 cup boiling water
- 1/2 cup California Chablis

Fry bacon in deep skillet, which has cover, until crisp. Remove and drain on paper toweling. Toss livers in flour seasoned with salt and pepper. Brown quickly in bacon fat remaining in skillet and remove. Sauté onions and mushrooms in remaining fat, until soft. Return livers to skillet, add broth and wine, cover and simmer 8 to 10 minutes until livers are just done. Serve immediately over rice or toast, crumbling crisp bacon over top.

My choice of wine to accompany this dish:
CALIFORNIA PETITE SIRAH OR BURGUNDY

NOTE: This delicious dish would be superb served over a combination of buttered wild rice and white rice, accompanied by fresh asparagus.

Turkey Lodi

(6 servings)

Mrs. James A. Beckman, Guild Wine Co., Lodi

- 3 pounds cooked turkey
- 1/4 cup flour
- 1 teaspoon salt
- 1/8 teaspoon pepper
- 1/4 cup olive oil
- 1/4 cup butter
- 1 cup California White Table Wine
  Pinch oregano
- 1/2 pound fresh mushrooms
- 1/4 cup butter
- 1/2 cup beef broth or consommé
- 1 egg yolk
- 1 tablespoon heavy cream

Slice meat thinly. Coat slices in flour seasoned with salt and pepper. Heat oil and butter in large frying pan. Lightly brown turkey slices. Pour off excess fat and return meat to pan with wine and oregano. Simmer over medium heat until almost dry, turning meat gently to coat all sides. Sauté mushrooms in butter (whole if small, or quartered or sliced). Add to turkey with consommé. Continue cooking until almost dry. Beat egg yolk and cream together. Remove turkey from heat. Pour egg-cream mixture over meat, turning gently to glaze all sides.

NOTE: With this dish, rich brown in color and flavor, serve a California Zinfandel.

GIBLET STEW from Miss Mary Lester, San Jose, is an original way to use these often neglected poultry parts. Combine 1 quart chicken stock, 1/4 cup garlic-flavor California wine vinegar, 1/2 cup California Burgundy, 1 cup catsup, 3 bay leaves, 1 teaspoon thyme, 1/2 teaspoon tarragon and a dash of Tabasco. Add 1 pound giblets cut in bite size pieces to stock. Simmer covered 1/2 hour, or until tender. Serve with boiled rice. Serves 4. Miss Lester likes California Gewürztraminer or Cabernet Sauvignon with this dish.

Squab and Weinkraut

(4 servings)

Mrs. Darrell Althausen, U. S. Dept. of Agriculture, Albany

I worked out this recipe before I knew there actually was a "Weinkraut."

- 1 pound sauerkraut, canned
- 1 medium apple, pared, cored and diced
- 1 tablespoon bacon grease
- 1/2 teaspoon caraway seed
- 2 tablespoons light brown sugar
- 1 cup California Black Muscat Wine

Rinse sauerkraut in sieve under cold water very briefly. Drain well. Add to kraut all other ingredients, bring to boil, lower heat and simmer uncovered 1/2 hour. Cover pan and simmer 20 to 30 minutes longer, stirring frequently.

SQUAB

- 4 squabs
  Salt
- 4 tablespoons butter
- 1/2 cup California White Table Wine or Vin Rosé
- 1/2 tablespoon flour
- 1 bay leaf

Truss squab, salt lightly and sauté in butter on all sides until golden brown. Remove to baking dish, placing breast side down. Pour pan drippings over birds, deglazing pan with California White Wine or Vin Rosé. Bake in 350° oven 35 to 45 minutes, until birds are tender, basting frequently with wine. Turn breast side up for last 10 minutes of cooking. Stir flour into pan juices until smooth and brown. Add wine or stock, a bay leaf and salt to taste. Cook until thickened, and pour over birds or serve separately.

My choice of wine to accompany this dish:
CALIFORNIA GEWÜRZTRAMINER, GREY RIESLING OR GREEN HUNGARIAN

NOTE: This dish can be attractively served, points out Mrs. Althausen, by nesting squab in ring of mashed potatoes, with an outer ring of weinkraut on platter. Two Rock Cornish Game Hens split in two may be substituted for squab with equally good results.

Mock Turtle Stew

(8 to 10 servings)

Mrs. Roy H. Richardson, Paul Masson Vineyard, Saratoga

This is an old "receipt" from a Savannah, Georgia lady who conducted a cooking school for young society matrons. Her terrapin stew was famous and this "mock terrapin" became another of her delicacies.

1	(4 to 5 lb.) stewing chicken
	Water to cover
2-1/2	cups California White Table Wine
6	egg yolks
2	tablespoons flour
1	cup butter, softened
2	cups milk
	Salt and white pepper to taste

Place chicken in large kettle and cover with water. Add 1 cup wine, bring to boil and simmer, covered 2-1/2 to 3 hours, until meat can easily be separated from bones. Remove all meat from bones, dice and place in serving casserole. Beat egg yolks well. Rub flour into butter and add to milk, which has been scalded. Cook over low heat, stirring until thickened. Add a little hot mixture to egg yolks and stir. Add egg mixture to white sauce off of heat, stirring constantly. Season, add chicken and remaining wine over low heat. Cook until heated through, but not boiling.

My choice of wine to accompany this dish:
CALIFORNIA PINOT CHARDONNAY OR EMERALD RIESLING

NOTE: If desired the flavor of this unctuous dish could be heightened by adding an onion, a carrot and a stalk of celery to the broth, which of course should be reserved for further use.

Squab Casserole

(6 servings)

Mrs. John G. Laucci, Franzia Brothers Winery, Ripon

This is a favorite dinner for New Year's Day, and easy to prepare.

1/2	cup onion, finely chopped
1/2	cup celery, finely chopped
3/4	cup butter (12 tablespoons)
2	cups soft bread crumbs
1	tablespoon parsley, chopped
1/2	teaspoon salt
1/4	teaspoon each pepper, thyme, oregano
6	squabs
1/2	pound mushrooms, diced
1	tablespoon olive oil
1	(12 oz.) can tiny peas, drained
1/4	cup California Dry Sherry

Sauté onion and celery in 4 tablespoons butter until soft, but not brown. Combine with bread crumbs, parsley, salt and seasonings. Stuff squabs and secure each with skewer or toothpicks. Rub squabs with 6 tablespoons softened butter and roast in shallow roasting pan in 350° oven 30 minutes, or until lightly brown. Meanwhile sauté mushrooms in 2 tablespoons butter and 1 tablespoon olive oil until golden. Combine peas, Sherry and mushrooms in casserole. Arrange squabs over peas and mushrooms and pour pan juices over all. Bake, uncovered, 15 or 20 minutes longer. Serve from casserole.

NOTE: Mrs. Laucci serves this company dish with green salad, curried rice, hot rolls, and for dessert, lemon pie. This menu would be enhanced by a California White Riesling.

Breast of Chicken Supreme

(4 servings)

Mrs. Angela Danisch, Brookside Vineyard Co., Bonita

2	whole chicken breasts, halved
1/3	cup flour
1	teaspoon salt
1/4	teaspoon pepper
1	tablespoon oil
1	(5 oz.) can water chestnuts, sliced
2	(10-1/2 oz.) cans cream of chicken soup
1	cup California Dry White Table Wine
	Rice, cooked according to package directions, substituting white wine for water
	Salted almonds or coconut

Coat chicken breasts thoroughly with flour seasoned with salt and pepper. Brown on all sides in oil and transfer to baking dish. Sprinkle with water chestnuts. Blend soup and wine, pour over chicken and bake uncovered in 350° oven 1 hour. Serve over rice, garnished with almonds or coconut.

NOTE: Mrs. Danisch serves this chicken with her own version of candied carrots. She boils carrots until tender in salted water, drains and arranges in shallow pan. She puts dots of butter over carrots, sprinkles on 1 tablespoon each of sugar and California Sherry and glazes carrots over medium heat, shaking pan to prevent scorching. A California Dry White Table Wine goes well with this menu.

DESSERTS

The sweet at the end of the meal rounds off dining pleasure and a delicious Dessert Wine of California to accompany it will inspire good conversation and render guests relaxed and happy. This wide selection of desserts from the tables of California winegrowers covers everything, starting with sophisticated versions of the humble baked apple. Ice cream and ices, by the way, should be allowed to ripen several hours before serving. If a baked pie shell is required, put a piece of foil over it and fill with dried beans during baking to prevent blistering. Be sure your cake is completely cool before frosting and don't whip the cream too far in advance of serving, for it will become watery at the bottom. Now raise a glass of California Port, Sherry or any of the other fine dessert wines available and toast the long labors in the vineyards that produced this liquid gold.

Steamed Raisin Pudding

(12 servings)

Mrs. John B. Cella II, United Vintners, San Francisco

2 cups dark seedless raisins	1 cup sifted all-purpose flour
1/3 cup California Sherry	1 tablespoon baking powder
1 cup butter	1 teaspoon salt
1-1/2 cups light brown sugar, firmly packed	2/3 cup milk
2 teaspoons vanilla extract	5 cups fine soft bread crumbs
2 eggs	1/2 cup pecans, chopped
	1/2 cup coconut, toasted

Chop raisins and add wine. Cream butter, sugar and vanilla together until light and fluffy. Beat in eggs. Resift flour with baking powder and salt. Blend into creamed mixture alternately with milk. Stir in crumbs, raisin-wine mixture, pecans and coconut. Spoon into well buttered 8-cup mold. Cover tightly, using foil if mold has no cover. Place on rack in large kettle. Add boiling water to half depth of mold. Cover kettle and steam for three hours, replenishing water as needed. Serve warm with brandied hard sauce.

NOTE: Serve California Cream Sherry with this pudding.

Pears in Port

(4 servings)

Mrs. Reginald Gianelli
East-Side Winery, Lodi

1	(1 lb. 4 oz.) can pear halves
1	(3-inch) stick cinnamon
	Whole cloves
1/4	cup California Port

Drain pear syrup into saucepan. Boil with cinnamon 5 minutes. Push 2 cloves into each pear half. Add wine to syrup, pour over pears and chill.

NOTE: These pears, served with a thin slice of fruitcake and a glass of California Port would make a refreshing dessert after roast turkey.

Refrigerator Cake

(10 to 12 servings)

Mrs. John M. Filice, San Martin Vineyards, San Martin

I experimented on this recipe with one of my dearest friends, Mrs. Warren L. Firenzi. She preferred Cream Sherry and our family chose Pale Dry. Either one will guarantee raves. No one will believe you haven't spent hours preparing this dessert.

    2   (3-1/2 oz.) packages vanilla flavor
        whipped dessert mix
    1   cup skim milk
    1   cup California Sherry, or apricot wine
    2   (2 oz.) packages whipped topping mix, or
        1/2 pint whipping cream
    1   cup skim milk, for use with topping mix
    2   packages lady fingers
        Apricot preserves or canned apricots,
        crushed and thickened with cornstarch

Prepare dessert mix as directed on package, using 1 cup milk and 1 cup wine. Prepare topping as directed on package and fold into pudding mix. Line 9-inch spring form pan with split lady fingers, on bottom as well as sides. Pour pudding mixture into lined pan and chill thoroughly before serving. If desired, a thin layer of apricot preserves, or crushed canned apricots may be spread over top of cake and finally a thin film of pudding over this.

My choice of wine to accompany this dish:
CALIFORNIA PALE DRY OR CREAM SHERRY

NOTE: The Sherry gives this cake a zabaglione-like flavor which is truly delicious.

Vanilla Wafer Cake

(12 servings)

Mrs. Tony Marusick, Calgrape Wineries, Delano

    2   cups sugar
    1   cup margarine
    6   eggs
    1/2 cup California Dry Sherry
    1   (12 oz.) box vanilla wafers,
        crushed fine (4-1/2 cups)
    1   (7 oz.) package shredded coconut
    1   cup pecans, chopped

Cream sugar and margarine together until fluffy. Add eggs, one at a time, beating well after each addition. Add wine, stirring well. Add crushed wafers, coconut and pecans, mixing thoroughly. Pour in greased 9 x 13 x 2-inch pan. Bake in 325° oven 1 hour. Cool in pan.

NOTE: This quickly done and deliciously chewy cake would be appetizing topped with Sherry-flavored whipped cream or ice cream and served with any California Dessert Wine.

Pot de Crème Parfaits

(8 servings)

Mrs. Don Rudolph, Cresta Blanca Wine Co., Livermore

This is a very rich dessert. It could be served as a late evening snack.

    1   (3-1/4 oz.) package chocolate pudding
        mix (not instant)
    1   (1 oz.) square unsweetened chocolate,
        grated
    2/3 cup sugar
    3   cups milk
    4   egg yolks
    2   tablespoons California Brandy
    1   (3-1/4 oz.) package coconut cream
        pudding mix (not instant)
    1/2 cup soft dried apricots, chopped
    1/8 teaspoon almond extract
    2   tablespoons California Sherry
    2   cups whipping cream

Combine chocolate pudding mix, unsweetened chocolate, 1/3 cup sugar in saucepan and stir in 1-1/2 cups milk. Cook, stirring constantly, over medium heat until mixture begins to thicken. Beat 2 egg yolks lightly and stir a little of the hot mixture into egg. Add Brandy. Stir egg-brandy mixture into pudding, return to heat and bring to a boil, stirring constantly. Remove from heat and chill. Combine coconut cream pudding mix with remaining sugar and milk in saucepan. Cook over medium heat, stirring constantly until mixture begins to thicken. Beat remaining egg yolks lightly, stir in a little hot pudding. Combine egg mixture with pudding and cook, stirring, until it reaches a boil. Remove from heat and stir in apricots, almond extract and Sherry. Chill. Whip cream until stiff. Divide in 2 equal parts. Fold half into each chilled pudding. Spoon into parfait glasses, alternating chocolate and coconut puddings.

My choice of wine to accompany this dish:
CALIFORNIA BRANDY OR SHERRY

California Berry Pie

(8 servings)

Mrs. Reese H. Vaughn, University of California, Davis

Dino Barengo introduced us to this delicious dessert many years ago, and gave us the recipe which has become a family favorite.

- 1/2 cup California Port
- 3/4 cup water
- 1 (3 oz.) package strawberry flavor gelatin
- 1 (12 oz.) package frozen sliced strawberries
- 2 teaspoons lemon juice
- 2 (3 oz.) packages cream cheese
- 2 tablespoons milk
- 1 (9-inch) baked pie shell
  Whipped cream

Heat wine and water to boiling. Add gelatin and stir until dissolved. Remove from heat. Add frozen strawberries and lemon juice, stirring to break up block of frozen berries. Chill until mixture begins to thicken. Meanwhile beat cream cheese and milk together and spread evenly over pie shell. Pour in gelatin mixture. Chill until firm. Garnish with whipped cream just before serving.

My choice of wine to accompany this dish:
CALIFORNIA PORT

Cherries Brandianne

(4 servings)

Mrs. William Perelli-Minetti, A Perelli-Minetti & Sons, Delano

This recipe only takes 3 minutes of your time and can be chilled in 30 minutes.

- 1 (8 oz.) jar red currant jelly
- 3 tablespoons California Brandy
- 1 (1 lb.) can pitted dark sweet cherries, drained and chilled
- 1/2 cup dairy sour cream

Blend jelly and Brandy. Stir in cherries. Refrigerate until serving time. Serve topped with dollops of sour cream.

NOTE: This excellent fruit combination could also be used to top pineapple or lemon sherbet, or ladle over baked custard. Gourmet results can be had with this recipe which is simplicity itself. Serve with any sweet California Dessert Wine.

Strawberries Romanoff

(6 servings)

Mrs. Catherine Soza, Wine Advisory Board, San Francisco

It is not wise to prepare this dessert far ahead of time because it tends to separate after sitting. It is basically simple to prepare, but taking the extra time to dress it up is worth the effort.

- 3 cups fresh strawberries, stemmed and rinsed
- 3/4 cup California Sherry
- 3/4 cup sugar
- 1 cup whipping cream
- 4 tablespoons orange Curaçao
- 2 tablespoons orange peel, grated
  Sprigs of fresh mint

Reserve 1/2 cup whole, perfect berries. Crush remaining berries, add Sherry and 1/2 cup sugar, stirring well. Chill thoroughly. Whip cream until soft peaks form, beat in remaining sugar. Cover and refrigerate. About 1/2 hour before serving time, pour off a little berry-Sherry syrup into shallow dish. Invert chilled, stemmed dessert dishes in syrup to coat their rims. Dip in sugar to frost them and return to refrigerator. Fold Curaçao and orange peel into cream. Drain berries briefly, saving syrup. Fold berries into cream and spoon into frosted glasses. Pour a small amount of reserved syrup over each serving. Top with whole strawberry and mint leaf. Serve immediately.

My choice of wine to accompany this dish:
CALIFORNIA CLARET OR BURGUNDY

NOTE: Mrs. Soza suggests serving this delicious dessert after barbecued steaks and fresh corn on the cob.

Pears Gertrude

(12 servings)

Mrs. George L. Marsh, University of California, Davis

- 12 perfect ripe pears
  Cold water
- 1 tablespoon lemon juice
- 4 cups brown sugar
- 6 cups water
- 1 cup California Sherry
- 1/3 cup Tang
  Heavy cream

Peel pears, leaving whole, with stems on. Place immediately in bowl of cold water with lemon juice, to keep fruit from turning brown while making syrup. Boil brown sugar and water 5 minutes, add pears. Cook slowly until tender and somewhat transparent. Do not overcook. Remove pears carefully from syrup and dip each one while still warm in Sherry. Place in dish. Boil syrup until thickened. Add Sherry mixed with Tang. Pour over pears and chill. Serve with cream, or if desired, freeze cream 1-1/2 hours until crystalized, but not stiff.

NOTE: Mrs. Marsh prefers to use Comice pears for this dessert, although Bartletts will do nicely. Serve with California Cream or Straight Sherry.

Pears Elwood

(4 servings)

Mr. Richard H. Elwood, Llords & Elwood Winery, Los Angeles

- 4 pears, peeled, not cored
- 2 cups California Sweet Semillon
- 1-1/2 cups strawberries
- 1-1/2 cups raspberries
- 2 cups powdered sugar
- 1/2 cup whipping cream
  Sugar and vanilla extract to taste,
  or vanilla sugar
- 1/4 cup California Port

Poach pears in Sweet Semillon until tender. Drain and cool. Rinse and crush berries, add powdered sugar to taste, and freeze to mushy consistency. Whip cream, adding sugar and vanilla to taste. Add Port slowly as cream begins to thicken. Mix well. For individual serving, on nest of cream place iced berries, the pear, more berries, and top with cream.

NOTE: Reserve the white wine used to poach pears for another dessert or cake sauce. If a purist about real vanilla flavor, make vanilla sugar by combining a 1 inch vanilla bean, cut in several pieces, with 1 cup granulated sugar and leave in jar until sugar absorbs vanilla flavor. Remove bean. Serve this rich and pretty dessert with California Ruby Port.

Gingerbread Pear Pudding

(9 servings)

Mrs. Jake Rheingans, Sanger Winery Association, Sanger

- 1/4 cup butter or margarine
- 1/2 cup brown sugar
- 1/4 cup California Muscatel
- 1 (1 lb. 13 oz.) can pears, drained and sliced, or equivalent fresh pears
- 1 (14-1/2 oz.) package gingerbread mix
- 1/3 cup California Muscatel
- 2/3 cup water
  Whipped cream

Melt butter in 9-inch square pan. Blend in sugar and 1/4 cup Muscatel. Arrange pear slices in rows in pan. Beat gingerbread mix, 1/3 cup wine and water together vigorously until blended. Carefully spoon over pears. Bake in 350° oven 30 minutes. Cut into 3-inch squares and serve warm topped with whipped cream.

NOTE: This version of upside-down cake could be served with the California Muscatel used in its preparation.

Pear Crisp

(8 servings)

Mrs. John B. Cella II, United Vintners, San Francisco

- 8 ripe pears
- 1/8 teaspoon salt
- 1/4 cup California Sherry
- 1/3 cup butter or margarine
- 1/3 cup light brown sugar
- 1 teaspoon nutmeg
- 1 teaspoon lemon peel, grated
- 2 cups raisin bran flakes, crushed to make 1-1/3 cups
  Whipped cream

Pare and core pears. Cut in eighths, lengthwise. Place in shallow baking dish, sprinkle with salt and add Sherry. Cover and bake in 350° oven 30 minutes. Meanwhile melt butter in heavy pan, add brown sugar, nutmeg and lemon peel. Heat until bubbly, stirring constantly. Add crushed cereal and stir to coat evenly. Spread evenly over pears. Bake, uncovered, 10 minutes longer, until lightly browned. Serve warm with whipped cream.

NOTE: A glass of California Sherry would go nicely with this attractive dessert.

Baked Apples Piedmont

(4 servings)

Mrs. Louis J. Foppiano, L. Foppiano Wine Co., Healdsburg

- 4 to 6 juicy apples
- 2 tablespoons lemon juice
- 4 tablespoons California Sherry or Marsala
- 1/2 cup California Chablis
- 1/4 cup butter, melted
- 1/2 cup brown sugar, or honey
  Sweetened whipped cream

Core and slice unpeeled apples. Add lemon juice and Sherry. Marinate 1/2 hour. Drain, reserving Sherry marinade, and arrange in well buttered baking dish. Pour over Chablis, butter and sugar. Bake in 375° oven until golden and bubbly, basting with marinade. Serve warm or cold with whipped cream.

NOTE: While this makes a delicious dessert with cream, sour cream, or for weight watchers, yogurt; it could also be served plain with roast pork or duck. Either California Sherry or White Table Wine could accompany this dish.

Applesauce

(6 to 8 servings)

Miss Mirjam van Gelderen, Oak Barrel Cellars, Berkeley

12 to 15 apples (Gravenstein or Red Delicious)
2/3 cup California Chablis
1/3 cup sugar

Rinse apples; peel, quarter, core and place in sauce pan with wine. Cover loosely, bring to boil, turn down heat and simmer 15 minutes, or until apples are tender, stirring thoroughly 2 or 3 times. Remove from heat and stir in sugar. Serve warm or cold.

My choice of wine to accompany this dish:
CALIFORNIA GREY RIESLING

Blossom Hill Baked Apples

(6 servings)

Mrs. E. Jeff Barnette, Martini & Prati Wines, Santa Rosa

We have an abundance of apples on our ranch. I bake as many apples as my large oven will hold. I freeze them and they are delicious for dessert in a hurry.

1ST RECIPE:

6 large apples
Strawberry or raspberry jam
1 cup California Tokay, Muscatel or Cream Sherry
1/2 cup light brown sugar

Remove cores, being careful not to bore all the way through bottoms. Fill centers with jam. Place in baking dish, pour over wine and sprinkle with sugar. Place layer of aluminum foil loosely over top of apples and bake in 350° oven for about 1 hour, or until done. Serve hot or cold, with or without whipped cream.

2ND RECIPE:

6 Roman Beauty apples
1 cup California Muscatel or Tokay
2 teaspoons orange rind, grated
2/3 cup orange juice
2 tablespoons lemon juice
1 cup sugar

Core and peel apples one quarter of the way down. Place in shallow baking dish. Combine wine, rind, orange and lemon juice, sugar, and bring to boil. Simmer 5 minutes and pour over apples. Bake in 350° oven 45 minutes, or until done, basting frequently. Serve warm or cold, plain or with cream.

My choice of wine to accompany these dishes:
ANY CALIFORNIA SWEET DESSERT WINE

BAKED APPLES DELANO is the superbly wine-flavored creation of Mrs. William Perelli-Minetti, A. Perelli-Minetti & Sons, Delano. Peel top third of 6 perfect apples and remove cores. Fill centers with mixture of 1/2 cup sugar, and 1/2 teaspoon cinnamon. Top each apple with 1 tablespoon butter. Pour 2 cups California Burgundy over them and bake in 325° oven 1 hour, or until tender, basting apples occasionally. Serves six happy people. A glass of California Ruby Port would make a pleasant accompaniment.

Vintner's Chiffon Pie

(6 servings)

Mrs. Joseph Grippi, The Christian Brothers, Napa

1 baked 9-inch pie shell
1 envelope unflavored gelatin
1/3 cup cold water
4 eggs, separated
3/4 cup sugar
2/3 cup California Cream Sherry
1/4 teaspoon salt
1/2 cup whipped cream
Dash nutmeg

Bake pie shell until nicely browned. Cool. Soften gelatin in cold water. Beat egg yolks until thick and lemon colored. Gradually beat in 1/2 cup sugar; add Sherry and salt. Cook over hot water, stirring constantly, until consistency of soft custard. Add gelatin, stirring until dissolved. Cool. Beat egg whites with 1/4 cup sugar until stiff. Fold into custard and spoon into pie shell. Chill until firm. Garnish with whipped cream and sprinkle with nutmeg, if desired.

NOTE: Another decorative garnish with this light sweet dessert would be a scattering of shaved bitter chocolate over the whipped cream. Serve pie with California Cream Sherry.

Rhubarb Zinfandel

(10 to 12 servings)

Mrs. John Franzia, Sr., Franzia Bros. Winery, Ripon

- 4 cups rhubarb
- 2 cups sugar
- 3/4 cup water
- 3/4 cup California Zinfandel

Wash rhubarb and cut into 1-1/2-inch pieces. Place rhubarb, sugar, water and Zinfandel in deep casserole. Cover and bake in 350° oven 30 minutes. Do not stir. Serve cold with sliced bananas.

NOTE: This dessert is equally delicious served by itself. Pass crisp cookies or pound cake. Also try it with vanilla ice cream. Serve a California Port with it.

Pears with Chocolate Sauce

(5 servings)

Mrs. John B. Cella II, United Vintners, San Francisco

- 1/3 cup California Sherry
- 1/2 cup water
- 1/3 cup sugar
-       Pinch salt
- 1 tablespoon lemon juice
- 5 ripe pears
- 5 baked tart shells
-       Chocolate sauce

Combine Sherry, water, sugar, salt and lemon juice and bring to boil, stirring. Simmer 5 minutes. Meanwhile peel and core pears from bottom, leaving stems intact. Poach fruit in syrup about 5 minutes, or until just barely tender. Baste frequently to poach evenly. Cool fruit in syrup. To serve, drain pears and place each in tart shell. Carefully pour chocolate sauce into shells around pears.

NOTE: Serve any sweet California Dessert Wine.

Rhubarb Wine Soup

(4 servings)

Mrs. Norman N. Fromm, Fromm and Sichel, San Francisco

- 1 tablespoon cornstarch
- 3/4 cup sugar
- 1/4 cup water
- 1 stick of cinnamon
- 1/2 teaspoon nutmeg
- 3 slices lemon
- 2 cups California Burgundy
- 2 cups rhubarb, cut in small pieces

Combine cornstarch, sugar, water and bring to boil. Add spices, lemon, wine and rhubarb and cook 5 minutes, or until rhubarb is soft. Remove cinnamon stick. Serve warm or cold.

NOTE: Serve a glass of California Ruby Port with this rosy dessert.

Prune Crisp

(6 servings)

Mrs. Leo Demostene, Soda Rock Winery, Healdsburg

- 1 cup prunes, cooked
- 1/4 cup sugar
- 1/2 cup California Sherry
- 1/2 teaspoon cinnamon
- 2/3 cup flour
- 1/4 teaspoon salt
- 1/3 cup brown sugar
- 1/3 cup butter
- 2/3 cup quick-cooking oats
- 2/3 cup coconut
-       Whipped cream

In saucepan combine pitted prunes, sugar, Sherry and cinnamon. Simmer 15 minutes, and set aside. Sift flour with salt. Add brown sugar, cut in butter, add oats and coconut. Spread half of dry mixture in 8-inch pan. Spoon prune mixture over this and top with remaining dry mixture. Bake in 325° oven 45 minutes. Cut into bars for cookies, or serve warm with whipped cream.

NOTE: Serve with California Light Muscat.

PRUNE BETTY is a variation of Mrs. Demostene's which she suggests as an alternative. Cook together 2 cups cooked prunes, 1/2 cup Sherry, 1/2 cup sugar, cinnamon to taste, for 15 minutes. Spread in 8-inch square pan and sprinkle with half a box of spice cake mix. Drizzle 6 tablespoons melted butter over this and, if desired, 1/2 cup chopped nuts. Bake in 350° oven 45 minutes. And for good measure she adds, "Try apricots and prunes or applesauce and prunes with yellow cake mix for more good variations."

CHEESE CHABLIS is a creamy invention from Mrs. Norman N. Fromm, Fromm and Sichel, San Francisco. Soften 1 envelope unflavored gelatin in 1/4 cup cold water. Heat 1 cup California Chablis to boiling; add gelatin, 1/4 cup sugar and stir until dissolved. When cool, stir in 1 cup each cottage cheese and whipping cream. Turn into a lightly oiled mold and chill until set. Serve with a berry, apricot or peach topping and California Port or Light Muscat. Serves 6.

California Cocktail

(6 servings)

Mrs. Alessandro Baccari, Baccari Wine Festival, San Francisco

   1 (1 lb. 14 oz.) can fruit cocktail
   1 large banana, sliced
   1 medium apple, thinly sliced
   2 fresh peaches, cut in small pieces, or
     3 halves canned clingstone peaches
 3/4 cup California Sherry
 1/8 cup California Sweet Vermouth
 1/8 cup Cointreau
   3 drops orange extract

Turn fruit cocktail into bowl. Add banana, apple, peaches, wines, liquor, and extract. Stir gently and chill well before serving.

NOTE: A California Sec Champagne would go nicely with this refreshing assemblage of fruits and flavors.

Pears au Vin

(4 servings)

Mrs. Stanford J. Wolf, Paul Masson Vineyards, Saratoga

   1 (1 lb.) can Bartlett pear halves
 1/3 cup golden raisins
 1/4 cup soft dried apricots
 1/2 cup California Chablis

Combine pear halves and syrup with raisins and apricots. Add wine and stir lightly, making sure all fruit is well covered with wine. Refrigerate, covered, several hours or overnight. Serve cold.

NOTE: Serve with California Port and a crisp butter cookie.

Marsala Orange Sauce

(2 cups)

Mrs. Louis J. Foppiano, L. Foppiano Wine Co., Healdsburg

 1/2 cup golden California raisins
   1 cup marmalade, or 1 (10 oz.) jar
   2 tablespoons orange juice
 1/2 cup California Sweet Sherry

Place all ingredients in a blender or electric mixer. Whip for 1 minute until very smooth. Chill in serving bowl. Serve this as a topping on puddings, cakes or vanilla ice cream.

NOTE: This sauce is also good with ingredients left unblended. After combining let stand for an hour to allow raisins to become mellow and plump. Serve with California Sweet Sherry.

Almond Bavarian

(6 servings)

Mrs. M. J. Filice, San Martin Vineyards, San Martin

   1 envelope unflavored gelatin
 1/4 cup water
   2 eggs, separated
1-1/4 cups milk
 1/2 cup sugar
 1/8 teaspoon salt
 1/3 cup California Sherry
   1 drop almond extract
   1 cup whipping cream
 1/4 cup slivered almonds
    Maraschino cherries

Soften gelatin in water. Beat egg yolks until thick; beat in milk, sugar and salt. Cook over hot water in top of double boiler until thickened, stirring often. Add softened gelatin, stirring to dissolve. Add wine, almond extract and chill until mixture thickens. Beat egg whites stiff and whip cream. Fold egg whites and 1/2 cup whipped cream into gelatin mixture and chill. Serve in sherbet glasses, garnishing with additional whipped cream, a sprinkling of almond slivers and top with maraschino cherries.

NOTE: This smooth Bavarian Cream would be good with a California Tokay.

Angel Nectar Dessert

(8 servings)

Mr. Evins R. Naman, Wine Institute, San Francisco

- 1 store-bought angel food cake
- 1 pint vanilla ice cream
- 1 cup coconut
- 1 cup sugar
- 3 cups apricot nectar
- 3 teaspoons lemon juice
- 1-1/2 tablespoons orange rind, grated
- 1/3 cup California Marsala or Sherry

Break cake into approximately 1-1/2-inch pieces. Shape ice cream into small balls, roll in coconut, place in flat pan and put in freezer. Combine sugar and apricot nectar. Boil rapidly 5 minutes. Remove from heat, stir in lemon juice and orange rind. Add wine. When ready to serve, heat nectar mixture in chafing dish, add angel food cake pieces. Place ice cream balls in sherbet glasses, cover with warmed cake and syrup. Serve immediately.

NOTE: Mr. Naman suggests a delectable dinner menu with this ambrosial creation for a finish: crown roast of lamb; peeled long green peppers, roasted, dressed with olive oil, wine vinegar and capers; and bulgur pilaf (cracked wheat.) Serve California Cream Sherry with dessert.

Strawberries Marsala

(6 servings)

Mrs. Robert Diana, Villa Armando Winery, Pleasanton

Strawberries and Marsala have an affinity for each other greater than that of strawberries and cream. This dessert being of Italian origin, the traditional berries used were the tiny wild ones which grow in the Alban Hills near Rome. Use fine domestic berries if you can't find wild ones, but on no account put sugar on them.

- 1 quart strawberries
- 1 cup California Marsala

Clean berries. If large, halve them. Place in serving bowl, pour over Marsala and marinate in refrigerator at least 1 hour. Serve cold with slices of sponge cake or Madeleines.

My choice of wine to accompany this dish:
CALIFORNIA CHABLIS OR SAUTERNE

Cherries Jubilee

(4 servings)

Brother Timothy, The Christian Brothers, Napa

- 3/4 cup red currant jelly
- 1 (1 lb. 14 oz.) can red pitted cherries, drained
- 1/2 cup California Brandy
- 1 pint vanilla ice cream

Melt jelly in chafing dish and add cherries. Blend and heat. Pour Brandy into center of cherries and heat without stirring. Ignite Brandy and spoon cherries and sauce over firm ice cream while still aflame.

NOTE: A quick simple version of a classic dessert. Serve with California Ruby Port or Madeira.

Ice Cream with Coconut

(1 serving)

Mrs. Jack L. Davies, Schramsberg Vineyards, Calistoga

This is a favorite standby to use when time is limited. Can be dressed up with mandarin orange slices or glacé fruits. Guests enjoy this sweet, without feeling too full after a heavy meal.

- 1 rounded tablespoon shredded coconut
- 1 large scoop vanilla ice cream
- 2 tablespoons sweet California Dessert Wine, of choice

Toast coconut over low heat until lightly and evenly browned, shaking pan often, or brown in 325° oven 10 minutes. Place ice cream in a dessert dish, top with wine and sprinkle with coconut.

My choice of wine to accompany this dish:
CALIFORNIA DESSERT WINE OR CHAMPAGNE

Pecan Candy

(about 30 candies)

Mr. J. W. Fleming, Lockeford Winery, Lockeford

- 1 cup brown sugar, firmly packed
- 1 cup white sugar
- 1/2 cup evaporated milk
- 2 cups pecans
- 2 tablespoons California Sweet Sherry

Mix well all ingredients except wine in heavy saucepan. Cook over medium heat to soft ball stage, 234° to 240° (a little syrup, dropped into very cold water forms a soft ball which flattens when removed from water). Stir constantly. Remove from heat and when mixture stops bubbling, add Sherry. Cool slightly, then beat until candy thickens. Drop from spoon onto small squares of wax paper in order to wrap each piece separately.

Canteloupe and Port

(1 serving)

Brother Timothy, The Christian Brothers, Napa

1/2 canteloupe
California Port

Scallop top of canteloupe with spoon and fill depressions with Port. Place in refrigerator several hours before serving.

NOTE: Dorothy Canet of Western Foods Associates uses a melon ball cutter instead of a spoon. After refrigerating melon with Port, she places scoop of vanilla ice cream in center. Served with a glass of California Port, this also makes an exciting dessert.

Rudy's Special

(6 servings)

Mr. and Mrs. Rudy Windmiller, Almaden Vineyard, Los Gatos

A light and delightful dessert, especially appreciated after a heavy meal.

1 (8-1/2 oz.) can applesauce
1 pint vanilla ice cream
California Port

Put 2 or 3 tablespoons applesauce into individual dessert dishes. On this place 1 scoop ice cream and pour 2 to 3 tablespoons Port over all.

NOTE: Serve with the same California Port, and pass crisp cookies.

Lemon Honey Bananas

(6 servings)

Miss Mary Lester, San Jose

In little silver compote dishes, this dessert looks elegant, or it can be served in parfait glasses with a touch of California Brandy or apricot brandy on top.

6 bananas, cut in halves lengthwise
2 tablespoons honey
2 teaspoons lemon juice
1-1/2 cups California White Table Wine
1/2 cup brown sugar

Arrange bananas in shallow baking dish. Drizzle on honey and lemon juice. Pour wine over bananas and sprinkle with brown sugar. Bake in 400° oven 15 to 20 minutes, until bananas are tender and glazed, basting once or twice.

My choice of wine to accompany this dish:
CALIFORNIA GEWÜRZTRAMINER, GREY RIESLING OR CREAM SHERRY

Peach and Cream Pudding

(6 servings)

Mrs. Edmund Friedrich, Paul Masson Vineyards, Saratoga

Prepare this easy dessert ahead of time to give flavors a chance to blend. It makes a light finish after a heavy meal.

1 (3-1/2 oz.) package vanilla flavor whipped dessert mix
1/2 cup California Sweet Vermouth
1 envelope whipped topping mix
1 (1 lb.) can sliced peaches

Prepare dessert mix according to package directions, substituting Vermouth for 1/2 cup water. Prepare topping mix, following package directions. Fold into pudding mix. Fold in well drained peaches. Spoon into sherbet or Champagne glasses and refrigerate 3 to 4 hours.

My choice of wine to accompany this dish:
CALIFORNIA SWEET OR DRY VERMOUTH

NOTE: Mrs. Friedrich adds, "For another good dessert, substitute strawberry whipped dessert mix plus crushed strawberries for vanilla and peach combination."

Orange Tapioca Cream

(5 servings)

Mrs. Jane Murphy, Wine Institute, San Francisco

This is perfect with Southern fried chicken and a vegetable aspic salad.

1-3/4 cups milk
1/4 cup sugar
1/4 teaspoon salt
3 tablespoons quick-cooking tapioca
1 egg, separated
1/4 cup California Muscatel
2 large oranges

Combine milk, 2 tablespoons sugar, salt, tapioca and lightly beaten egg yolk. Cook, stirring constantly until mixture just reaches boiling. Remove from heat. Beat remaining sugar into egg white until stiff. Fold into hot pudding. Stir in wine. Cool, stirring once after 15 minutes. Peel oranges and section, removing all white membrane. Fold oranges into cream mixture and chill thoroughly before serving.

My choice of wine to accompany this dish:
CALIFORNIA CHABLIS

Lemon Prune Delight

(6 servings)

Mr. D. C. Turrentine, Wine Advisory Board, San Francisco

My sister, Marge, whose recipe this is, is a venturesome cook. She has a keen sense of taste and everything she tries turns out well.

      1 (12 oz.) package pitted prunes
      2 cups water, or less
    2/3 cup seedless raisins
      1 lemon
      1 cup sugar
        California Brandy
        California Sherry
        Whipped cream

Cook prunes in sufficient water to cover just until tender. Remove from syrup. Add raisins, juice and peel of lemon cut into very thin strips, and sugar to syrup. Boil down to about half its volume. Add to prunes. Chill. After spooning into individual serving dishes, add 1 teaspoon Brandy and 1 tablespoon Sherry to each. Top with whipped cream.

My choice of wine to accompany this dish:
CALIFORNIA CREAM SHERRY OR RUBY PORT

Editor's note: To enhance wine flavor 1 cup California Sherry may be substituted for a cup of the water in which prunes are cooked.

Sauterne Ice

(6 to 8 servings)

Mr. Fred Weibel, Weibel Champagne Vineyards, Mission San Jose

The recipe was invented by one of our associates and other students in a cooking school class. They said, "Let's make an unusual but elegant and simple wine dish." This is it.

      2 cups sugar
      4 cups water
      1 tablespoon lemon rind, freshly grated
      1 cup California Sauterne

Combine sugar, water, bring to boil and boil 5 minutes. Cool. Add lemon rind and wine. Freeze in refrigerator tray, stirring several times during freezing. (A hand-turned or electric ice cream freezer will turn out a smoother product.)

My choice of wine to accompany this dish:
**CALIFORNIA SAUTERNE, CHENIN BLANC
OR GREEN HUNGARIAN**

NOTE: Mr. Weibel further comments, "This is so light and refreshing it could be served on a picnic or to conclude a many-course meal. The flavor puzzles guests who can rarely guess its simple ingredients."

Almond-Stuffed Peaches

(6 servings)

Mrs. Louis J. Foppiano, L. Foppiano Wine Co., Healdsburg

      6 large firm peaches, or
        12 canned halves, drained
    1/2 cup toasted almonds
  1-1/3 cups powdered sugar
      1 tablespoon candied orange peel or
        citron, chopped
    1/2 cup California Dry Sherry

Peel and halve peaches, removing pits. Chop almonds until pulverized and mealy. (Can be done, a few at a time, in a blender.) Add 2/3 cup sugar and mix thoroughly. Add orange peel and blend. Fill peach halves with mixture. Place peaches in shallow baking dish, sprinkle with remaining sugar and pour in Sherry. Bake in 350° oven 10 to 15 minutes, until hot and bubbly.

NOTE: Serve this luscious combination warm or cold, plain, or topped with sour cream or vanilla ice cream, along with a glass of California Cream Sherry.

Gina Fruit Cup

(4 servings)

Mrs. William Bonetti, Charles Krug Winery, St. Helena

      1 cup strawberries
      2 tablespoons sugar
      2 tablespoons lemon juice
      1 cup fresh apricots, sliced
      2 tablespoons orange juice
      4 slices light cake, or
        12 lady fingers
    1/2 cup California Port
      8 scoops vanilla ice cream
      2 cups whipped cream
      4 almond macaroons, crumbled

Sprinkle strawberries with 1 tablespoon sugar and lemon juice. Sprinkle apricots with remaining sugar and orange juice. Refrigerate at least 2 hours. Sprinkle cake with Port. Arrange in chilled parfait glasses in following order: 1/2 slice cake; 1 scoop ice cream; 1/4 cup strawberries; 1/2 slice cake; 1/4 cup whipped cream; 1/4 cup apricots; 1 scoop ice cream; 1/4 cup whipped cream. Sprinkle tops with macaroon crumbs.

NOTE: This rich party dessert could be served with California Chenin Blanc.

ICE CREAM PUDDING is not a case of gilding the lily, but is just another example of how things can be made better with wine. Mrs. Leonard Maullin, Milford Co. of California, Los Angeles, softens a quart of rich French vanilla ice cream, beats in 1-1/2 cups of any sweet California Dessert Wine until well blended and pours mixture into parfait glasses. They are frozen for at least 6 hours. Before serving decorate as desired from a wide choice of garnishes: whipped cream, chopped nuts, glacé fruits, macaroon crumbs, pitted dates or prunes chopped fine, compatible fresh fruits crushed, or your own inspiration. The same California Dessert Wine as used in pudding will complement it. Serves 8.

Brandy Pudding

(6 servings)

Mr. and Mrs. Dinsmoor Webb, University of California, Davis

  1/4 teaspoon salt
    3 eggs, separated
    6 tablespoons sugar
    1 envelope unflavored gelatin
  2/3 cup milk
    3 tablespoons California Brandy
       or Sherry
    1 cup whipping cream

Add salt to egg yolks; beat until thick and lemon colored. Gradually beat in sugar. Soften gelatin in milk; heat until gelatin dissolves and cool slightly. Add milk mixture to egg yolks, beating constantly. Add Brandy. Chill until mixture thickens. Fold in whipped cream and stiffly beaten egg whites. Turn into 1-1/2 quart mold and chill until set. To serve, unmold on platter. Can be topped with diced fresh or frozen fruit which has been marinated in a little Brandy or Sherry to which a little sugar has been added.

My choice of wine to accompany this dish:
CALIFORNIA CREAM SHERRY OR PORT

Peaches in Cream

(6 to 8 servings)

Mrs. August Sebastiani, Samuele Sebastiani Winery, Sonoma

My family is especially fond of this easy dessert which will complement any meal.

      1 (1 lb. 13 oz.) can peaches,
         halved or sliced
      1 (3-5/8 oz.) package instant
         vanilla pudding
  1-1/4 cups milk
    1/2 pint whipping cream
    1/3 cup California Sherry
         Nutmeg

Drain peaches well, arrange in serving dish and refrigerate. Make pudding according to package directions, using 1-1/4 cups milk instead of 2 cups. Refrigerate 5 minutes. Fold in stiffly beaten cream. Refrigerate 10 minutes. Add Sherry, mixing well. Spread over peaches and fleck with nutmeg.

My choice of wine to accompany this dish:
CALIFORNIA CHAMPAGNE

COFFEE FLAVORED SUNDAE is from Mrs. B. C. Solari, United Vintners, San Francisco. She says this is the simplest possible dessert, but an interesting and delicious taste combination. To a large scoop of good quality vanilla ice cream add 1/4 cup Special Natural Wine flavored with cocoa and coffee. Sprinkle with slivered almonds and serve with a crisp cookie and a glass of any California Dessert Wine.

Saratoga Trifle

(8 servings)

Mrs. Otto E. Meyer, Paul Masson Vineyards, Saratoga

      1 (3-1/4 oz.) package vanilla pudding mix
      2 cups milk
      8 macaroons
      1 cup California Sweet Sauterne
      8 lady fingers
    1/2 cup blanched almonds, coarsely chopped
    1/2 pint whipping cream
    1/3 cup California Madeira or Sherry

Prepare pudding with milk according to package directions. Chill. Crumble macaroons in glass serving dish with sides, and drench with 1/2 cup Sauterne. Cover with half the pudding. Arrange lady fingers on top and moisten with remaining wine. Spread with other half of pudding. Sprinkle with almonds. Whip cream until it forms soft peaks, blend in Madeira and spread over trifle. Chill several hours and serve very cold.

NOTE: The memory of this dessert, descended from Colonial times, might have come to California via covered wagon. Serve it with California Madeira or Sherry.

Sherry Orange Cake

(12 to 15 servings)

Mrs. Carol Lee Ashimine, Wine Institute, San Francisco

- 1 package orange cake mix
- 1 envelope whipped topping mix
  (do not whip — use direct from package)
- 1 teaspoon cinnamon
- 1/2 teaspoon nutmeg
- 1/2 teaspoon ground cloves
- 1 tablespoon orange peel, grated
- 4 eggs
- 1/4 cup orange juice
- 3/4 cup California Dry Sherry

Combine all ingredients in large bowl. Blend until thoroughly moistened. Beat with electric mixer at medium speed 4 minutes. Pour into two greased and floured layer cake pans, or an angel food cake pan. Bake in 350° oven 50 minutes, or until done. Allow cakes to cool slightly in pans before turning out on cake rack. Frost with following:

CHOCOLATE SHERRY FROSTING

- 3 squares (3 oz.) unsweetened chocolate
- 1/4 cup California Medium Sherry
- 1/4 cup strong coffee
- 1 teaspoon vanilla
- 1/4 cup butter, softened
- 3-1/2 cups powdered sugar
- 1/2 cup walnuts

Melt chocolate with Sherry and coffee over hot water. Add all other ingredients except nuts and beat with electric mixer until smooth. Add chopped or ground nuts, reserving a few whole nutmeats for garnish. Frost both layers and sides of cake.

NOTE: Mrs. Ashimine has also given us a variation on this superb cake. Substitute devil's food cake mix for the orange cake and glaze with a simple mixture of 1-1/2 cups sifted, powdered sugar and 2 tablespoons California Dry Sherry. A glass of California Cream Sherry could accompany either cake, and give your guests pleasure.

Chocolate Cake

(6 servings)

Mr. Rex Malloy, Mont La Salle Vineyards, Napa

This is an original recipe.

- 1-1/4 cups sifted all purpose flour
- 2 teaspoons baking powder
- 1/2 teaspoon salt
- 1 cup brown sugar, firmly packed
- 2 eggs, separated
- 1/4 cup milk
- 1/4 cup California Red Table Wine
- 1/3 cup cooking oil
- 2 squares (2 oz.) unsweetened chocolate, melted
- 1-1/2 teaspoons vanilla extract
- 1/2 cup white corn syrup
- 1/4 cup California Brandy
- 2/3 cup whipping cream
  Semisweet chocolate, grated

Sift together flour, baking powder and salt. Stir in brown sugar. In another bowl beat together egg yolks, milk, wine, oil, melted chocolate and vanilla. Mix gradually into flour mixture, beating until well blended. Fold in stiffly beaten egg whites. Turn into greased 9-inch round cake pan, which has been lined with a 9-inch round of wax paper. Bake in 375° oven about 30 minutes, until cake tester comes out clean. Place cooled cake in shallow dish. Pierce with toothpick all over top. Combine corn syrup with Brandy and pour over cake. Let stand overnight, covered, in refrigerator. Cover top and sides of cake with whipped cream and decorate with grated chocolate.

NOTE: A noble glass of California Port would complement this rich and fine cake.

Crunchy Fruit Cobbler

(8 to 10 servings)

Miss Erma Tolstonage, CVA Company, San Francisco

Serve with coffee after a luncheon of chef's salad, and finger sandwiches.

- 1 (1 lb. 4 oz.) can crushed pineapple
- 1 (1 lb. 5 oz.) can cherry pie filling
- 1/2 cup brown sugar, firmly packed
- 1/2 cup California Sherry
- 1/4 teaspoon salt
- 1 (1 lb. 2-1/2 oz.) package lemon flavor cake mix
- 1/2 cup chopped walnuts
- 1/2 cup butter

Combine fruits, brown sugar, wine and salt in bottom of well buttered 2-quart baking pan. Sprinkle dry cake mix and walnuts over fruit mixture. Cut butter in small pieces and dot over top. Bake in 300° oven about 1 hour. Serve warm or cold, topped with whipped cream or sour cream, if desired.

My choice of wine to accompany this dish:
CALIFORNIA CHAMPAGNE

Lemon Ice Box Cake

(10 servings)

Mrs. Louis W. Pellegrini, Sr., Italian Swiss Colony, Asti

- 1 cup sugar
  Juice of 1 lemon
  Pinch salt
- 3/4 cup water
- 4 eggs, separated
  Rind of 1 lemon, grated
- 1 (3 oz.) package lemon gelatin
- 1/4 cup Special Natural Wine, citrus-flavored
  Lady fingers
  Sponge Cake
  Whipped Cream
  Chopped Nuts

Combine 1/2 cup sugar, lemon juice, salt, water and beaten egg yolks in double boiler. Cook, stirring until slightly thickened. Add grated rind and gelatin while hot. Stir occasionally while cooling. Add wine. When gelatin begins to set, fold in egg whites, which have been stiffly beaten with remaining sugar. Line sides of 9-inch layer cake pan with lady fingers, line bottom with thin layer of sponge cake (or use lady fingers). Fill lined pan with gelatin mixture and refrigerate for a minimum of 2 hours. Serve with whipped cream sprinkled with chopped nuts.

NOTE: Serve this California descendant of Charlotte Russe with a sweet California Dessert Wine to taste.

Peaches en Gelée

(6 servings)

Mrs. Alexis Farafontoff, California Wine Association, Lodi

- 1 (1 lb. 13 oz.) can clingstone peach halves
- 1 envelope unflavored gelatin
- 3/4 cup water
- 1 cup California Port
- 2 tablespoons sugar
  Whipped cream

Drain peaches. Soften gelatin in 1/4 cup peach juice. Combine water, wine and sugar in saucepan. Bring to boil, add peaches and simmer 3 minutes. Remove peaches and arrange in large, shallow serving bowl. Add gelatin to hot wine mixture, stirring until dissolved. Pour over peaches and chill until firm. Top with whipped cream.

My choice of wine to accompany this dish:
CALIFORNIA PORT

Jean's No-Bake Fruitcake

(12 servings)

Mrs. Fred Snyde, Woodridge Vineyard Association, Lodi

- 1 pound marshmallows
- 3/4 cup milk
- 1 teaspoon cinnamon
- 1/4 teaspoon each nutmeg and ground cloves
- 1/4 cup California Sherry or Brandy
- 1 pound seedless raisins
- 1 pint mixed dried fruit, chopped
- 4 cups walnuts or pecans, coarsely chopped
- 1 pound crushed graham crackers
  California Sherry

Melt marshmallows in milk. Add spices and Sherry or Brandy. Add fruits, nuts and cracker crumbs. Press into lightly buttered container. Cover and refrigerate for 1 month. Sprinkle 2 tablespoons Sherry over cake twice a week.

NOTE: Serve a slice of this easy cake with the same California Sherry used to moisten it.

Sherry Apple Pie

(6 servings)

Mrs. E. Jeff Barnette, Martini & Prati Wines, Santa Rosa

- 1 (9-1/2 oz.) package pie crust mix (for 2-crust pie)
- 2 tablespoons sugar
- 4 to 6 tart cooking apples
- 2/3 cup granulated sugar
- 2 tablespoons flour
- 1/8 teaspoon each, salt and cinnamon
- 1/4 cup California Sherry
- 1 teaspoon lemon juice
- 1/4 cup sugar
- 1/4 cup Cheddar cheese, shredded, or walnuts, chopped
- 1 tablespoon California Sherry
- 1 tablespoon butter, melted

Prepare half of pie crust mix to make 9-inch shell. Reserve remaining mix for topping. Line 9-inch pie pan with pastry, flute edge and brush lightly if desired with slightly beaten egg white. Sprinkle 2 tablespoons sugar over bottom crust and set aside. Peel, core and slice apples. Mix together sugar, flour, seasonings, wine and lemon juice. Arrange layers of sliced apples and sugar-flour mixture to fill crust. To remaining pie crust mix add sugar, cheese or walnuts, Sherry and butter. Mix until crumbly and spread over apples. Cover loosely with foil and bake in 425° oven 15 minutes. Remove foil, reduce heat to 350° and bake 30 to 40 minutes, or until well done and topping is brown.

My choice of wine to accompany this dish:
CALIFORNIA DESSERT WINE

Peach Cake

(8 servings)

Mrs. Leo Demostene, Soda Rock Winery, Healdsburg

For years I've been making a quick prune cake, using spice cake mix, prunes and Sherry. I didn't have any cooked prunes one day so I tried it with peaches instead. The family liked it — so a new recipe!

- 1 package yellow cake mix
- 1 (1 lb. 13 oz.) can sliced peaches, well drained
- 3/4 cup California Sherry, sweet or dry
- 3 eggs
- 1-1/2 cups powdered sugar, sifted
- 2 tablespoons lemon juice

With electric mixer, using low speed, combine cake mix, peaches and Sherry. Add eggs and beat until blended, about 1 minute. Pour batter into buttered 9 x 13 inch pan. Bake in 350° oven for 35 to 40 minutes. While still warm, frost with lemon icing, made by mixing sugar and lemon juice until smooth.

My choice of wine to accompany this dish:
ANY CALIFORNIA WHITE TABLE WINE

NOTE: Mrs. Demostene has given us two recipes for the price of one. Try the prune spice cake as well as the delicious peach cake above.

Saint's Delight

(8 servings)

Mrs. Earl Harrah, Wine Advisory Board, San Francisco

- 1 store-bought angel food cake, or lemon or orange chiffon cake mix
- 1 (3-1/4 oz.) package vanilla pudding mix
- 1/2 cup California Sherry
- 1 cup blanched almonds, chopped coarsely
- 1 cup whipping cream
- 1 tablespoon sugar
- 8 tablespoons California Sherry
- 1 teaspoon vanilla extract

Cut cake into three even layers. Make custard with pudding mix according to package directions substituting 1/2 cup Sherry for part of the liquid called for. Cool custard, stirring occasionally and chill. Toast almonds in oven until golden. Beat cream with sugar until it stands in soft peaks. Add 2 tablespoons Sherry and vanilla. To assemble, place 1 layer of cake in glass serving dish with sides and sprinkle with 2 tablespoons Sherry and some of the toasted almonds. Spread a layer of custard over this and cover with next slice of cake. Sprinkle with 2 tablespoons Sherry and a scattering of almonds; cover with another layer of custard. Top with third slice, sprinkle with Sherry; frost top and sides with whipped cream. Decorate with rosettes of cream using a pastry tube, if desired. Pat remaining almonds around sides of dessert and pour any remaining custard around cake. Refrigerate until serving time.

My choice of wine to accompany this dish:
CALIFORNIA CREAM SHERRY OR PORT

NOTE: Using store-bought cake and pudding mix, you will have a grand company dessert with practically no work.

Candy Cake

(2 9-inch loaves)

Mrs. Edmund Friedrich, Paul Masson Vineyards, Saratoga

This cake serves as an excellent and different substitute for the traditional Christmas fruitcake. It is a rich cake which requires no frosting or garnishes. I recommend it highly.

- 1 cup butter or margarine
- 2 cups sugar
- 5 eggs
- 1 tablespoon vanilla extract
- 1/2 cup buttermilk
- 1/2 cup California Cream Sherry
- 1 cup dates, cut up
- 1 pound orange candy slices
- 1 cup nuts, chopped
- 1 cup coconut (4 oz. can)
- 4 cups sifted all-purpose flour
- 1/2 teaspoon baking soda
- 1 teaspoon salt

Cream butter and sugar together until fluffy. Beat in eggs, one at a time. Stir in vanilla, buttermilk and Sherry. In another bowl mix together dates, candy, nuts and coconut with 1/2 cup flour. Sift remaining flour with soda and salt. Add to creamed mixture, blending until smooth. Stir in candy mixture. Spoon into well greased 9 x 5 x 2-inch loaf pans. Bake in 325° oven 1 hour.

My choice of wine to accompany this dish:
CALIFORNIA CREAM SHERRY

NOTE: This cake keeps well and freezes well. It could be made well before Christmas, dosed with California Brandy, wrapped in cheesecloth and then foil, and dosed two or three times more to become a fragrant treat for the holiday.

Brandy Cheesecake

(10 servings)

Mrs. Paul L. Halpern, Italian Swiss Colony, Madera

This recipe was given to me minus the Brandy by Siri Cereghino, one of our fine office girls. It was so delicious I decided to add the grape brandy and send it on to you.

- 20 graham crackers
- 1/4 cup butter, melted
- 1 (3 oz.) package lemon-flavor gelatin
- 1 cup boiling water
- 1 envelope unflavored gelatin
- 3/4 cup cold water
- 1 (4-1/4 oz.) package whipped topping mix
- 1 cup milk
- 2 teaspoons vanilla extract
- 4 tablespoons California Brandy
- 1 (8 oz.) package cream cheese, softened
- 3/4 cup sugar

Roll graham crackers into crumbs, add butter, mixing well. Press 3/4 of mixture onto bottom of (2 qt.) flat pyrex baking dish. Dissolve lemon gelatin in boiling water. Cool. Soften plain gelatin in cold water. Set over hot water to dissolve. Beat topping mix with milk. Add vanilla and Brandy. Beat cream cheese until fluffy. Add sugar gradually, continuing beating. Beat plain gelatin and lemon gelatin into cream cheese mixture. Fold in whipped topping thoroughly. Spoon into dish lined with crumbs. Cover top with remaining crumbs. Cover and refrigerate overnight.

NOTE: Mrs. Halpern comments, "This is light and airy and goes with any menu. It is easy and can be made a day or two ahead. Serve with good hot coffee and California Brandy."

Cherry Cake

(2 loaves)

Mrs. A. J. Winkler, University of California, Davis

- 1/4 cup California Sherry or Brandy
- 1 pound candied cherries
- 1 pound pitted dates
- 2 slices candied pineapple, cut in small pieces
- 1 pound pecans
- 4 eggs
- 1 cup sugar
- 1 cup sifted all purpose flour
- 1 teaspoon baking powder
- 1/2 teaspoon salt
- 1 teaspoon vanilla extract

Pour Sherry over fruits and pecans. Beat eggs lightly, add sugar and beat well. Resift flour with baking powder and salt. Add to egg mixture and mix thoroughly. Stir in vanilla and Sherry-fruit-nut mixture. Turn into 2 greased loaf pans (8-1/2 x 4-1/2 x 2-1/2 inches.) Bake in 300° oven 1-1/2 to 2 hours, or until done and brown on top.

NOTE: A slice of this cake would be pleasant with vanilla ice cream and a glass of California Cream Sherry.

Poor Man's Fruitcake

(1 8-inch square cake)

Mrs. Edmund Friedrich, Paul Masson Vineyards, Saratoga

The title of this recipe attracted me when I was a thrifty service wife. It is not half as time- or money-consuming as the regular fruitcake, yet it has eye and taste appeal.

- 1 cup sugar
- 3/4 cup shortening
- 1 cup seedless raisins
- 1 cup broken walnuts
- 1 teaspoon cinnamon
- 1/2 teaspoon each ground cloves and ground ginger
- 1/2 cup strong coffee (instant coffee may be used)
- 1/2 cup California Brandy
- 2 eggs, well beaten
- 2 cups flour
- 1 teaspoon baking powder
- 1 teaspoon baking soda

Combine all ingredients except eggs, flour, baking powder and soda. Boil 5 minutes and cool 15 minutes. Add eggs. Sift together flour, baking powder and soda and mix with other ingredients. Pour in greased pan and bake in 350° oven 30 minutes.

My choice of wine to accompany this dish:
CALIFORNIA SHERRY

NOTE: Mrs. Friedrich frosts her cake with lemon butter frosting, made with 2 cups confectioner's sugar, 2 tablespoons lemon juice, grated lemon rind and 2 or 3 tablespoons softened butter, beaten together.

Nutmeg Cookies

(3 dozen cookies)

Mrs. Vincent Indelicato, Sam-Jasper Winery, Manteca

- 1 (1 lb. 3 oz.) package yellow cake mix
- 1 teaspoon nutmeg
- 1/2 cup soft butter or margarine
- 1 egg, beaten
- 1/4 cup California Sherry
- 1 cup walnuts, chopped

Combine cake mix and nutmeg. Add butter, egg, and Sherry. Beat until smooth. Add walnuts. Drop teaspoonsful of mixture on lightly buttered baking sheet. Bake in 350° oven 12 to 15 minutes, until lightly browned. Remove to wire rack to cool.

My choice of wine to accompany this dish:
CALIFORNIA VIN ROSÉ

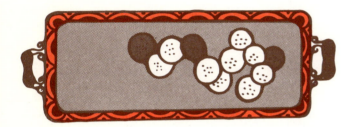

Lebkuchen

(50 to 80 cookies)

Mrs. Kay Martin, California Growers Wineries, Cutler

This is one of our favorite Christmas cookies. They store well in air tight containers and can be made several weeks ahead of the holidays. They also freeze well.

- 4 eggs
- 1 pound brown sugar (2-1/3 cups)
- 1 teaspoon cinnamon
- 1/2 teaspoon ground cloves
- 1-1/2 cups sifted all-purpose flour
- 1 teaspoon baking powder
- 1/2 teaspoon salt
- 3/4 cup California Muscatel
- 3/4 cup raisins
- 3/4 cup nuts, chopped
- 2 tablespoons flour

Beat eggs thoroughly. Beat in sugar and spices. Resift flour with baking powder and salt. Add to egg mixture alternately with wine. Mix raisins and nuts together, sprinkling with 2 tablespoons flour. Combine thoroughly with batter. Turn into flat, greased 11 x 16-inch jelly roll pan and bake in 400° oven about 15 minutes. When cool, cut into squares or bars.

NOTE: The traditional German ancestor of this American version of Lebkuchen is always frosted with a hard white sugar glaze. Serve with California Muscatel.

Tutti-Frutti Bombe

(8 servings)

Mrs. Earl Harrah, Wine Advisory Board, San Francisco

- 1-1/2 cups whipping cream
- 1/4 cup sugar
- 4 tablespoons California Brandy
- 1 (30 oz.) can crushed pineapple
- 1/4 cup citron, finely chopped
- 2 tablespoons each red and green glacé cherries, finely chopped
- 9 pitted dates, cut into small pieces
- 1/2 cup California Port
- 2-1/2 pints vanilla ice cream

Set a 2-quart melon mold in freezer until very cold. Whip cream with sugar until thick and glossy. Fold in Brandy. Spread cream evenly all over inside of mold. (If mold is not sufficiently cold, cream will slide down the sides.) Freeze until very firm, 2 to 3 hours. Meanwhile, drain pineapple well. Add chopped glacé fruits — 1/2 cup fruitcake mix can be substituted to save time and trouble — and dates. Cover with Port and let stand 1/2 hour, stirring occasionally. Allow ice cream to soften sufficiently to be easily stirred. Add fruit mixture, mix well and pour into freezing trays. Freeze until almost solid. Pack firmly into melon mold. Freeze until firm. Unmold 10 minutes before serving, keeping in freezer until it is carried to table.

NOTE: It is always preferable, if not imperative, to allow frozen desserts to remain in freezer overnight to ripen flavors. With this elegant dinner party dessert, serve a California Sec Champagne.

Anise Cookies

(6 to 8 dozen cookies)

Mrs. Walter E. Kite, Guild Wine Company, San Francisco

- 4 cups sifted flour
- 4 teaspoons baking powder
- 3 teaspoons salt
- 2 eggs
- 1 cup sugar
- 1 teaspoon vanilla extract
- 2 teaspoons anise
- 1/4 cup California Cream Sherry
- 3/4 cup butter, melted
- 2 cups walnuts, coarsely chopped

Resift flour with baking powder and salt. Beat eggs well. Beat in sugar. Add dry ingredients, mixing well. Add vanilla, anise, wine, butter and walnuts, mixing well after each addition. Divide dough into halves. Roll lengthwise on floured board to 1/2 inch thickness. Grease 2 cookie sheets lightly. Place cookie dough halves on sheets and bake in pre-heated 350° oven approximately 20 minutes, until dough has risen and is pale brown. Remove from oven. Slice across length of dough in 1-inch slices. Turn each slice on its side, to allow all sides to brown. Return to oven and bake 10 minutes longer, until golden brown. Cool and store in cookie jars.

NOTE: These would be appealing for an afternoon snack accompanied by a glass of California Cream Sherry.

Fun With Wine Accessories

Wine can be delightful no matter how simply it is served. What's more, wine really doesn't need any accessories to go with it. There are, however, wine-related articles that give beauty to the table or that added extra interest, excitement, and convenience to the service and enjoyment of wine.

Salt and Pepper Shakers

A little touch of elegance for the dinner table can be had with glass salt and pepper shakers shaped like grape clusters, which hang on a silver-plated grapevine. They seldom fail to draw appreciative comments from guests.

Sommelier Chain and Key

An item that adds interest to service of wine at gatherings is the Sommelier Chain and Key, the traditional symbol of the sommelier, or wine steward, who has charge of the wine cellar and the service of wines. Sommeliers are to be found in many of the world's famous clubs and restaurants. Members of some groups devoted to tasting, appreciation, and the study of wine wear Sommelier Chains and Keys during meetings as part of their pleasant ritual.

The key, of course, is symbolic of the key to the wine cellar. The Chain is usually about 40 inches long and the key nine inches. This device is frequently used as a trophy in a wine tasting contest, as a gift to a wine knowledgeable friend, to decorate a home wine cellar, recreation or dining room, or home bar.

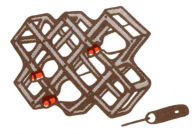

Bottle Racks and Cork Pops

Many of those who live in modern homes and apartments have a wine "cellar" in a closet or some other cool spot. For this purpose, bottle racks of wood, or other material, are available in order to store corked bottles on their sides; this is done to keep the corks moist and airtight. Most of these racks hold ten bottles, and they fold up when they're not in use. They fit into most cabinets and cupboards and, as many a housewife has discovered, a bottle rack makes a decorative conversation piece on the back of a bar or on a counter top.

The new and revolutionary way to remove a cork from a bottle of wine is not to pull it at all, but to push it. This is accomplished by a cork remover known as "Cork Pops." It requires a minimum of effort — and it fascinates all, young and old. It's a real fun gadget, as well as being highly practical.

Simply thrust the "Cork Pops" needle all the way through the cork, and then lightly press the top of the capsule. The gas in the capsule pushes the cork out with a satisfying "pop!" No tug, no strain, no broken corks. (Just be careful not to press so long that the cork comes out with excess force accompanied by some of the wine.)

The Wine Advisory Board has published four large wine cookbooks, below listed, in addition to the one you are reading. They are practical accessories to add to the enjoyment of wine, and they contain many recipes for flavorful dishes and interesting wine information.

Recipes from the Winemakers

EPICUREAN RECIPES OF CALIFORNIA WINEMAKERS, illustrated with drawings in two colors, tells you how to prepare world-famous gastronomical treats in your own home and in most cases, inexpensively. These wine-cooked dishes include such savory foods as Roast Suckling Pig and Boeuf à la Bourguignonne. Most of the recipes, submitted by California winemakers, their wives, and associates, are easy to prepare, but produce unforgettable taste experiences.

ADVENTURES IN WINE COOKERY BY CALIFORNIA WINEMAKERS shows that winemakers are among the most food and flavor-conscious people in the world. The more than 500 recipes and food ideas in this book reflect that background. Its features tell you about the winemaker's favorite wines, the health values of wine, bottle sizes, jiffy cookery, wine and food combinations, a basic cellar, entertaining with wine, and toasts and quotations that have been inspired by wine.

FAVORITE RECIPES OF CALIFORNIA WINEMAKERS was based upon the simple truth, known for thousands of years in countless countries that good food is made even better with wine. Featured information includes wine uses, quick tips on cooking, a wine cookery chart, wine glassware, and wine in the diet.

GOURMET WINE COOKING THE EASY WAY is especially designed for the cook who wants to spend a minimum of time in the kitchen. It features convenience foods — frozen, mixed, freeze-dried, canned and other packaged foods. With these foods, the manufacturer has done part of the work ordinarily done in the kitchen and the addition of wine makes these dishes truly fit for a gourmet. For instance, you will find from this book that a small amount of Sherry transforms canned pea or bean soup into a rich and aromatic dish for your menu. Port turns raspberry-flavored gelatin into a distinctive dessert.

If any of these items is not available in your local retail stores, write for help in locating them to: Wine Advisory Board, 717 Market Street, San Francisco, California 94103.

Wine Terms

Acidity

In wine, acidity is the word normally used to indicate the quality of tartness or sharpness to the taste, the presence of agreeable fruit acids, an important favorable element in wine quality. Not to be confused with sourness, dryness or astringency.

Aroma

That part of the fragrance of wine which originates from the grapes used, as distinguished from "bouquet."

Astringency

The quality of causing the mouth to pucker. The degree of astringency of a wine depends primarily upon the amount of tannin it has absorbed from the skins and seeds of the grapes. Moderate astringency is a desirable quality in many wine types.

Body

Consistency, thickness or substance of a wine, as opposed to the lack of body in a thin wine. Body of wine reflects the quantity of solid matter, or "extract," in solution in the liquid.

Bouquet

That part of the fragrance of wine which originates from fermentation and aging, as distinguished from "aroma."

Fruity

Having the fragrance and flavor of the grape; sometimes used to designate a combination of tartness and sweetness; "grapy."

Generic

Wine type names which stand for definite type characteristics are called generic names. Generic names of geographic origin originally applied to the wines of specific Old World grape and wine districts. As those wines became famous, their names, through the centuries came to designate any wines with similar characteristics, wherever grown. Burgundy, Champagne, Port, Rhine Wine, Sauterne and Sherry are the best known generic wine type names of geographic origin. Claret and Vermouth, on the other hand, are generic names without geographic significance.

Varietal

When a wine is named for the principal grape variety from which it is made, it is said to have a varietal name. Cabernet, Chardonnay, Muscatel, Pinot Noir, Riesling and Zinfandel are among the best known varietal names for wine types in the United States. Most wines with varietal names fit also into the broad generic name groups; for instance, Riesling is a Rhine Wine, Zinfandel and Cabernet are Clarets.

Vintage

The gathering of grapes and their fermentation into wine; also the crop of grapes or wine of one season. A vintage wine is one labeled with the year in which all its grapes were gathered and crushed, and the juice therefrom fermented.

Wine

The naturally fermented juice of fresh ripe grapes.

RECIPE INDEX

First printing Nov., 1970

Second printing Feb., 1972